How to Be Good at Science,
Technology & Engineering

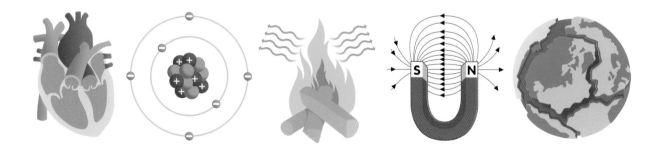

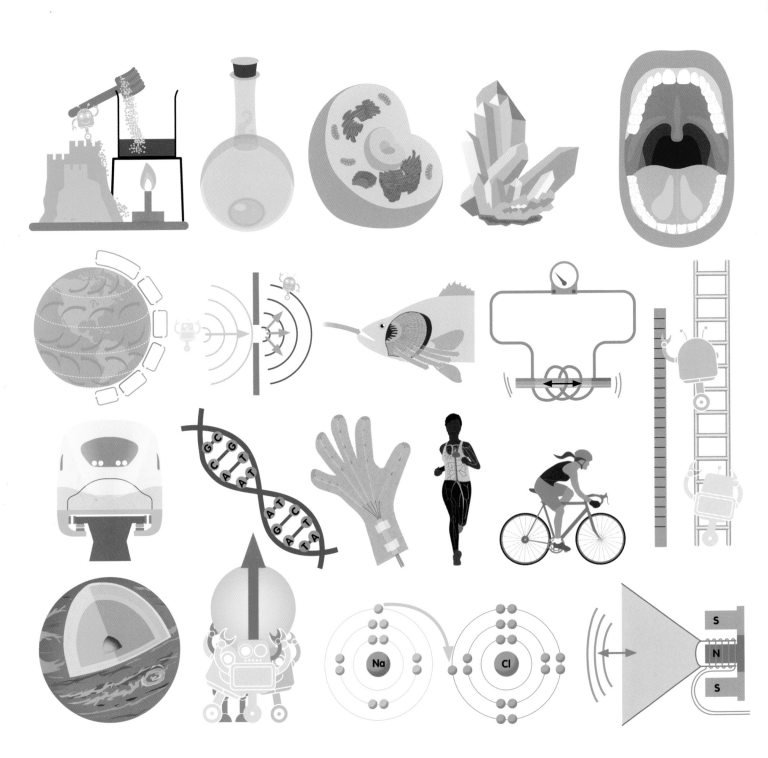

How to Be Good at Science, Technology & Engineering

DK

Penguin Random House

Senior editor Ben Morgan
Senior art editors Sunita Gahir, Peter Radcliffe

Editors Shaila Brown, Laura Sandford, Amanda Wyatt
Illustrators Acute Graphics, Sunita Gahir,
Karen Morgan, Peter Radcliffe
US editor Kayla Dugger
US executive editor Lori Hand

Authors Robert Dinwiddie, John Farndon, Clive Gifford,
Derek Harvey, Peter Morris, Anne Rooney, Steve Setford
Consultants Derek Harvey, Penny Johnson

Managing editor Lisa Gillespie
Managing art editor Owen Peyton Jones

Production editor Gillian Reid
Production controller Francesca Sturiale
Jacket editor Claire Gell
Jacket designers Juji Sheth, Surabhi Wadhwa-Gandhi, Jomin Johny
Senior DTP designer Harish Aggarwal
Jackets editorial coordinator Priyanka Sharma
Managing jackets editor Saloni Singh
Design development manager Sophia MTT

Publisher Andrew Macintyre
Art director Karen Self
Design director Phil Ormerod
Publishing director Jonathan Metcalf
Special sale & custom publishing manager Michelle Baxter

This Paperback Edition, 2020
First American Edition, 2018
Published in the United States by DK Publishing
1450 Broadway, Suite 801, New York, NY 10018

A catalog record for this book is available from the Library of Congress.
ISBN 978-0-7440-2937-6

Printed and bound in China

FOR THE CURIOUS
www.dk.com

Contents

1 Introduction

2 Life

3 Matter

4 Energy

Science is the key to understanding the world.
Scientists come up with theories and test them
with experiments to help us answer all kinds
of questions—from how living things survive
to why planes don't just fall to the ground.
Engineers use science and math to invent new
technologies that make our lives easier.

INTRODUCTION

How science works

Science is more than just a collection of facts. It's also a way of discovering new facts by having ideas and then testing them with experiments.

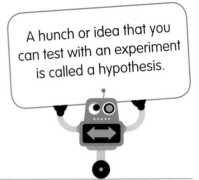

A hunch or idea that you can test with an experiment is called a hypothesis.

The scientific method

Most scientists carry out experiments to test their ideas. An experiment is just one step in a sequence of steps that form what's known as the scientific method. This is how it works.

1 Make an observation
The first step is to notice, or observe, an interesting pattern. For instance, you might notice that the grass growing in old cow pies is taller and greener than the grass elsewhere.

The grass in old cow pies is taller and greener.

2 Form a hypothesis
The next step is to form a scientific idea that explains the pattern. This idea is called a hypothesis. You might think, for example, that something in cow pies helps plants grow taller.

3 Carry out an experiment
Next you test your hypothesis by carrying out an experiment. In this case, you might grow plants in three types of soil: soil with lots of cow manure; soil with a little cow manure; and soil with none. To improve your experiment, you might grow lots of plants in each type of soil, not just one of each.

No manure in the soil

Small amount of manure in the soil

Lots of manure in the soil

4 Collect data

Scientists collect results (called data) from experiments very carefully, often using measuring instruments such as rulers, thermometers, or weighing scales. To compare how well different plants grow, you might measure their height with a ruler.

A ruler shows exactly how tall the plant has grown.

Every measurement is recorded.

5 Analyze results

To make the results easier to understand, you might plot them on a graph. The graph here shows the average height plants grew to in the different kinds of soil. Growing lots of plants and working out an average for each type of soil makes the results more reliable. In this case, the results support the hypothesis that manure helps plants grow.

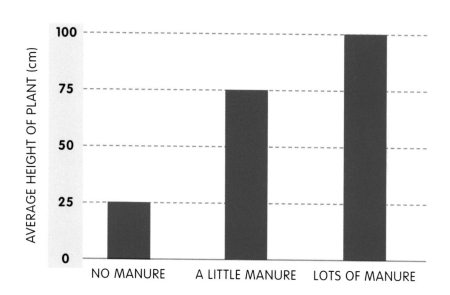

To find out if manure helps other kinds of plants grow, you need to repeat the experiment.

6 Repeat the experiment

A single experiment doesn't prove a hypothesis is true—it just provides evidence that it might be true. Scientists usually share their results so that others can repeat the experiment. After many successful results, a hypothesis may eventually be accepted as a fact.

Working scientifically

Working scientifically means working in a careful and
methodical way that makes errors less likely to happen.
Scientists take great care to avoid errors when they carry
out experiments.

Taking measurements

Many experiments involve measuring things. For instance,
in a chemistry experiment you might measure a liquid's
temperature. To be confident of getting the right answer, it
would be wise to measure the temperature several times,
but this could give you several different readings.

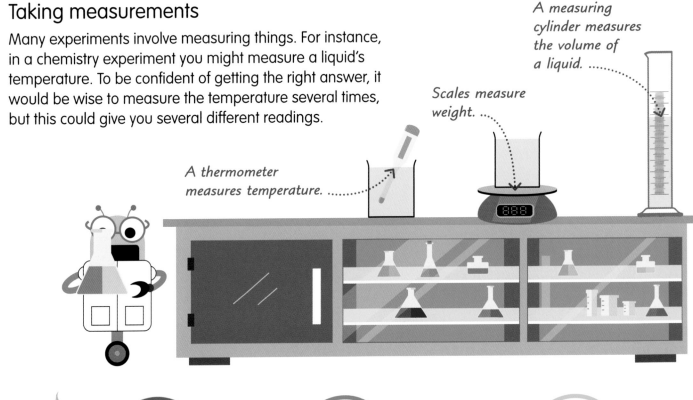

*A measuring
cylinder measures
the volume of
a liquid.*

*Scales measure
weight.*

*A thermometer
measures temperature.*

1 Precise but not accurate
Imagine you take the
temperature four times and all
four readings show the same
number to two decimal places,
but the thermometer is faulty.
The readings are precise but
not accurate.

2 Accurate but not precise
Now imagine you use a
different thermometer that isn't
faulty but the readings are all
slightly different—perhaps the
tip of the thermometer was in
a different place each time. The
readings are accurate but they
aren't precise.

3 Accurate and precise
Finally you stir the liquid
before taking the temperature,
and all four readings are about
the same and all correct. They
are accurate and precise.
Whenever scientists take
measurements, they try to
be accurate and precise.

Bias

Scientists also strive to avoid something called "bias," which causes errors to creep into measurements. For instance, imagine you use a stopwatch to time how long a chemical reaction takes. The stopwatch might be perfectly accurate and precise, but because it takes you half a second to press the button, all your readings are incorrect by the same amount.

Working with variables

The most important things a scientist measures during an experiment are called variables. There are three important types of variables: independent, dependent, and control.

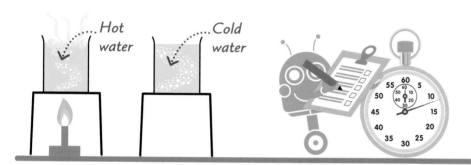

Hot water

Cold water

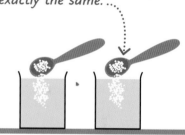

The amount of salt and water in both beakers has to be exactly the same.

1 Independent variable
This is something a scientist deliberately changes as part of an experiment. In an experiment to see if salt dissolves faster in hot or cold water, you might use two beakers of water, one hot and one cold. The water's temperature is the independent variable.

2 Dependent variable
This is the variable you measure to get your results. In the salt test, for instance, the dependent variable is the time salt takes to dissolve. It's called dependent because it might depend on another variable, such as how hot the water is.

3 Control variables
These are variables you keep carefully controlled so they don't harm an experiment. In the salt test, they include the amount of salt and the amount of water. These must be kept constant in both beakers so they don't affect the dependent variable.

Working together

Teamwork is important in science. All scientists build on the work of earlier scientists, either strengthening their ideas with new evidence or overturning theories altogether. Scientists work in groups to pool their skills and expertise, and they share findings by publishing them. But different teams also compete to be the first to carry out a successful experiment.

Fields of science

There are hundreds of different fields (areas) of science, but most of them belong to one of three main groups: biology, chemistry, and physics.

All scientists build on the work and discoveries of previous scientists.

Studying life

The scientific study of living things, from the tiniest cells to the largest whales, is called biology. Biologists study the internal workings of organisms, how organisms develop, grow, and interact, and how different species (types of organisms) change over time.

GRASSHOPPER   SONG THRUSH

1 Animals
The study of animals, including how their bodies work and how they behave, is called zoology.

2 Plants
The study of plants, from tiny clumps of moss to the tallest trees, is called botany.

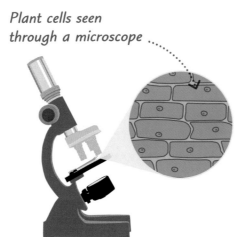

Plant cells seen through a microscope

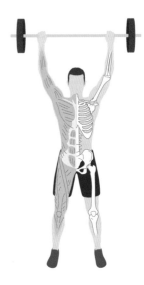

3 Environment
Some biologists study how living things interact with each other and the natural world around them in order to survive. We call this field of science ecology.

4 Cells
All living things are made of tiny cells that you can only see through a microscope. Microbiologists study these cells and how they work.

5 Human body
Some biologists specialize in studying the human body and keeping it healthy. Medicine is the scientific study and treatment of diseases.

Studying matter

The scientific study of matter is called chemistry. Chemists study the way particles called atoms and molecules interact to form different substances.

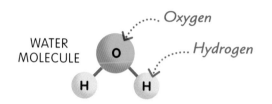

WATER MOLECULE

Oxygen

Hydrogen

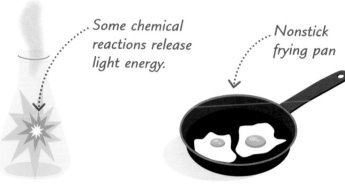

Some chemical reactions release light energy.

Nonstick frying pan

1 Atoms and molecules
Atoms and molecules are the building blocks of all chemicals. A water molecule, for example, has one oxygen atom and two hydrogen atoms.

2 Chemical reactions
When two or more chemicals are put together, their atoms may rearrange to form new chemicals. We call this a chemical reaction.

3 Materials
Chemists have created many useful materials that don't exist in nature, such as the nonstick lining used to make saucepans.

Studying forces and energy

Physics is the scientific study of forces and energy and the way these affect everything from atoms to the whole universe.

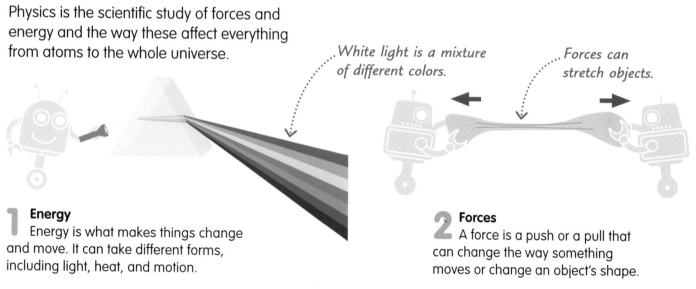

White light is a mixture of different colors.

Forces can stretch objects.

1 Energy
Energy is what makes things change and move. It can take different forms, including light, heat, and motion.

2 Forces
A force is a push or a pull that can change the way something moves or change an object's shape.

Studying Earth and space

Some scientists study the structure of planet Earth or the more distant planets and stars we can see in space. Earth science (geology) and space science (astronomy) overlap with many areas of physics, chemistry, and even biology.

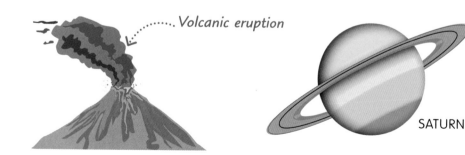

Volcanic eruption

SATURN

1 Earth
Earth scientists (geologists) study rocks and minerals, Earth's inner structure, and the processes that cause earthquakes and volcanoes.

2 Space
Space scientists (astronomers) use telescopes to study moons, planets, stars (including our Sun), and the vast, swirling clouds of stars we call galaxies.

How engineering works

Engineers work in a similar way to scientists, but their job is different. While scientists perform experiments to test theories about the world, engineers aim to solve specific human problems by inventing or constructing something.

Types of engineers

Most engineers specialize in a particular type of engineering, allowing them to build up expert knowledge and experience. There are many branches of engineering, but most belong to one of four main classes: civil, mechanical, electrical, and chemical engineering.

1 Civil engineering

Civil engineers work with large structures, such as buildings, roads, bridges, and tunnels. They use math and physics to ensure that designs are safe and strong. Many also need to know about materials science and earth science.

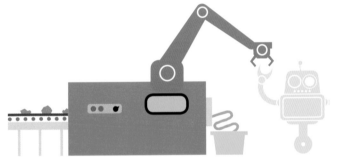

2 Mechanical engineering

Mechanical engineers create machinery, from cars and aircraft to robots. They need a good knowledge of math, physics, and materials science, and like many other engineers they use CAD (computer-aided design) for making models.

3 Electrical engineering

Electrical engineers design and manufacture electrical devices, from tiny microprocessor chips in electronic devices to the heavy-duty machinery used to generate electricity. Understanding math and physics is essential for electrical engineers.

4 Chemical engineering

Chemical engineers use their knowledge of chemistry and other sciences to design, build, and run factories that manufacture chemicals on a large scale. They work in many different fields, including oil refining and drug manufacturing.

The engineering design process

All kinds of engineers follow the same basic process when solving a problem. This involves a series of steps, some of which are repeated over and over as a design or model is tested and improved.

1 Ask
The first step is to ask what the problem is and find out as much detail about it as possible. For instance, the problem might be to create a new river crossing. How many people need to travel and how often? Are there any nearby roads? How wide and deep is the river?

2 Imagine
The next step is to think up lots of possible solutions. Use your imagination. You could build a bridge, dig a tunnel, or use boats to ferry cars over the river. Consider the merits, drawbacks, and costs of each idea, and choose the best one to develop further.

3 Plan
After deciding which idea to work on, you need to do some planning. If you want to build a bridge, draw sketches. How large will it be, how will it be supported, and what materials will you use to build it?

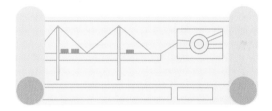

4 Model
Next you need to build a model of your chosen design. This could be a scale model made from plastic, wood, or metal, or it might be a digital model made on a computer using a CAD program.

5 Test and improve
Once the model is built, test it to see how well it works. Is there a problem? If so, revise the model and test again. Many cycles of testing and revising might be needed. The models that go through testing are called prototypes.

6 Share
The final step is to share your results by writing a report or doing a presentation. Professional engineers present their results to the client that hired them to solve the problem. If the client decides to go ahead and build and manufacture the object, the engineer helps with that process too.

Earth is home to an incredible variety of living things, but they all have certain features in common. They are all made of tiny building blocks called cells, which are controlled by genes stored in DNA. All kinds of living things strive to produce offspring, and over long periods of time, all forms of life change by a process called evolution.

LIFE

What is life?

There are millions of different kinds of living things, from germs that are too small to see to elephants, whales, and towering trees. Living things are also known as organisms.

One study estimates that there are about 9 million species of complex organisms on Earth.

Characteristics of life

Most of the living things we see around us are animals and plants. Although animals and plants look very different, they share certain characteristics in common with all organisms. These are the characteristics of life.

Plants use the Sun's energy to make their own food.

1 Getting food
All organisms need food, which gives them both energy and the raw materials they need to grow. Animals get food by eating other organisms. Plants get food by making it, using sunlight, air, and water.

Urinating is one of the main ways animals excrete harmful waste chemicals.

Horses breathe in air to bring oxygen into the body for respiration.

2 Getting energy
All living things use energy. They get it from food by a chemical process known as respiration, which takes place inside cells. Most organisms need a continual supply of oxygen from the air for respiration, which is why they need to breathe.

3 Sensing
All organisms can sense things in their surroundings. Animals can sense light with their eyes, sound with their ears, smells with their nose, touch and heat with their skin, and the taste of food with their tongue.

4 Removing waste
Lots of processes happening inside an organism produce waste products that must be removed from the body in a process called excretion. This is because the waste products may harm the body if they are allowed to build up.

Count the species

See how many different types of organisms you can identify in a backyard in only one minute. A good place to find small animals is under rocks or plant pots, where small creatures like to hide and keep out of the sun.

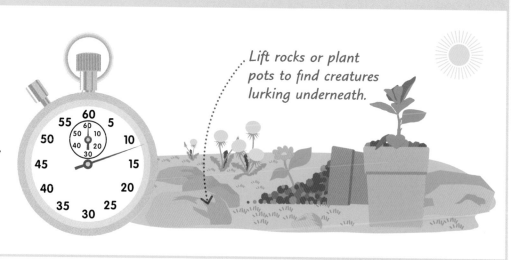

Lift rocks or plant pots to find creatures lurking underneath.

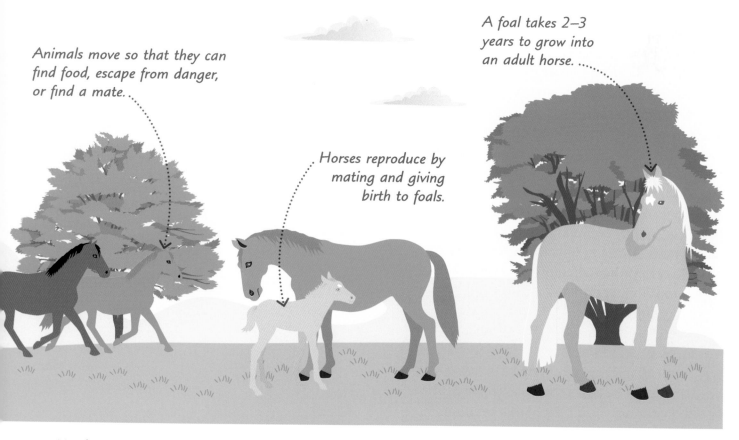

Animals move so that they can find food, escape from danger, or find a mate.

Horses reproduce by mating and giving birth to foals.

A foal takes 2–3 years to grow into an adult horse.

5 Moving
All living things move, though some move so slowly that we hardly notice. Animals move quickly by using their muscles. Plants move by growing—their shoots grow upward to the light and their roots grow down into the soil.

6 Reproducing
All organisms strive to create new organisms by a process called reproduction. Plants, for example, create seeds that grow into new plants. Animals lay eggs or give birth to babies.

7 Growing
Young organisms grow into mature ones, getting larger as they age. Some organisms simply get bigger as they age, but others also change. An acorn, for instance, grows into an oak tree and a caterpillar grows into a butterfly.

Classification

There are nearly two million known species (types of organisms) on Earth. These species are classified into groups based on the common ancestors they share, just like a family tree.

More than 95 percent of animal species are invertebrates.

Divisions of life

Every organism on Earth belongs to one of several major divisions of life, such as the animal kingdom and the plant kingdom.

1 Animal kingdom

Animals are multicellular organisms that eat other organisms. They have sense organs to detect changes in their surroundings, and nervous systems and muscles so they can respond quickly.

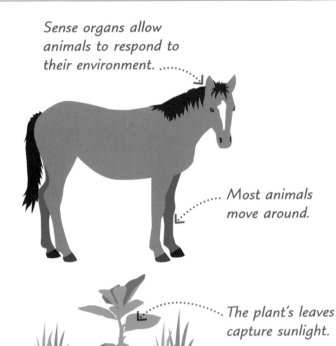

Sense organs allow animals to respond to their environment.

Most animals move around.

2 Plant kingdom

Plants are multicellular organisms that produce food by capturing sunlight. Most plants have leaves to absorb sunlight and roots to anchor them in place and absorb water from the ground.

The plant's leaves capture sunlight.

Roots

3 Fungus kingdom

Fungi absorb food from dead or living organic matter, such as soil, rotting wood, or dead animals. Members of this kingdom include mushrooms, toadstools, and molds.

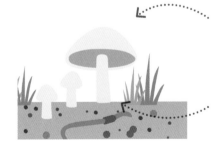

Mushrooms are the reproductive parts of fungi that live in soil.

Fungus

4 Microorganisms

Microorganisms are so tiny they can only be seen with a microscope. Many types consist of just a single cell. Microorganisms can be divided into three kingdoms.

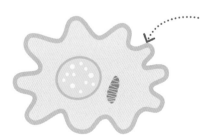

Amoebas are single-celled organisms less than a millimeter wide.

Classifying animals

Earth's animals are divided into two major groups: animals with backbones (vertebrates) and animals without backbones (invertebrates). These are then divided into even more groups.

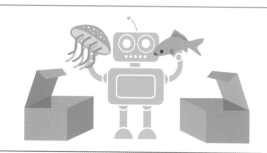

INVERTEBRATES

Sponges
Sponges are simple animals that live on the seabed and filter food from the water.

Flatworms
Flatworms are worms with flat bodies and no segments.

Annelids
Annelids are worms with segmented bodies. Earthworms are annelids.

Echinoderms
Echinoderms are sea creatures such as starfish and sea urchins.

Cnidarians
Cnidarians include jellyfish and anemones. They have stinging tentacles and their bodies are symmetrical.

Arthropods
These creatures have hard, external skeletons. They include insects and spiders.

Mollusks
Most mollusks are soft-bodied animals with a protective shell. Snails are mollusks.

VERTEBRATES

Fish
Fish have gills for breathing and scaly skin. They are cold-blooded, which means their body temperature varies with their surroundings.

Reptiles
These cold-blooded creatures have dry, scaly skin and most lay eggs on land.

Mammals
Mammals are warm-blooded animals with fur or hair. They feed their young with milk.

Amphibians
These cold-blooded animals have moist, slimy skin and most lay eggs in water.

Birds
Birds are warm-blooded, which means they maintain a constant body temperature. They have feathers and most can fly.

Cells

All living things are made up of microscopic units called cells.
The smallest living things have only one cell each, but animals
and plants are made up of millions of cells working together.

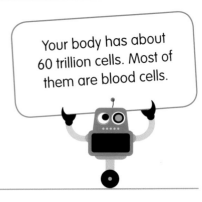

Your body has about
60 trillion cells. Most of
them are blood cells.

Animal cells

Animal cells and plant cells have many features in
common, but animal cells lack a sturdy wall and so are
often irregular in shape. All cells work like miniature
factories, performing hundreds of different tasks every
second of the day. Many of these tasks are carried out
by tiny bodies called organelles inside the cell.

1 Cell membrane
This is the outer barrier of a cell. Like a film of
oil, it stops water from leaking through. However,
tiny gateways allow other substances to cross it.

2 Mitochondria
These are rod-shaped organelles that provide
cells with power. To work, they need a continual
supply of sugar and oxygen.

3 Nucleus
The instructions that tell a
cell how to work and grow are
stored here as molecules of
DNA (deoxyribonucleic acid).

4 Cytoplasm
A jellylike fluid called
cytoplasm fills much of the cell. It
is mostly water but many other
substances are dissolved in it.

5 Endoplasmic reticulum
Large organic molecules
such as proteins and fats are
manufactured on this network
of folded tubes and sacs.

Cell size

Most cells are just a fraction of a millimeter
long. This is too small for the human eye to
see, so scientists use microscopes to study
cells. On average, plant cells are slightly
larger than animal cells.

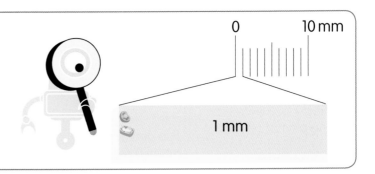

0   10 mm

1 mm

Plant cells

Plant cells have many of the same organelles as animal cells, but they also have a fluid store called a vacuole and bright green organelles called chloroplasts, which capture and store energy from sunlight. Plant cells also have tough outer walls that make them more rigid than animal cells.

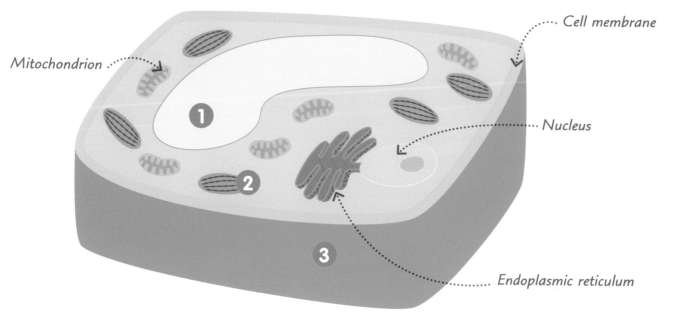

Mitochondrion

Cell membrane

Nucleus

Endoplasmic reticulum

1 A vacuole in the center of the cell stores water. When you water a plant, its vacuoles swell with water, making the plant's stem and leaves sturdy and firm.

2 Chloroplasts use the energy in sunlight to create energy-rich sugar molecules from air and water. This process is called photosynthesis.

3 A cell wall surrounds and supports a plant cell. It is made of a tough, fibrous material called cellulose—the main ingredient in paper, cotton, and wood.

REAL WORLD TECHNOLOGY

Microscopes

Microscopes are viewing devices that make it possible to see tiny objects such as cells. Using a series of curved glass lenses that work like magnifying glasses, they can make objects look hundreds of times bigger. The sample of cells is placed on a thin piece of glass, and a light is shined through this to help make the cells visible.

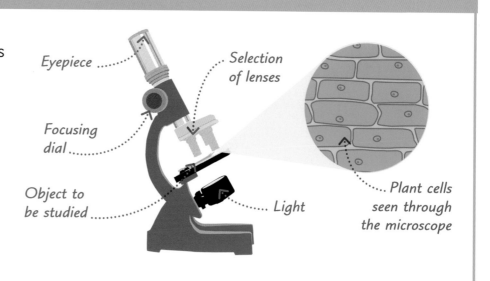

Eyepiece

Selection of lenses

Focusing dial

Object to be studied

Light

Plant cells seen through the microscope

Cells, tissues, and organs

The cells in the human body are joined in groups that work together, known as tissues. Different tissues are joined to form organs, and organs work together in groups called systems.

Types of cells

There are many different shapes and types of cells, each one specialized to do a specific role. Every cell has the same basic structure: an outer coating called a membrane; a jellylike cytoplasm containing many structures called organelles, which bring the cell to life; and a nucleus—the cell's control center.

> Tiny organelles called mitochondria power a cell so it can do its job.

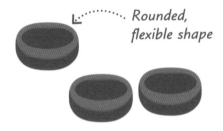

Rounded, flexible shape

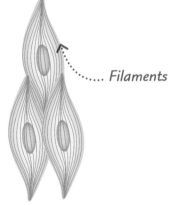

Flexible shape so the cell can engulf germs

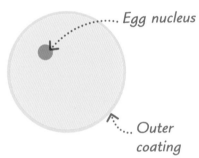

Egg nucleus

Outer coating

1 Red blood cells
These disk-shaped cells are found in the blood. They transport oxygen around the body.

2 White blood cells
White blood cells patrol the body for germs and destroy them.

3 Egg cells
An egg cell is the female sex cell. When fertilized by sperm, it grows into a baby.

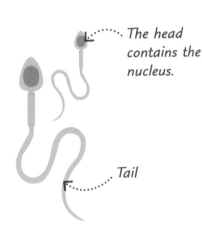

The head contains the nucleus.

Tail

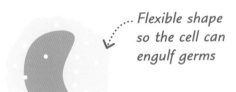

Filaments

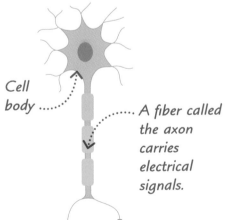

Cell body

A fiber called the axon carries electrical signals.

4 Sperm cells
The male sex cell has a head and a powerful tail so it can swim toward the egg.

5 Muscle cells
Filaments in muscle cells contract to produce movement.

6 Nerve cells
A network of nerve cells form the nervous system. They carry signals around the body.

Tissues

Most cells are joined together in layers to form tissues. Epithelial cells, for instance, are tightly packed together to form a protective wall of tissue that lines the inside of the mouth, stomach, and intestines.

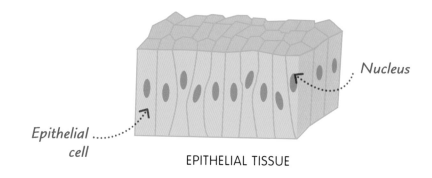

Nucleus

Epithelial cell

EPITHELIAL TISSUE

Organs

Different types of tissue combine to form organs. The stomach is an organ that stores food and digests it. It is lined with epithelial tissue, but its wall also contains muscle tissue and glandular tissue that secretes digestive juices.

HUMAN STOMACH

Outer protective lining (pink)

Muscle tissues (red)

Glandular tissues (brown)

The stomach's inner lining is made up of epithelial tissue.

HUMAN DIGESTIVE SYSTEM

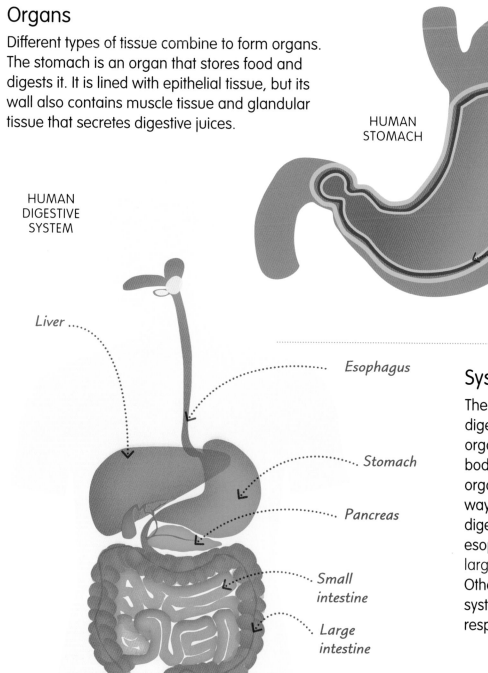

Liver

Esophagus

Stomach

Pancreas

Small intestine

Large intestine

Systems

The stomach is just one organ in the digestive system—the collection of organs that break down food so the body can absorb it. Groups of organs that work together in this way are called organ systems. The digestive system includes the esophagus, stomach, small and large intestines, liver, and pancreas. Other systems include the muscular system, nervous system, and respiratory (breathing) system.

Nutrition

All living things need food. Food contains chemicals called nutrients that provide the body's cells with energy and with essential materials needed for growth and repair.

As well as needing nutrients from food, your body needs a regular supply of water.

Nutrients

There are six main types of nutrients that the human body needs to stay healthy. Three of these—proteins, carbohydrates, and lipids—are needed in larger amounts than the others. Eating a balanced, varied diet is the best way to make sure your body gets all the nutrients and water it needs.

Nuts are a good vegetarian source of protein.

Spaghetti is high in carbohydrates.

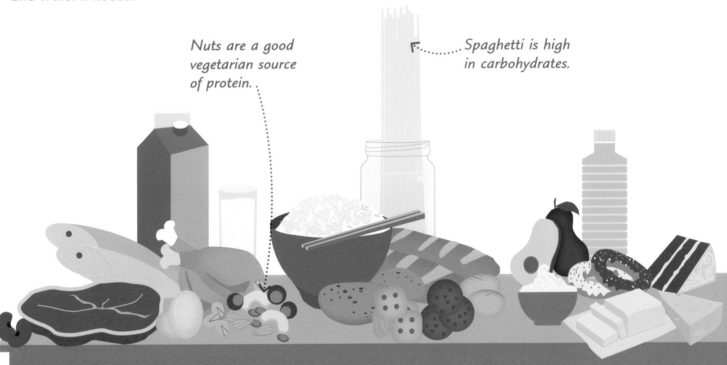

1 Proteins
The body's most important building blocks, proteins are used to build new tissue and to repair existing tissue. Meat, fish, eggs, beans, and nuts are all high in protein.

2 Carbohydrates
These work like fuel and are used in respiration to provide cells with energy. Foods high in carbohydrates include bread, potatoes, rice, pasta, and sugary foods such as honey.

3 Lipids
Fats and oils (lipids) supply large amounts of energy in a form that the body can store. They are also a vital part of all cells. Oil, butter, cheese, and avocados are rich in lipids.

Energy from food

Your body is fueled by the chemical energy in food, just as a car is fueled by gasoline. A banana has enough energy to keep you running for about 12 minutes, but other foods have more energy. If you take in more energy than you use, your body stores energy as fat.

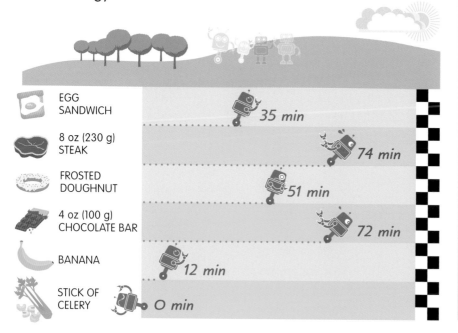

EGG SANDWICH — 35 min

8 oz (230 g) STEAK — 74 min

FROSTED DOUGHNUT — 51 min

4 oz (100 g) CHOCOLATE BAR — 72 min

BANANA — 12 min

STICK OF CELERY — 0 min

Look at the labels

Look at the packaging on different foods—you'll see tables showing the amount of each nutrient and the quantity of energy, measured in kilojoules (kJ). Which foods have the most energy? Which do you think are the most healthy?

Nutrition Information		
Typical values	**Per serving**	**% daily value**
Energy kJ	1,800	22%
Energy kcal	430	20%
Fat	12 g	18%
Carbohydrate	31 g	10%
Protein	7.9 g	53%
Fiber	0 g	0%
Salt	0.5 g	20%

4 Vitamins

Vitamins are organic compounds that the body needs in tiny amounts to stay healthy. Humans need 13 vitamins. Many come from fresh fruit and vegetables.

5 Minerals

Minerals are inorganic chemicals that the body needs in small amounts. Calcium, for instance, is needed to make teeth and bones. Most fresh vegetables are rich in minerals.

6 Fiber

Fiber comes from the cell walls of plants. Most fiber isn't digested, but it helps keep the digestive system healthy. Vegetables and whole-grain foods are rich in fiber.

Human digestive system

Your digestive system helps your body break down
food until the nutrients it contains are small enough
to be absorbed into your bloodstream.

1 Mouth
Inside the mouth, food is mashed into
smaller pieces by the teeth and moistened
by saliva (spit) from the salivary glands.

2 Esophagus
The esophagus connects the mouth to
the stomach. Muscles in its wall alternately
contract (squeeze) and relax to push food
down. This is called peristalsis.

3 Stomach
Inside the stomach, food is
churned up and mixed with stomach
acid. Digestive enzymes start to break
down proteins.

4 Small intestine
This 23-foot- (7-meter-) long tube is
coiled to provide an enormous surface area
for nutrients to be absorbed into the blood.
Enzymes secreted into the small intestine
digest proteins, fats, and carbohydrates.

5 Large intestine
Bacteria in the large intestine feed on
undigested food, releasing more nutrients. Water
is absorbed from the undigested remains, which
leave the body through the anus as feces (poop).

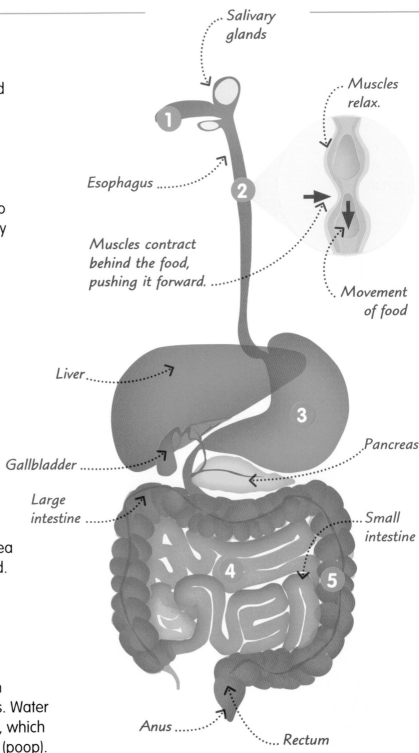

Salivary
glands

Muscles
relax.

Esophagus

Muscles contract
behind the food,
pushing it forward.

Movement
of food

Liver

Pancreas

Gallbladder

Large
intestine

Small
intestine

Anus

Rectum

Model intestines

You can make a model of the intestines using an old pair of tights, orange juice, crackers, a banana, and scissors. Be sure to do this activity over a tray, since it gets a bit messy.

1 Put one banana and five crackers into a bowl, then pour in one cup of orange juice. Mash them into a pulp.

2 Spoon the mixture into one leg of an old pair of tights. Holding the tights over a tray, squeeze the food along. The juice will seep out of the tights, just as the nutrients pass into the blood through the intestinal wall.

3 Keep pushing the food through the tights until the undigested remains get stuck at the end. Using scissors, snip off the toe of the tights, and push the food through the hole.

How enzymes work

Food nutrients are made up of long, chainlike molecules too large for the body to absorb. Chemicals known as enzymes attack the links in these chains, separating the molecules into particles small enough to enter the bloodstream. Each enzyme targets a particular type of food molecule.

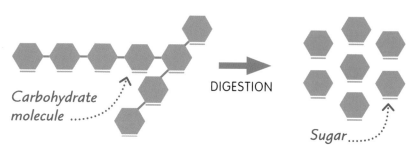

Carbohydrate molecule ......   DIGESTION   *Sugar* ....

1 Carbohydrate molecules
Carbohydrate molecules are broken down into sugars by enzymes, such as amylase, that work in the mouth and small intestine. Bread, pasta, and rice are rich in carbohydrates.

Protein molecule .....   DIGESTION   *Amino acid* ....

2 Protein molecules
Protease enzymes working in the stomach and small intestine break down protein molecules into amino acids. Protein is found in foods such as meat and cheese.

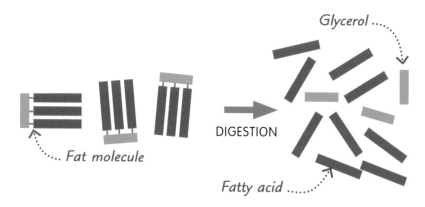

Glycerol ....   DIGESTION   *Fat molecule*   *Fatty acid* ....

3 Fat molecules
Bile, a digestive juice made by the liver, turns fats into small droplets. These droplets are then broken down into fatty acids and glycerol by lipase enzymes working in the small intestine.

Teeth

Animals use their teeth, set inside their jaws, to help break down food. Muscles allow their jaws to bite and chew, while teeth provide the hard edges to slice, tear, or grind food.

Teeth are coated in enamel, which is the hardest substance in the human body.

Human teeth

Teeth with different shapes perform different jobs. Humans are omnivores, which means we eat a variety of foods, including plants and animals, so our teeth are not specialized for one type of diet.

1 Molars
Flat-topped teeth in the cheeks have ridges, or cusps, and are used to crunch and grind food.

2 Premolars
Premolars help the larger molars grind food into a paste.

3 Canines
Pointed canine teeth grip, bite, and tear food into smaller shreds.

4 Incisors
Chisel-like incisors are at the front of the mouth, and are used for nibbling and cutting food.

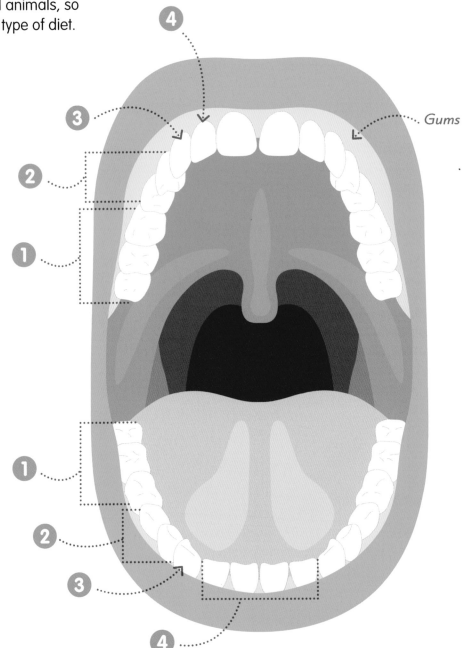

Gums

Carnivore teeth

Carnivores, such as cats and dogs, eat meat. This means they need teeth that can kill their prey and cut it into pieces.

1 Canines for grabbing
Extra-big, daggerlike canines grab and stab prey. They pierce flesh, helping the carnivore to both kill their prey and eat the meat.

2 Molars for slicing
Carnivores' molars have sharp, knifelike edges that slice meat. They are strong with deep roots to crunch through bones.

DOG SKULL

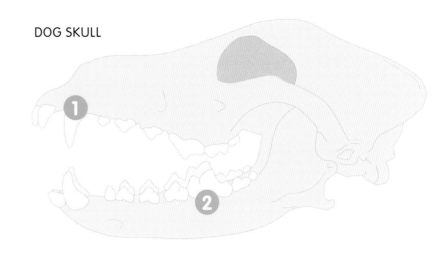

Herbivore teeth

Herbivores, such as rabbits and horses, eat plants. This means they need teeth that can cut and chew vegetation.

1 Incisors for grazing
Long, sharp incisors at the front of the mouth cut through vegetation. Canines aren't needed for eating plants, so some herbivores don't have them.

2 Molars for grinding
Vegetation is much tougher than meat, so herbivores' molars have rough surfaces with sharp ridges that grind down vegetation.

HORSE SKULL

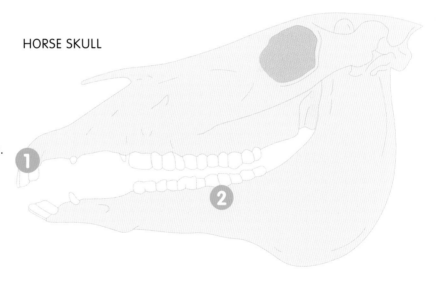

REAL WORLD TECHNOLOGY

Dental implants

If a person loses an adult tooth, a dental implant can be used to help replace the tooth. An implant is an artificial titanium tooth root. It is placed into the jawbone, below the gums, with a connector on top, so that the dentist can attach a replacement tooth to it.

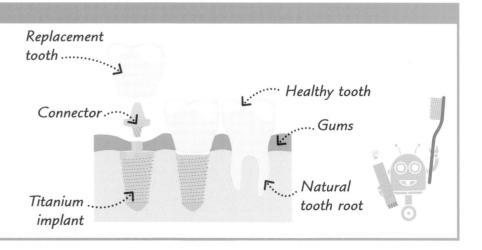

Replacement tooth
Connector
Healthy tooth
Gums
Titanium implant
Natural tooth root

Respiration

All living cells need energy. They obtain it using the process of respiration, which releases the chemical energy stored in food molecules and turns it into a form cells can use.

Running makes your body require more oxygen, so you breathe deeper and faster.

Aerobic respiration

Most organisms use oxygen to release energy. This is called aerobic respiration. Living cells need a continuous supply of oxygen to stay alive, but extra oxygen is needed when animals are more active.

1 Getting oxygen
The human body gets the oxygen it requires by breathing air into the lungs through the nose and mouth.

2 Inside the lungs
Oxygen is transferred from the lungs into the blood. Carbon dioxide, the waste product of respiration, is transferred from the blood into the lungs to be breathed out.

3 Through the blood
Oxygen is carried around the body by hemoglobin in the blood. Hemoglobin is a bright red substance that gives blood its color.

4 Muscle cells
Inside muscle cells, a chemical reaction turns glucose (sugar molecules from food) and oxygen into water and carbon dioxide, releasing the energy that powers muscle contraction.

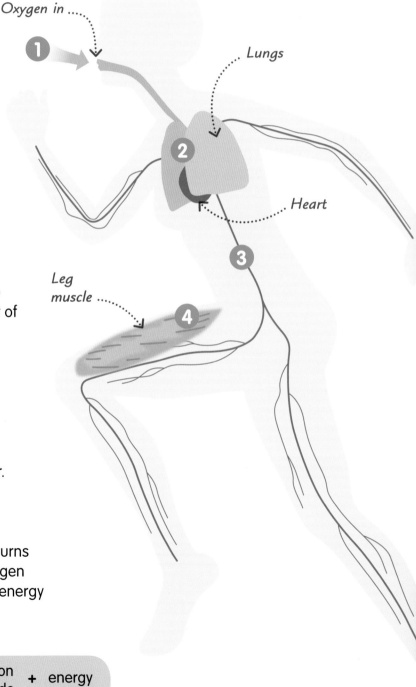

Oxygen in ......

Lungs

Heart

Leg muscle ......

glucose + oxygen → water + carbon dioxide + energy

Anaerobic respiration

If a cell cannot get enough oxygen for aerobic respiration, it switches to anaerobic respiration (meaning "without air"). Anaerobic respiration releases less energy than aerobic respiration. In the human body, it creates a waste product called lactic acid, which builds up during exercise. Microorganisms such as yeast use anaerobic respiration in places where there is no oxygen—for example, inside rotting fruit.

Rotting fruit

Gas exchange

All living organisms have gas exchange surfaces, which let oxygen enter the body and waste carbon dioxide leave. To help the gases enter and leave the body, gas exchange surfaces have a large surface area and thin walls. Insect tracheae (tubes that hold air), fish gills, and mammal lungs are examples of gas exchange surfaces.

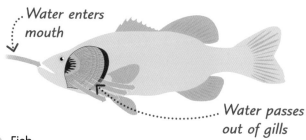
Water enters mouth
Water passes out of gills

3 Fish
Oxygen-rich water enters a fish's mouth and passes over its gills. The gills contain filaments full of tiny blood vessels that absorb oxygen.

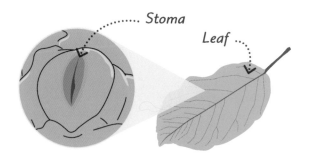
Stoma
Leaf

1 Plants
The undersides of plant leaves have thousands of tiny openings called stomata. Each stoma can open and close to let gases pass in and out of the leaf.

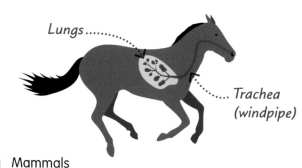
Lungs
Trachea (windpipe)

4 Mammals
When mammals breathe, they inhale, filling their lungs with oxygen-rich air, and then exhale, removing waste carbon dioxide.

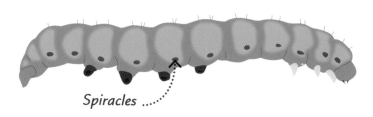
Spiracles

2 Insects
Tiny holes called spiracles in an insect's body let it take in air. The holes lead to a network of tubes called tracheae, which run throughout the body.

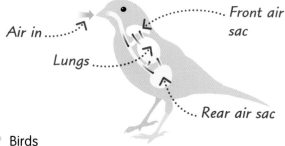
Air in
Front air sac
Lungs
Rear air sac

5 Birds
In birds, air travels through the lungs in one direction only. It moves between various air sacs that are connected to different parts of the body.

Lungs and breathing

The cells in your body need a continual supply of oxygen to stay alive. Your lungs take in air with every breath, bringing oxygen to your blood so that it can be transported around the body.

There are around 480 million air sacs (alveoli) inside your lungs.

Breathing in

1 The diaphragm is a large muscle between the chest and stomach. It flattens and moves down, while muscles between the ribs pull the rib cage up. These movements make the lungs expand.

2 Air is sucked in through the nose and mouth and passes down the trachea, or windpipe, into the lungs.

3 The trachea branches out into thousands of small tubes, known as bronchioles, which end in tiny sacs called alveoli. The alveoli fill with air.

4 Oxygen moves through the walls of the alveoli into the blood by diffusion, and waste carbon dioxide diffuses from the blood into the air to be breathed out. There are millions of alveoli, providing a huge surface area for gas exchange.

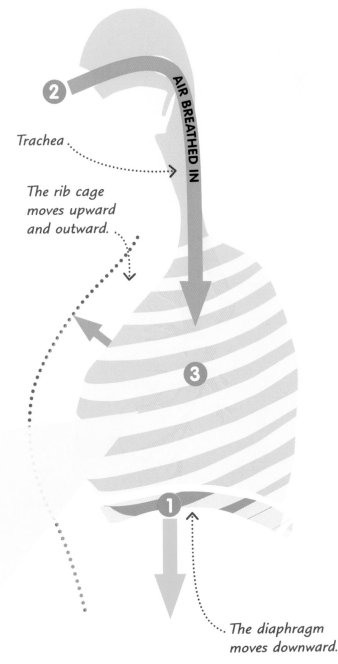

AIR BREATHED IN

Trachea

The rib cage moves upward and outward.

The diaphragm moves downward.

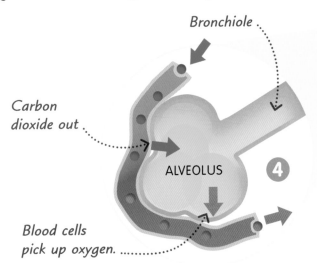

Bronchiole

Carbon dioxide out

ALVEOLUS

Blood cells pick up oxygen.

Asthma

If a person has asthma, the muscles in their bronchiole walls sometimes contract and become inflamed (swollen). The bronchioles narrow and it becomes harder for the person to breathe.

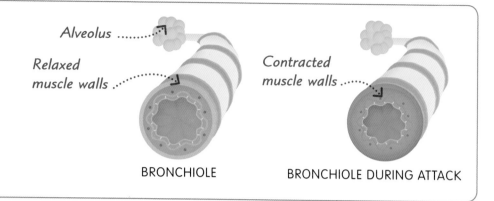

Alveolus

Relaxed muscle walls

Contracted muscle walls

BRONCHIOLE

BRONCHIOLE DURING ATTACK

Breathing out

1 The diaphragm springs back into its natural arched shape, squeezing the lungs.

2 The rib cage moves down, which also squeezes the lungs.

3 The air inside the lungs is pushed up through the bronchioles and trachea and leaves the body through the nose and mouth.

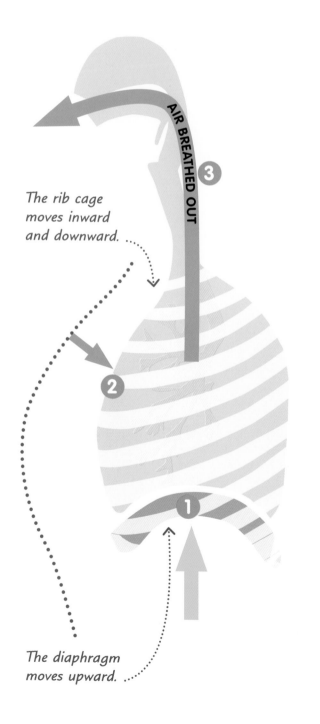

AIR BREATHED OUT

3

The rib cage moves inward and downward.

2

1

The diaphragm moves upward.

TRY IT OUT

Measure your lung capacity

Fill a plastic water bottle and place it upside down in a bowl of water with its neck underwater. Remove the cap and put a long flexible straw into the neck. Now take a deep breath and blow into the straw for as long as you can. The volume of air that collects in the bottle shows your lung capacity.

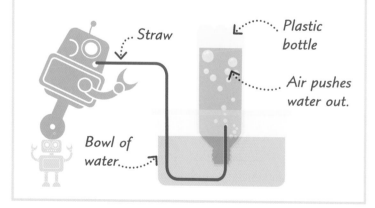

Straw

Plastic bottle

Air pushes water out.

Bowl of water

Blood

Blood is a liquid that flows around the bodies of animals, delivering oxygen and nutrients and carrying away wastes. Pumped by the heart, it flows through a vast network of tubes that reach every part of the body.

Blood transport system

All large animals use blood as their transport system for oxygen, nutrients, and waste. Tubes called blood vessels allow blood to flow around the body. A muscular heart pumps regularly to keep the blood flowing through these vessels in one direction.

Blood returns to the heart through veins.

Blood leaves the heart through arteries.

The heart pumps to keep blood flowing.

1 Heart
The heart contains blood-filled chambers. Each chamber's walls are packed with muscles. As the muscles contract, they squeeze the chamber, pushing blood to the rest of the body.

2 Arteries
Strong vessels leading away from the heart are called arteries. They carry blood to the body's tissues. Arteries have thick walls because the blood inside is at high pressure.

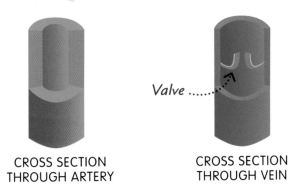

Valve

CROSS SECTION
THROUGH ARTERY

CROSS SECTION
THROUGH VEIN

3 Capillaries
Inside the tissues, the arteries split into billions of microscopic, thin-walled vessels called capillaries. Nutrients, oxygen, and waste pass from the blood into the tissue cells by diffusion.

4 Veins
Veins take blood back to the heart. They have valves to stop blood from flowing backward. Their walls are thinner than artery walls since the blood inside is at a lower pressure.

How blood works

Blood is a living liquid made of billions of tiny cells. It has four components: red blood cells, white blood cells, platelets, and plasma. Each component has a different function.

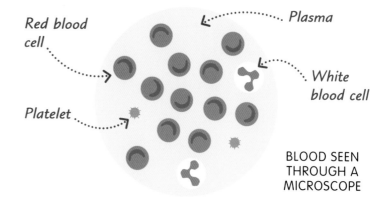

Red blood cell

Plasma

Platelet

White blood cell

BLOOD SEEN THROUGH A MICROSCOPE

1 Red blood cells are the most numerous in blood. They contain hemoglobin, which carries oxygen collected from the lungs. They have no nuclei.

2 White blood cells are larger than red blood cells. They don't transport substances. Instead, they protect the body from infection by killing germs.

3 Platelets are cell fragments that become spiky to stop bleeding after injury. They help blood leaking from a vessel to clot (thicken).

4 Plasma is a pale yellow liquid, mostly made of water. It carries dissolved nutrients and waste products, such as carbon dioxide, around the body.

Diffusion

Capillaries carry oxygen and nutrients in the blood to every cell in the body. These substances move into the cells by diffusion—a process that lets a substance spread from an area of high concentration to an area of low concentration. Waste products, such as carbon dioxide, pass in the opposite direction. Capillary walls are just one cell thick, so the diffusion distance is very short.

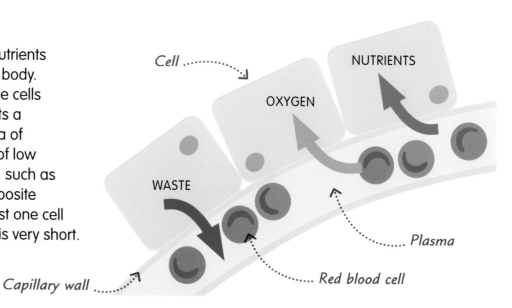

Cell

NUTRIENTS

OXYGEN

WASTE

Plasma

Red blood cell

Capillary wall

Blood transfusions

A blood transfusion is when blood from a healthy person (donor) is given to a person who is ill or seriously injured. Blood is taken through a plastic tube inserted into a vein in the donor's arm. Before it is given to the patient, it is tested to make sure it matches the patient's blood type.

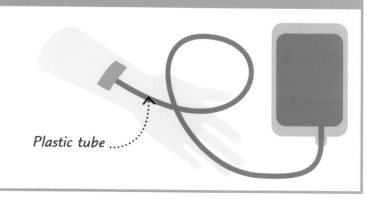

Plastic tube

The heart

The heart is a strong, muscular pump that keeps blood flowing around the body. Unlike other muscles, your heart works nonstop, beating constantly throughout your life.

The sound of a heartbeat is caused by the valves inside the heart snapping shut.

Inside the heart

There are four chambers inside the heart—two at the top, called atria, and two at the bottom, known as ventricles. Each time the heart relaxes, the atria and ventricles fill with blood. When the heart contracts (squeezes), the blood is forced out. Flaps called valves open and close with each heartbeat to keep the blood flowing in the right direction.

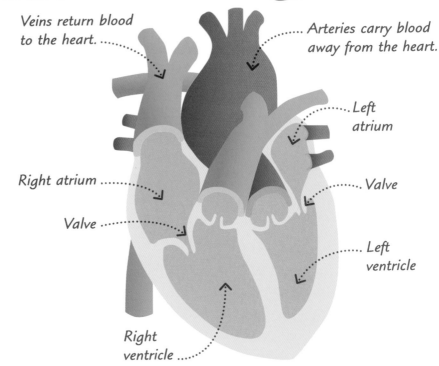

Veins return blood to the heart.

Arteries carry blood away from the heart.

Left atrium

Right atrium

Valve

Valve

Left ventricle

Right ventricle

Stages of a heartbeat

The heart beats tirelessly—70 times in a minute and 40 million times in a year. Each heartbeat is a carefully timed sequence of steps.

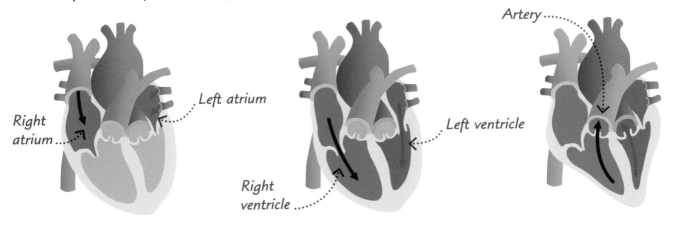

Right atrium

Left atrium

Right ventricle

Left ventricle

Artery

1 When the heart relaxes, blood from the veins fills its top two chambers (atria).

2 The atrium walls contract, squeezing blood into the two lower chambers (ventricles).

3 The ventricle walls contract, pumping blood out of the heart to the arteries.

Double circulation system

The left and right sides of the heart pump blood through two different routes. One route takes blood to the lungs to collect oxygen, and the other takes blood to the rest of the body to deliver oxygen to the body's organs.

1 The right side of the heart pumps blood to the lungs, where the blood picks up oxygen from the air and releases the waste gas carbon dioxide.

2 The oxygen-rich blood, shown here in red, returns to the left side of the heart.

3 The blood is then pumped to the rest of the body's organs to deliver vital oxygen and pick up carbon dioxide.

4 Now low in oxygen, the used blood returns to the heart and the cycle begins again.

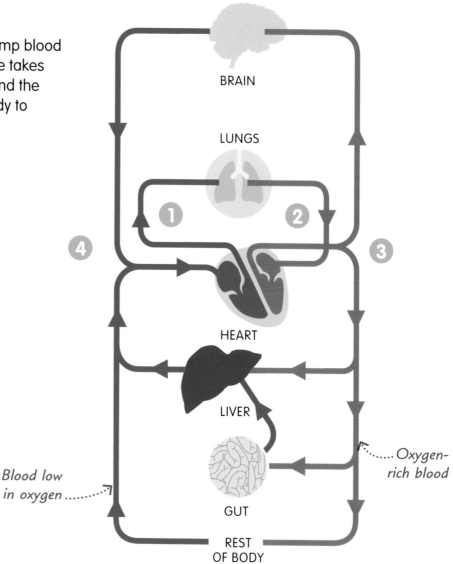

BRAIN

LUNGS

HEART

LIVER

GUT

REST OF BODY

Blood low in oxygen

Oxygen-rich blood

REAL WORLD TECHNOLOGY

Repairing the heart

If a person has an unhealthy diet, fat can build up in the coronary arteries that supply blood to the heart's own muscle. The arteries become narrow and stop working properly. In some cases, the artery is repaired by inserting a metal tube called a stent to widen the narrowed artery.

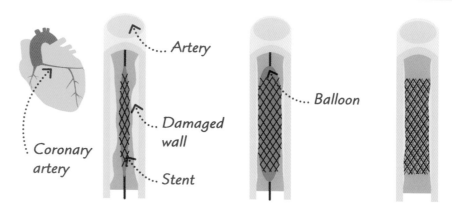

Coronary artery

Artery

Damaged wall

Stent

Balloon

1 The stent is inserted into the damaged artery. Inside the stent is a balloon.

2 The balloon is inflated. This opens up the stent and widens the faulty artery.

3 The balloon is removed and the stent is left in place. Blood can now flow freely.

Excretion

Many of the processes that happen in living cells produce waste chemicals. Removing these unwanted chemicals from the body is called excretion.

Excretion in humans

The most important organs of excretion in the human body are the kidneys. However, several other organs play an important role in excretion too.

1 Skin
Sweat secreted by skin serves mainly to cool the body down, but it also removes water and salts from the body.

2 Lungs
The gas carbon dioxide is a waste product of respiration. It is carried to the lungs by the blood and breathed out.

3 Liver
The liver breaks down excess proteins, producing a nitrogen-rich waste chemical called urea. It also breaks down old blood cells to make a waste called bile.

4 Kidneys
The kidneys filter urea, excess water, and many other wastes out of the blood to create a liquid called urine.

5 Bladder
The bladder stores urine from the kidneys and expands as it fills. When it's full, nerve endings in its wall trigger the urge to urinate.

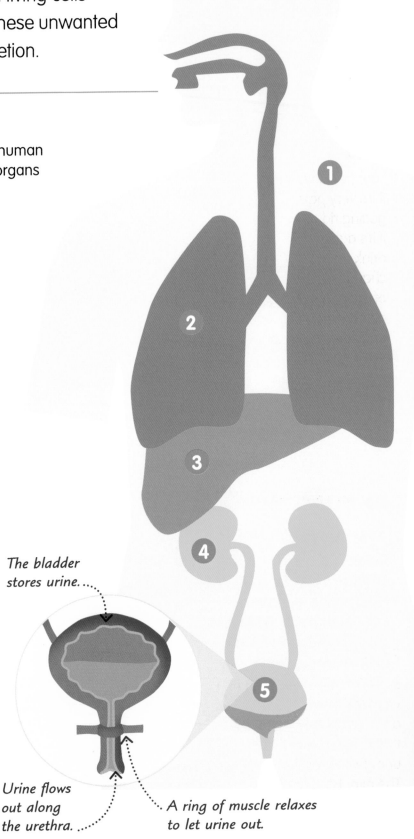

The bladder stores urine.

Urine flows out along the urethra.

A ring of muscle relaxes to let urine out.

Color test

Your pee says a lot about you.
If it's very pale, your body is
getting rid of excess water.
If it's dark, you may need to
drink more water. Some foods
change the color or smell
of urine. Try eating beets,
blackberries, and asparagus
and see what happens!

Excretion in plants

Plants excrete waste chemicals through their leaves. Waste
carbon dioxide from respiration is released into the air or used
up in photosynthesis. Other wastes are stored inside cells until
the leaves die and fall off the plant.

NIGHT   DAY

At night, plants
excrete waste carbon
dioxide from
respiration. ···· CO_2

O_2 CO_2 O_2

···· In the daytime
they excrete waste
oxygen from
photosynthesis.

···· Salt glands

···· Ducts

···· Nostril

Salt glands

Seawater is too salty for us to drink, but some
animals can drink it thanks to special organs that
secrete salt. Seabirds have salt glands that filter the
blood and remove excess salt from seawater. The
waste trickles out of their nostrils as a salty liquid.
Sea turtles secrete salt in their tears.

Egestion

Excretion means getting rid of chemical
wastes that come from living cells. Many
animals also have to get rid of wastes
that are not from cells, such as feces—
undigested food from the intestines.
The expulsion of feces from the body
is called egestion, not excretion.

Feces ····

Fighting infections

The human body is under continual attack from harmful microorganisms (germs). The immune system identifies these invaders, destroys them, and remembers them for the future.

> Some diseases, such as asthma, are caused by the immune system overreacting.

Building immunity

Each time the body encounters a new germ, it learns how to attack it swiftly. This gives long-lasting immunity.

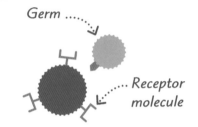

Germ ....

Receptor molecule

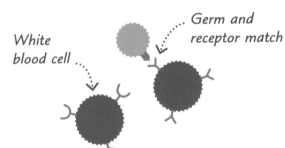

White blood cell ....

Germ and receptor match

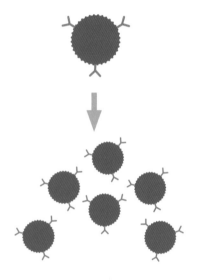

1 Some germs spread from person to person in the air. When breathed in, these germs may get into the bloodstream or other body fluids.

2 White blood cells try to lock on to the germs with a wide range of different receptor molecules on their surface. Eventually a match is found.

3 Triggered by the match, the successful white blood cell divides to make thousands of new cells, all with matching receptor molecules.

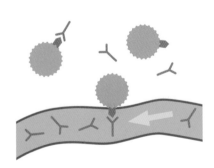

Phagocyte

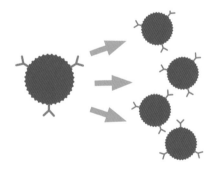

4 The new cells release their receptor molecules in huge amounts. The molecules, called antibodies, travel throughout the body and cling to germs.

5 The antibodies act as beacons to another kind of white blood cell, called a phagocyte. Phagocytes swallow and destroy the germs.

6 The blood cell that detected the germ also makes memory cells. These stay in the body for years, ready to mount a faster attack if the germ returns.

Body barriers

The first lines of defense against most germs are physical and chemical barriers that stop germs from entering the body's soft internal tissues.

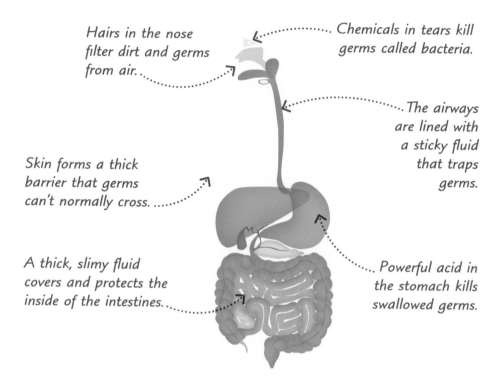

Hairs in the nose filter dirt and germs from air.

Chemicals in tears kill germs called bacteria.

The airways are lined with a sticky fluid that traps germs.

Skin forms a thick barrier that germs can't normally cross.

A thick, slimy fluid covers and protects the inside of the intestines.

Powerful acid in the stomach kills swallowed germs.

REAL WORLD TECHNOLOGY

Vaccines

Vaccines make people immune to diseases. They are created from germs that have been modified to make them harmless. When injected into the body, the modified germs trigger white blood cells to produce antibodies and remember the germs.

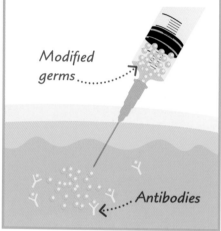

Modified germs

Antibodies

Inflammation

If your skin is injured, germs can get in. To block their path, the area around the wound becomes swollen, painful, and red. This is called inflammation.

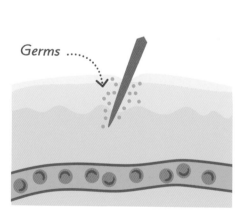

Germs

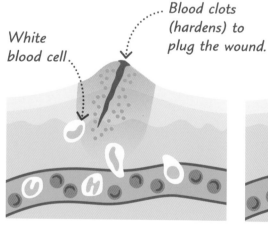

White blood cell

Blood clots (hardens) to plug the wound.

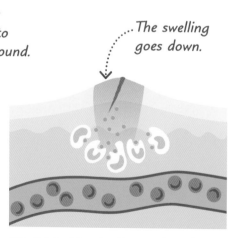

The swelling goes down.

1 A sharp object pierces the skin, allowing germs in. Damaged cells around the wound release chemicals that trigger inflammation.

2 Nearby blood vessels widen, making the skin red. They let fluid leak out, causing swelling, and white blood cells invade the damaged area.

3 White blood cells attack and consume the germs. The damaged tissue begins to heal and the swelling goes down.

Sensing and responding

To survive, organisms must sense their surroundings and respond to food or danger. Animals sense and respond faster than plants thanks to their nervous system and muscles.

> The human nervous system carries messages at speeds of up to 220 mph (360 km/h).

Staying alive

The brain is the control center of an animal's nervous system. It decides how the animal will respond to changes in its surroundings through a five-step process.

The rabbit's brain receives and processes information about the stimulus.

... The fox is a stimulus for the rabbit.

1 Stimulus
A stimulus is any change in the surroundings that triggers a response in an organism. The sight and smell of a predator, such as a fox, is a powerful stimulus for a rabbit.

2 Receptors
The rabbit has different receptors (such as eyes, nose, and ears) to detect different types of stimulus. Its receptors gather information, which is then sent to the brain.

3 Control center
The rabbit's brain processes the information from the receptors. It recognizes the fox as a danger and decides how the rabbit should respond.

How plants sense and respond

Plants can detect light or water, but they don't have a nervous system or muscles to help them respond quickly. Instead, they respond very slowly over time in the way that they grow.

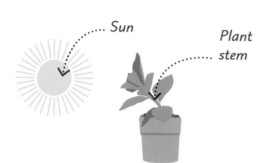

Sun
Plant stem

Tendrils

Seed
Root

1 Light
Light is a stimulus for the stems of plants. One side of the stem grows faster than the other, making it bend toward the light.

2 Touch
When the tendrils or stems of climbing plants touch something, they respond by bending. This makes them wrap around a support as they grow.

3 Gravity
Plant roots sense gravity and respond by growing down into the soil. Whichever way up a seed is when it sprouts, its root will bend to grow down.

Nerve

Messages travel from the brain to the muscles via nerves.

4 Effectors
The rabbit's brain sends messages to organs called effectors—the parts of the body, such as muscles, that will produce a response. The brain tells the rabbit's leg muscles to contract.

5 Response
Within a split second of seeing the fox, the rabbit bolts and disappears into its burrow, where the fox cannot reach it.

TRY IT OUT

Sensitive skin

Some parts of human skin are more sensitive than other parts. These extra-sensitive parts contain more touch receptors (nerve cells that detect touch). Try touching a fingertip with both ends of a hairpin or paper clip held close together. Does it feel like one object or two? Try other parts of your skin. The parts where you feel both ends are where you have the most touch receptors.

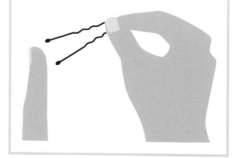

Human nervous system

The nervous system is your body's control network—an intricate web of billions of nerve cells that carry high-speed electrical signals between your brain and the rest of your body.

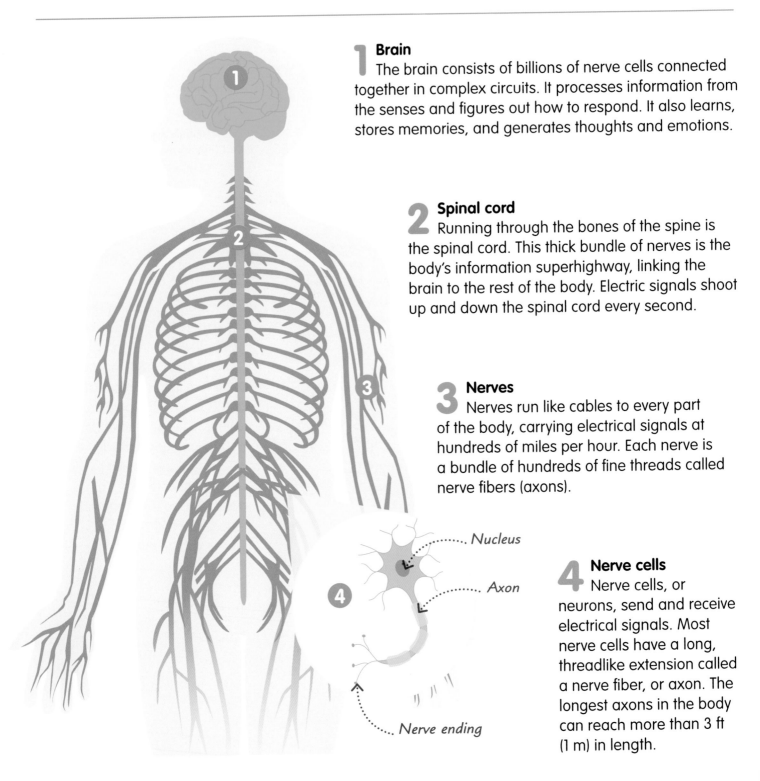

1 Brain
The brain consists of billions of nerve cells connected together in complex circuits. It processes information from the senses and figures out how to respond. It also learns, stores memories, and generates thoughts and emotions.

2 Spinal cord
Running through the bones of the spine is the spinal cord. This thick bundle of nerves is the body's information superhighway, linking the brain to the rest of the body. Electric signals shoot up and down the spinal cord every second.

3 Nerves
Nerves run like cables to every part of the body, carrying electrical signals at hundreds of miles per hour. Each nerve is a bundle of hundreds of fine threads called nerve fibers (axons).

Nucleus

Axon

Nerve ending

4 Nerve cells
Nerve cells, or neurons, send and receive electrical signals. Most nerve cells have a long, threadlike extension called a nerve fiber, or axon. The longest axons in the body can reach more than 3 ft (1 m) in length.

Sending nerve signals

Neurons meet each other at junctions called synapses. A synapse contains a tiny gap that stops an electrical signal from passing directly from one cell to another. Instead, chemicals called neurotransmitters carry the signals across the gaps.

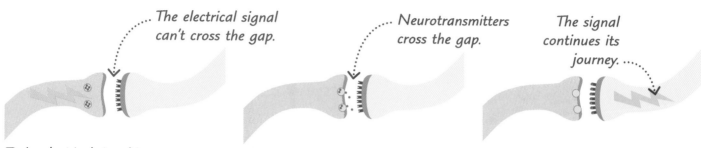

The electrical signal can't cross the gap.

Neurotransmitters cross the gap.

The signal continues its journey.

1 An electrical signal (a nerve impulse) travels along a neuron until it reaches the end of the cell.

2 The signal triggers the release of a neurotransmitter from tiny stores at the end of the nerve cell.

3 The chemicals bind to receptors on the next cell, triggering a new electrical signal.

Cerebral cortex

The outermost part of the brain is called the cerebral cortex. Humans have an unusually large cerebral cortex. Deep grooves divide it into areas called lobes. Some mental tasks, such as processing language, are concentrated in specific lobes. However, most mental tasks involve many parts of the brain working together in ways that are not yet understood.

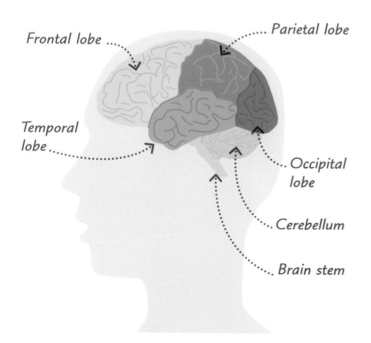

Frontal lobe

Parietal lobe

Temporal lobe

Occipital lobe

Cerebellum

Brain stem

REAL WORLD TECHNOLOGY

Prosthetic arm

An artificial replacement for a missing limb is called a prosthesis. Modern prosthetic arms have sensors that pick up nerve signals in muscles, allowing the user to move the mechanical hand by thought.

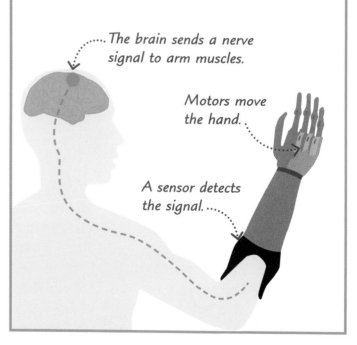

The brain sends a nerve signal to arm muscles.

Motors move the hand.

A sensor detects the signal.

The human eye

Eyes are the sense organs that allow us to see the world. Stimulated by light, they send nerve signals to your brain, where the information is processed into images.

> Your brain combines the images from both eyes to create 3D vision.

How the eye works

Your eye works like a camera, focusing the light rays until a clear image is made. Light reaches your eye directly from a light source, such as the sun or a light bulb. But it can also come from light reflecting (bouncing) off an object.

The retina is the inner lining of the eyeball.

Iris

Lens

1

2

3

Pupil

Cornea

This muscle controls the shape of the lens to focus on near and far objects.

The outer, white layer of the eye is called the sclera.

1 Letting in the light
Light enters the eye through the clear front part of the eye called the cornea. Here, the rays are slightly bent before passing through the pupil, a hole in the middle of the iris.

2 Focusing the light
Eye muscles automatically change the shape of the lens to focus the light rays. These fall on the retina at the back of the eye, where a clear but upside-down image is formed.

3 Detecting the light
There are millions of light-sensitive cells at the back of the retina: cone cells that detect color in bright light, and rod cells that enable you to see in dim light.

Focusing

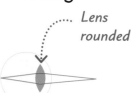

Lens rounded

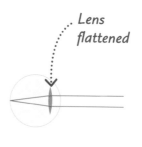

Lens flattened

1 Near vision
When you look at nearby objects, muscles around the lens contract, making the lenses fatter and increasing their focusing power. Distant objects become blurred.

2 Distant vision
When you look at distant objects, the muscles relax and the lenses get flatter. Distant objects become sharp and nearby objects become blurred.

The iris reflex

The iris (the colored part of your eye) controls how much light enters the eye by making the pupil smaller or bigger. In bright light the pupil gets smaller and in dim light it gets bigger.

EYE IN VERY
BRIGHT LIGHT

EYE IN VERY
DIM LIGHT

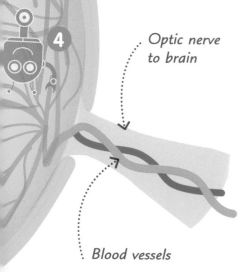

Optic nerve to brain

Blood vessels

4 **Forming an image**
The retina converts the light rays into nerve impulses. These then travel along the optic nerve to the brain, where they are processed into a detailed, upright image of the object.

REAL WORLD TECHNOLOGY

Glasses and contact lenses

In some people, the eyes do not properly focus light rays on their retinas, so they see a blurry view of the world. Glasses and contact lenses correct the work of the natural lens by bending the light rays when they enter the eye.

If you're near-sighted, rays from a distant object fall short of the retina.

NEAR-SIGHTED

A lens that curves inward corrects near-sightedness.

If you're far-sighted, rays from a near object focus beyond the retina.

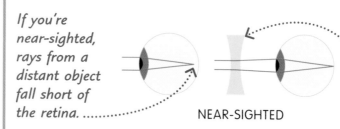

FAR-SIGHTED

A lens that curves outward corrects far-sightedness.

The human ear

Your ears are your body's organs of hearing. They detect sound waves traveling in the air and then send nerve signals to your brain, which creates the sense of hearing.

The human ear has three zones: the outer ear, which is the largest, the middle ear, and the inner ear.

How the ear works

Sound waves are given off by objects when they vibrate (move rapidly back and forth). These waves travel through air to your ear, where they are turned back into vibrations and then into waves traveling though liquid.

1 Outer ear
The outer ear collects sound waves and funnels them toward the eardrum—a thin flap of skin that vibrates when sound hits it.

2 Middle ear
Vibrations from the eardrum pass through three tiny bones in the middle ear. Called ossicles, they pivot back and forth like levers. They amplify sound (make it stronger) and pass the vibrations to the inner ear.

3 Inner ear
The sound now travels as waves through the fluid inside the inner ear. The waves enter a snail-shaped tube, called the cochlea, which is filled with tiny hairlike cells that can detect movement.

4 Messaging the brain
Sound waves inside the cochlea bend the hair cells by different amounts. These patterns of movements are sent as nerve signals to the brain.

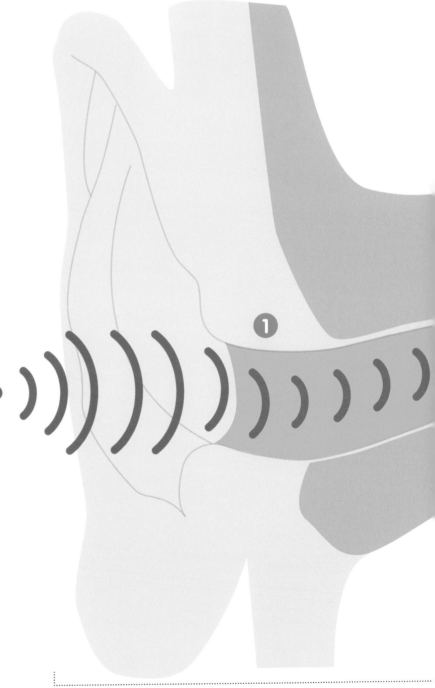

OUTER EAR

Detecting pitch

Our ears can hear whether sounds are deep or high because hair cells in different parts of the cochlea sense different pitches. Deep sounds like thunder are detected in the cochlea's center, while high sounds like birdsong are detected near its entrance.

Sense of balance

Ears give us a sense of balance. When you move your head, it causes fluid to slosh around inside a complex set of tubes and chambers next to the cochlea. The moving fluid triggers motion sensors, which send signals to the brain, telling the brain the head's position and movement.

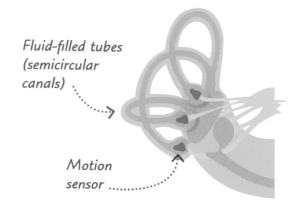

Fluid-filled tubes (semicircular canals)

Motion sensor

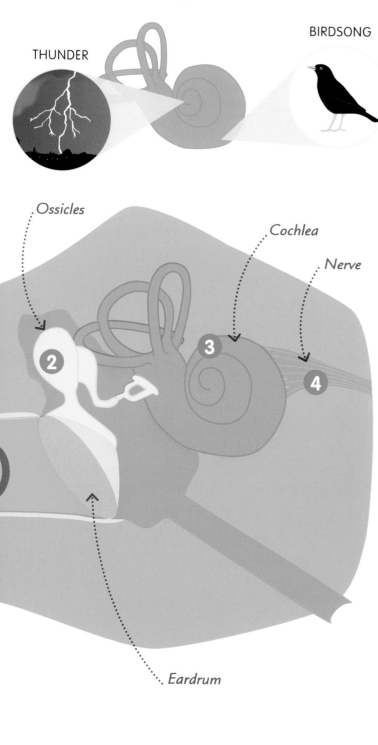

THUNDER

BIRDSONG

Ossicles

Cochlea

Nerve

2

3

4

Eardrum

MIDDLE EAR   INNER EAR

Cochlear implant

Cochlear implants are electronic devices that can restore hearing in deaf people. A microphone picks up sound and transmits a radio signal to a receiver surgically placed under the skin. The receiver sends electric signals along a wire to electrodes implanted in the cochlea, stimulating the hair cells.

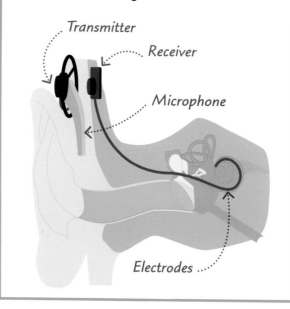

Transmitter

Receiver

Microphone

Electrodes

How animals move

All living things can move, but animals move more than plants. This is because animals have muscles and a nervous system, which control bigger, faster movements.

Animals need to move around to find food and mates, or to escape danger.

Movement in animals

Animals move by contracting their muscles. When muscles contract, they pull on parts of the body, helping the animal change position or move from one place to another. Moving uses energy, and this energy comes from respiration. Some animals have muscles that can contract very fast, which means they can move really quickly.

Circular muscles contract, pushing the front part of the body forward.

Other muscles make the worm bunch up, pulling the rest of the body behind.

1 Swimming
A fish swims by contracting strong muscles in the sides of its body. These make the body bend from side to side, helping the fish move through the water with its tail, while the fins keep its body balanced.

2 Wrigglers and burrowers
Many soft-bodied animals are packed with lots of muscles to help them move. Although earthworms move forward quite slowly, their muscles give them enough strength to push through soil, creating a burrow as they push forward.

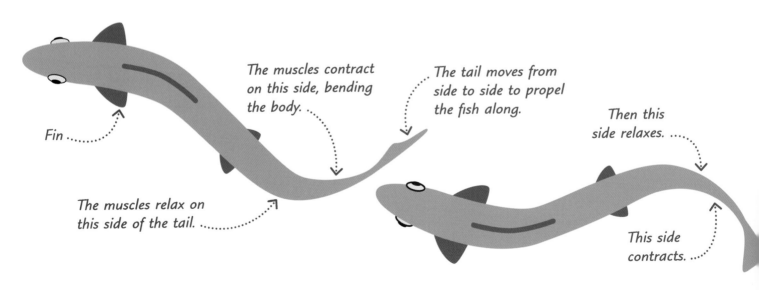

Fin

The muscles contract on this side, bending the body.

The tail moves from side to side to propel the fish along.

Then this side relaxes.

The muscles relax on this side of the tail.

This side contracts.

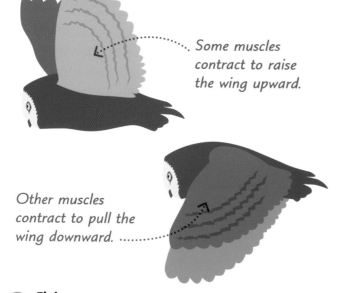

Some muscles contract to raise the wing upward.

Other muscles contract to pull the wing downward.

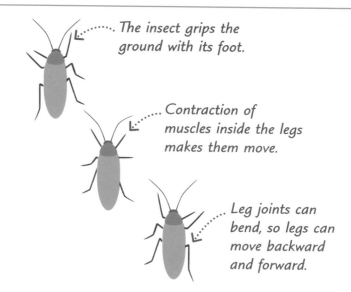

The insect grips the ground with its foot.

Contraction of muscles inside the legs makes them move.

Leg joints can bend, so legs can move backward and forward.

3 Flying

Animals that fly have strong muscles that move their wings up and down. Insects have wings on their back that are separate from their limbs. But birds use their front "arms" as wings for flying.

4 Walking and running

Animals that have legs use them to walk, run, burrow, climb, or even swim. Insects, spiders, lizards, birds, and mammals all have legs that contain strong muscles. When these muscles contract, the legs bend at their joints, helping the animal move along. Cheetahs are the fastest runners of all animals.

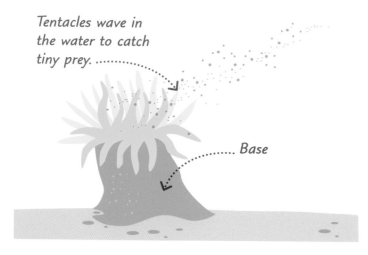

Tentacles wave in the water to catch tiny prey.

Base

5 Mobile tentacles

Although they may look like plants, sea anemones are carnivorous animals. For most of the time, their base (foot) stays fixed to the seafloor, so they feed by using their muscular tentacles to catch passing prey, transferring it to a mouth at the center of their body.

TRY IT OUT

Wobble walk

When we walk or run, we swing each arm with the opposite leg. Try swinging your right arm with your right leg and your left arm with your left leg instead. This will feel very odd. Swinging the opposite arm balances the twist generated when our legs step forward.

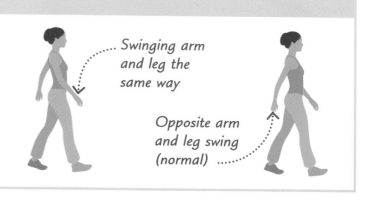

Swinging arm and leg the same way

Opposite arm and leg swing (normal)

Muscles

Muscles are the parts of the body that cause movement. All muscles work by contracting (getting shorter) to squeeze or pull on something.

Your fastest muscle is the one that makes you blink. It can work five times per second.

Opposite pairs

Muscles can pull bones but they can't push them back. To solve this problem, muscles are often arranged in opposite pairs that pull bones in two different directions.

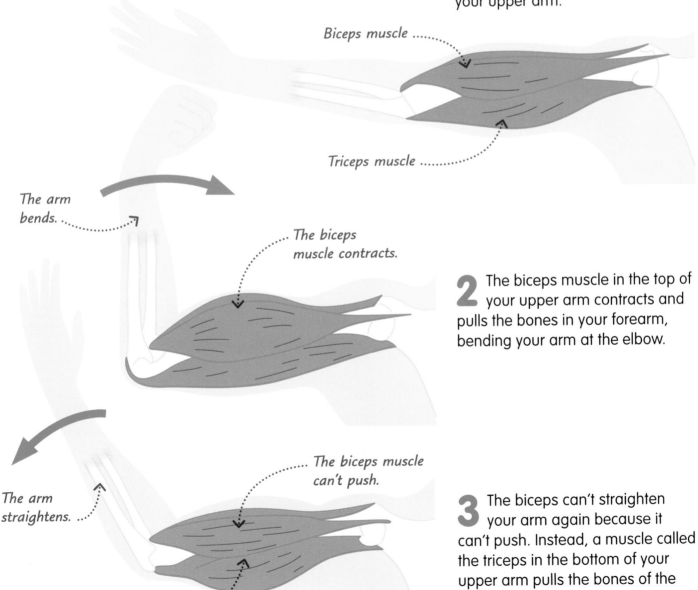

Biceps muscle ....

Triceps muscle ....

The arm bends. ....

... The biceps muscle contracts.

The arm straightens. ....

.... The biceps muscle can't push.

The triceps muscle contracts. ....

1 If you want to bend your forearm, your brain first sends a nerve signal to the biceps muscle in your upper arm.

2 The biceps muscle in the top of your upper arm contracts and pulls the bones in your forearm, bending your arm at the elbow.

3 The biceps can't straighten your arm again because it can't push. Instead, a muscle called the triceps in the bottom of your upper arm pulls the bones of the forearm in the opposite direction.

Types of muscles

The human body contains three main types of muscles. The muscles attached to the skeleton are called skeletal muscles or voluntary muscles because we can consciously control them. However, other muscles are involuntary and work automatically, without us thinking.

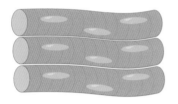

1 Skeletal muscle
Skeletal muscles consist of very long, slender cells called muscle fibers. They contract powerfully, but they can get tired after repeated use and need to rest to recover.

2 Smooth muscle
Smooth muscles are found in the walls of your intestines and stomach. They work automatically, squeezing food through your digestive system without you having to think.

3 Cardiac muscle
The heart's muscular wall is made of cardiac muscle, which consists of branched cells. These contract about once a second and keep working nonstop.

TRY IT OUT

Robot hand

Muscles are attached to bones by tough, stringy bands of tissue called tendons. Your fingers, for instance, are pulled by muscles in your forearm via tendons that run under the skin of your palm. You can see how they work by making a robot hand from cardboard, string, and straws.

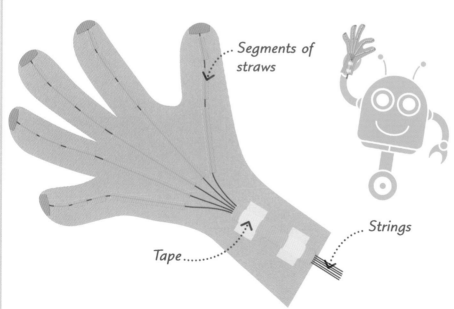

Segments of straws

Strings

Tape

1 Draw the outline of your hand on cardboard and cut it out.

2 Cut straws into segments and tape them on the "palm" of the hand and fingers, with gaps for the knuckles and finger joints. Make folds in the cardboard where the joints are.

3 Thread pieces of string or yarn through a straw at the wrist to the tip of each finger and secure the ends with tape.

4 Try pulling each string at the wrist to bend each finger separately.

Skeleton

The human skeleton is a flexible framework made up of more than 200 bones. These are connected in a way that supports the body while also allowing it to move.

1 Skull
The skull is made up of 22 bones that lock together firmly, forming a protective helmet around the brain.

2 Backbone
A column of 33 interlocking bones called vertebrae form the backbone, or spine, which supports the upper body.

3 Ribs
The 24 ribs form a curved cage around the chest. They help you breathe and they protect the heart and lungs.

4 Hip bones
The large hip bones provide anchorage for powerful leg muscles and form a bony cradle to support soft organs inside the belly.

5 Limb bones
The longest and strongest bones are in the limbs. These have highly flexible joints that help the body move.

6 Inside a bone
The largest bones are not completely solid. A honeycomb pattern of internal spaces makes them lightweight yet sturdy.

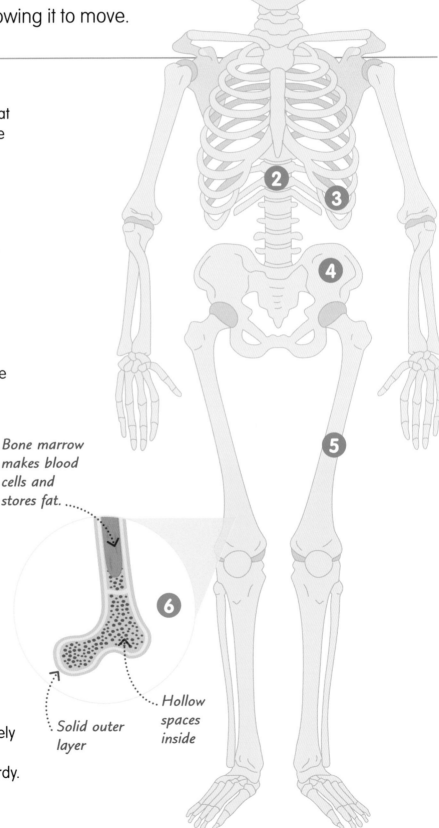

Bone marrow makes blood cells and stores fat.

Solid outer layer

Hollow spaces inside

Joints

Where two or more bones meet, they form a joint. Joints are held together by bands of fibrous tissue and muscle, but many allow the bones to move in particular ways.

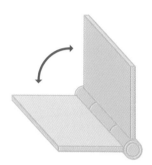

1 Pivot
When you turn your head, you use a pivot joint. This kind of joint allows one bone to rotate around another.

2 Hinge
If you bend a finger, you use a hinge joint. Like door hinges (above), these let bones move one way only.

3 Ball-and-socket
Your hips and shoulders have ball-and-socket joints that allow your arms and legs to swing any way.

Animal skeletons

Animal skeletons work in various ways. Some are made of bones inside the body, like ours, but others are on the outside. Some soft-bodied animals use liquid as a kind of skeleton.

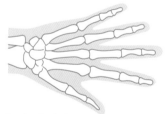

1 Endoskeleton
Humans and most other large animals have an internal skeleton, also called an endoskeleton.

2 Exoskeleton
Small animals such as insects have an exoskeleton—an external skeleton. It doubles as body armor.

3 Hydrostatic skeleton
A long, liquid-filled chamber enclosed tightly in muscle forms the hydrostatic skeleton of a worm.

REAL WORLD TECHNOLOGY

Artificial hips

Joints can wear down as people age, making movement painful—especially in the hips. In a hip replacement operation, the ball-and-socket hip joint is replaced with an artificial one made of a metal ball and a plastic cup.

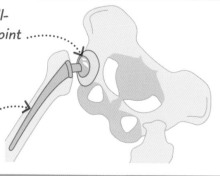

Artificial ball-and-socket joint ....

Metal shaft anchored in thigh bone ....

Staying healthy

The way you live affects your health. Staying in shape and eating a balanced diet keeps your body strong and helps stop you from getting sick.

Physical games and sports are just as good for your body as exercise workouts.

What does exercise do?

When you're physically active—whether playing or doing exercises—your heart, lungs, and muscles all work harder. Regular activity causes your body to adapt. Your heart, lungs, muscles, and even bones become stronger, making you physically fitter.

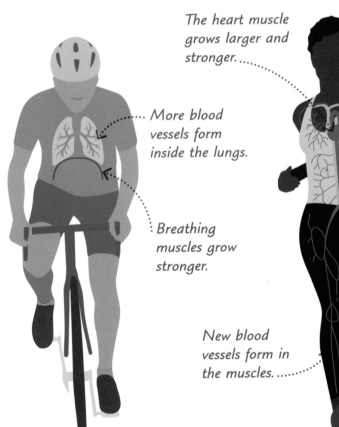

The heart muscle grows larger and stronger.

More blood vessels form inside the lungs.

Breathing muscles grow stronger.

Muscles enlarge and can work harder for longer.

Bone density increases.

The number of oxygen-carrying blood cells rises.

New blood vessels form in the muscles.

1 Respiratory system
Regular exercise strengthens breathing muscles and makes new blood vessels form in the lungs. These changes help your body take in oxygen faster.

2 Circulatory system
Your heart grows larger and stronger to pump more blood. Your circulatory system becomes more efficient at carrying oxygen, and your resting pulse rate falls.

3 Muscles and bones
Muscles, tendons, and ligaments all grow larger and stronger. Bones become wider and denser to withstand strain, and joints become more flexible.

Different types of exercise

There are two main types of exercise: aerobic and anaerobic exercise. Aerobic exercise makes you get out of breath for long periods, which benefits your respiratory and circulatory systems. Anaerobic exercise involves short bursts of physical effort, which strengthen muscles and bones.

AEROBIC

1 Ball games
Soccer and many other competitive sports provide plenty of aerobic exercise but make it seem fun rather than hard work.

2 Jogging
Regular gentle running is good for the heart and lungs and improves stamina—the ability to stay physically active for long periods.

3 Cycling
Cycling mainly benefits the heart and lungs. It puts less strain on muscles, bones, and joints than most other forms of exercise.

ANAEROBIC

4 Weight training
Lifting weights increases the strength and size of particular body muscles and improves bone density.

5 Gymnastics
The various disciplines of gymnastics improve strength, flexibility, and balance.

6 Sprinting
Sprinting strengthens muscles in the lower body and arms, as well as exercising the heart and lungs.

Smoking and health

Smoking harms health in many different ways. Cigarette smoke changes the cells lining the airways in the lungs and leaves tar in the alveoli, making the lungs less efficient. Smoking also damages blood vessels, causing heart attacks and strokes, and toxic chemicals in smoke can cause cancer in almost every part of the body.

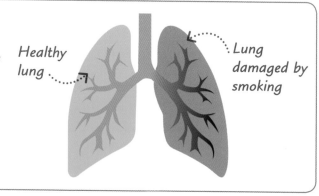

Healthy lung

Lung damaged by smoking

Animal reproduction

When animals have grown into adults, they can produce offspring. This is called reproduction. There are two different ways that living things reproduce: sexually and asexually.

> A cloned organism is an exact genetic copy of another organism.

Sexual reproduction

Sexual reproduction happens when males and females produce sex cells, and these sex cells join to make offspring. Each offspring inherits different characteristics from both parents, making all the offspring unique.

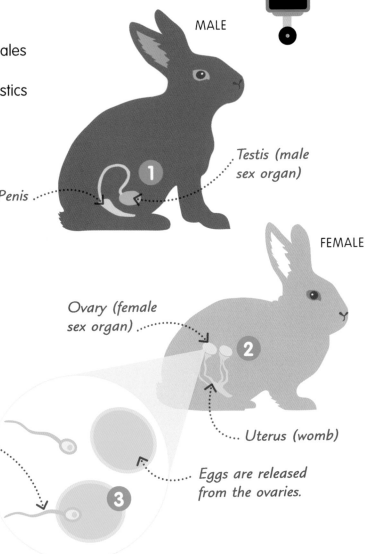

MALE

1 Male sex cells
Sex cells are produced inside sex organs. Males have sex organs called testes, which produce swimming sex cells called sperm.

Testis (male sex organ)

Penis ·········

FEMALE

2 Female sex cells
Females have sex organs called ovaries. They produce sex cells called eggs, which contain a store of nutrients to help the new offspring develop.

Ovary (female sex organ) ·········

Only one sperm is needed to fertilize an egg. ·····

3 Fertilization
In rabbits and other mammals, sperm from the testes enter the female's body when the male and female mate. The sex cells join in a process called fertilization.

Uterus (womb)

Eggs are released from the ovaries.

4 Babies
After an egg cell has been fertilized, it divides many times, growing to form a new individual called an embryo. Some animals lay eggs in which the embryo develops outside the mother's body, but in mammals the embryo develops into a baby inside the mother's uterus.

Each fertilized egg can develop into a baby rabbit.

Asexual reproduction

In asexual reproduction there is just one parent. Many small animals and microorganisms reproduce asexually. The offspring has all the same genes as the parent, making it genetically identical (a clone). There are three common ways of reproducing asexually: asexual birth, dividing in two, and fragmentation.

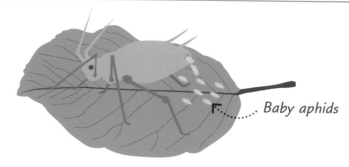

Baby aphids

1 Asexual birth
Aphids give birth to clones without having to mate, which allows them to multiply in number very quickly. The babies are born already pregnant with the next generation of babies.

2 Dividing
Sea anemones can reproduce by splitting in two, forming identical animals that share the same genes. The division starts at the mouth, then the rest of the body splits. The process can take from five minutes to several hours.

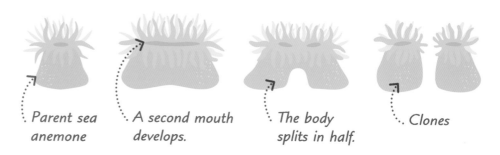

Parent sea anemone · *A second mouth develops.* · *The body splits in half.* · *Clones*

3 Fragmentation
When some animals are broken into fragments, the fragments can grow into whole new bodies. If a flatworm is cut into pieces, for example, each one becomes a new flatworm.

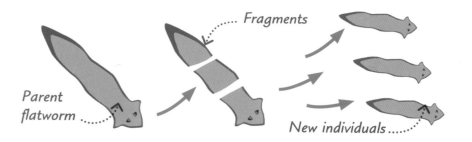

Fragments · *Parent flatworm* · *New individuals*

REAL WORLD TECHNOLOGY

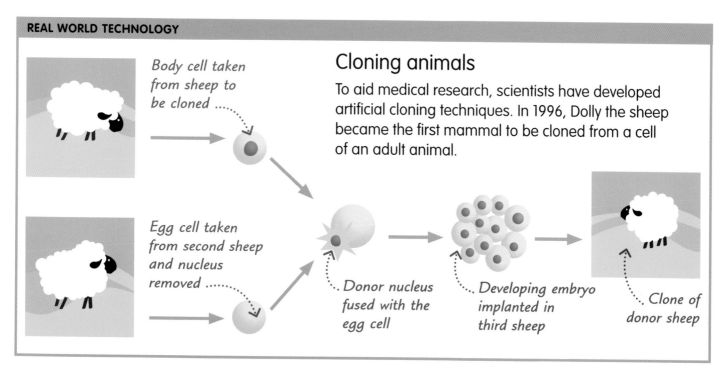

Body cell taken from sheep to be cloned

Cloning animals

To aid medical research, scientists have developed artificial cloning techniques. In 1996, Dolly the sheep became the first mammal to be cloned from a cell of an adult animal.

Egg cell taken from second sheep and nucleus removed · *Donor nucleus fused with the egg cell* · *Developing embryo implanted in third sheep* · *Clone of donor sheep*

Life cycle of mammals

Animals pass through different stages of a life cycle as they grow up and reproduce. Most mammals, including humans, spend the first part of the life cycle in their mother's body.

A few very unusual mammals—platypuses and echidnas—lay eggs.

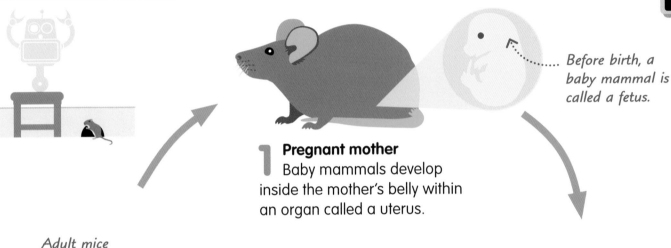

Before birth, a baby mammal is called a fetus.

1 Pregnant mother
Baby mammals develop inside the mother's belly within an organ called a uterus.

Adult mice can breed.

Mice give birth to a litter of several babies at once.

4 Adult mice
When mammals reach adulthood, they find partners so they can reproduce and have offspring of their own.

2 Babies
Newborn mammals feed on milk, a liquid produced by glands on the mother's body. Milk contains all the nutrients they need to grow.

3 Growing up
As young mammals grow bigger, they become curious and playful, which helps them learn about the world around them.

Life cycle of birds

Unlike mammals, baby birds develop inside eggs, which are usually laid in a nest. Like mammals, however, most birds rely on parents to care for them in the early part of their life cycle.

One ostrich egg weighs as much as 500 sparrow eggs.

Male and female birds often have different colors.

Chicks that are fully feathered are called fledglings.

1 Adult birds
Many birds, including sparrows, find partners by singing. Male and female sparrows cooperate to build a nest.

Sparrows' nests are made of twigs, grass, leaves, and feathers.

2 Eggs
The mother lays eggs, and both parents take turns sitting on the eggs to keep them warm.

4 Leaving nest
When the chicks are big enough to fly, they leave the nest. The parents keep feeding them for a week or so.

3 Chicks
Chicks (baby birds) hatch from the eggs. The parents feed them caterpillars and other insects.

How eggs work

Unlike mammals, which give birth to live young, birds develop inside eggs. An egg starts out as one huge cell that divides over time to form the different tissues and organs of the chick.

A chick has a tooth on its beak (an egg tooth) to chip its way out of the shell.

1 Shell
The egg's outer shell has tiny holes that let in air.

2 Air sac
The air sac helps the chick start to breathe just before it hatches.

3 Chalazae
Two rope-like strands join to each end of the egg and secure the yolk in place.

4 Yolk
The yolk is mostly made of lipids (oil and fat) and protein. It nourishes the developing embryo and is used up as the embryo grows.

5 Embryo
The embryo starts out as a cluster of cells. These divide and multiply, eventually becoming a chick.

6 White
The white, or albumen, cushions the embryo and also helps to nourish it. It is mostly water, but also contains protein.

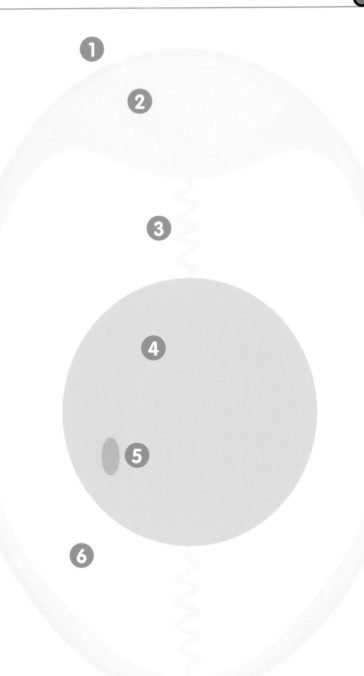

The developing chick

It takes 21 days for a chick to develop fully inside its egg. The parent bird sits on the egg during this time to keep it warm.

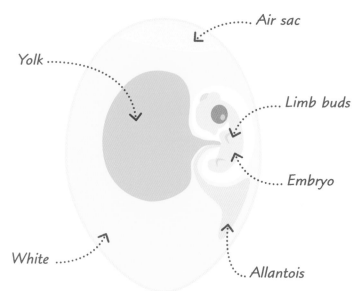

Air sac

Yolk

Limb buds

Embryo

White

Allantois

1 Day 5
The embryo's limbs have started to grow. A delicate pouch called an allantois grows from the embryo and attaches to the shell's lining. It carries oxygen and carbon dioxide, which pass through the shell, to and from the embryo.

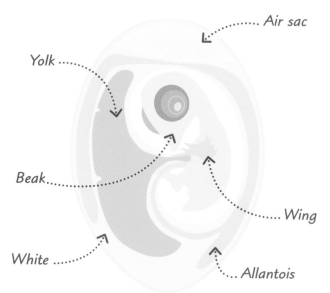

Air sac

Yolk

Beak

Wing

White

Allantois

2 Day 9
The embryo grows bigger. Its wings are developing and its beak has appeared. The allantois expands until it covers the entire lining of the shell.

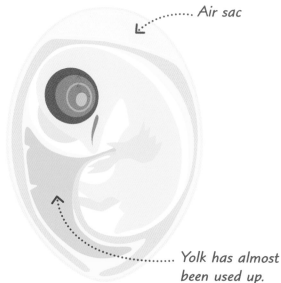

Air sac

Yolk has almost been used up.

3 Day 12
The limbs have grown longer, and the claws and nostrils are developing. Soft feathers called down cover the chick, and it has scales on its legs.

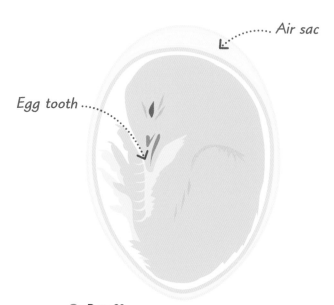

Air sac

Egg tooth

4 Day 21
The chick takes its first breath from the air sac and wriggles inside the shell, which cracks. It chips away at the shell with a tooth on its beak, until it can push one end of the egg away.

Life cycle of amphibians

Frogs belong to a group of animals called amphibians. Many amphibians spend their early life in water and their adult life on land. Their bodies go through a dramatic change, called metamorphosis, as they prepare for life on land.

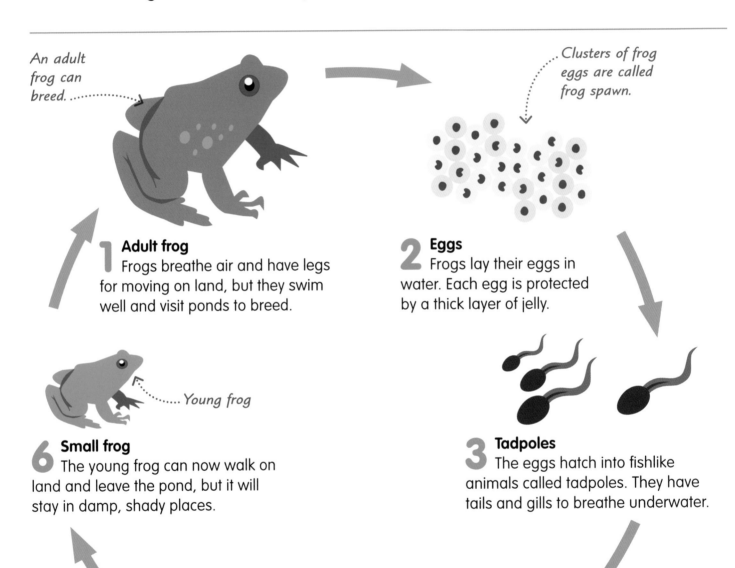

An adult frog can breed.

Clusters of frog eggs are called frog spawn.

1 Adult frog
Frogs breathe air and have legs for moving on land, but they swim well and visit ponds to breed.

2 Eggs
Frogs lay their eggs in water. Each egg is protected by a thick layer of jelly.

Young frog

6 Small frog
The young frog can now walk on land and leave the pond, but it will stay in damp, shady places.

3 Tadpoles
The eggs hatch into fishlike animals called tadpoles. They have tails and gills to breathe underwater.

Front legs

The back legs appear first.

5 Froglet
The front legs appear, and the tail shrinks as the body reabsorbs it. The tadpole is now a froglet.

4 Developing legs
As the tadpoles grow, their legs develop. Their gills disappear and they start to gulp air from the surface.

Life cycle of insects

Many insects undergo metamorphosis as they develop into adults. The change takes place during a motionless stage in the life cycle, when an insect is called a pupa.

> Some insects are larvae for almost their whole life and die within hours of becoming adults.

Butterflies have two pairs of wings.

The pupa of a butterfly is also called a chrysalis.

1 Butterfly
Adult butterflies can only eat liquids and are unable to grow. Most live for only a few weeks.

2 Egg
Butterflies usually lay their eggs on the underside of leaves, where they are hidden from view.

6 Pupa
The caterpillar stops eating or moving and becomes a pupa. Over a few days or weeks, the body changes into a butterfly.

3 Hatching out
Caterpillars hatch out and begin feeding. They eat the egg case first and then start eating leaves.

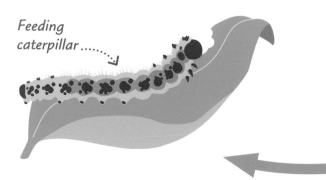

Feeding caterpillar

Growing caterpillar

5 Growing larger
Caterpillars eat almost nonstop and grow quickly. They shed their skin several times so their bodies can expand.

4 Larva
Young insects with grublike, wriggling bodies are called larvae. Caterpillars are the larvae of butterflies.

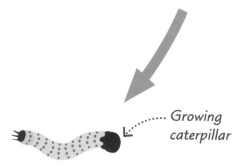

Human reproduction

Human reproduction happens when sperm from a man fertilizes (joins with) an egg from a woman. The fused cells produce an embryo, which develops into a baby over nine months.

The ovaries release about 400 eggs in a woman's lifetime.

Human reproductive systems

The male and female reproductive systems both include organs specialized to produce gametes—male and female sex cells. The female reproductive system also includes the uterus, a muscular organ that carries the developing baby until it is born.

1 Male reproductive system
The main organs in the male reproductive system are the penis and the two testicles (testes). The testicles (testes) hang outside the body, inside the scrotum. Inside the testes, millions of sperm cells are made every day.

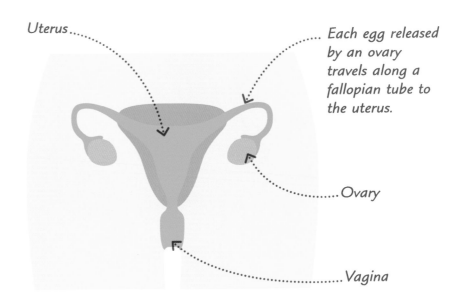

Bladder

Penis

The sperm duct takes sperm from the testes to a tube called the urethra, which runs through the penis.

Urethra

Testicle

Scrotum

2 Female reproductive system
The main parts of the female reproductive system are the uterus (womb), the vagina, and two ovaries. The ovaries store and release eggs. If an egg is fertilized, it develops into a baby, which is carried inside the uterus for nine months. Once it has developed, the baby leaves the body through the vagina, during birth.

Uterus

Each egg released by an ovary travels along a fallopian tube to the uterus.

Ovary

Vagina

The menstrual cycle

The menstrual cycle is the process that prepares a woman's body to make a baby. It has four stages, which last about 28 days all together.

28-DAY REPEATING CYCLE

DAY 6–13 ➔ DAY 14 ➔ DAY 15–28 ➔ DAY 1–5

Egg

1 The uterus lining thickens in preparation for the release of an egg, which is maturing in one of the ovaries. The body is getting ready for a possible pregnancy.

2 The egg is released from the ovary. This is called ovulation. The egg travels along the fallopian tube to the uterus. If the egg is fertilized, the uterus lining keeps thickening.

3 The thickened uterus lining is no longer needed if the egg is not fertilized. The egg breaks down and leaves the body through the vagina.

4 The uterus sheds its lining, which leaves the body as blood through the vagina. This is called menstruation or a "period."

Fertilization

When the man releases sperm into the woman's vagina during sexual intercourse, the sperm swim toward the egg. Fertilization is when a sperm successfully reaches and joins with the egg. The fused cells then start to multiply to form a cluster of cells, which develops over several weeks into an embryo.

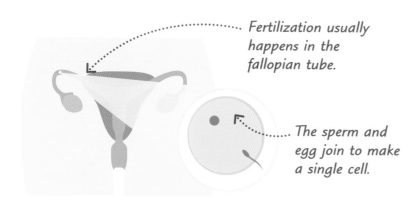

Fertilization usually happens in the fallopian tube.

The sperm and egg join to make a single cell.

In vitro fertilization (IVF)

In vitro fertilization (IVF) is a method used to help people who find it difficult to conceive (get pregnant). Sperm and egg cells are taken from the parents' bodies and mixed in a laboratory until fertilization occurs. In some cases, sperm may be injected into the egg. The fertilized egg is placed into the woman's uterus and a pregnancy begins.

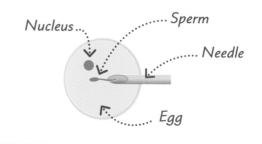

Nucleus

Sperm

Needle

Egg

Gestation and birth

After a human egg cell is fertilized, it can develop into a baby inside a woman's uterus. This is called gestation or pregnancy. The mother's body provides everything the baby needs to grow.

Gestation lasts 9 months in humans but 21 months in elephants.

Fallopian tube ....

Ovary

Zygote ....

Wall of uterus

1 Zygote
When a sperm and egg cell fuse, they form a single cell called a zygote. This happens inside a part of the woman's body called a fallopian tube, which runs between an ovary (where eggs are made) and the uterus (where the baby grows).

2 Embryo
As the zygote travels toward the uterus, it divides into two cells, then four, eight, and so on. It is now called an embryo.

3 In the uterus
After 4–5 days, the embryo reaches the uterus. It is now a cluster of dozens of cells and looks like a berry, but has a hollow center.

4 Implantation
About 6 days after fertilization, the embryo embeds itself in the wall of the uterus. Inside it is a cluster of cells that will eventually form a body. The outer cells begin to form an organ called a placenta, which will feed the baby.

REAL WORLD TECHNOLOGY

Ultrasound scanning

Doctors can check that unborn babies are healthy by using a technique called ultrasound scanning. An ultrasound machine transmits high-pitched sound waves from a probe pressed against the mother's skin. The probe also picks up echoes of the sound waves from the baby, and the machine converts these echoes into a moving image.

Probe ....

Screen

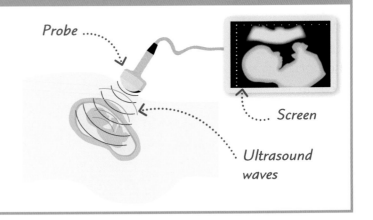

Ultrasound waves

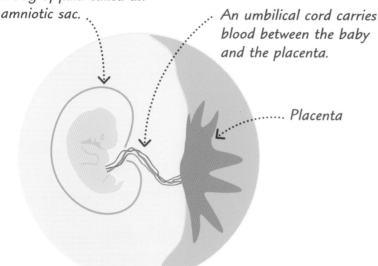

The baby develops inside a bag of fluid called an amniotic sac.

An umbilical cord carries blood between the baby and the placenta.

.... *Placenta*

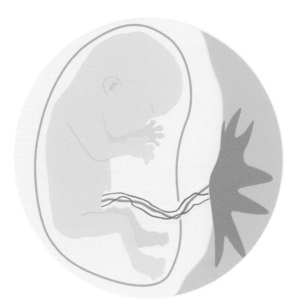

5 Developing body

By about 3 weeks after fertilization, a tiny body has formed. A mere ½ in (1 cm) long, it has a large head, buds where limbs will grow, and a tail. Its heart is beating and pumps blood to the placenta, which absorbs food from the mother's blood.

6 Fetus

From about nine weeks after fertilization, the baby looks human and is called a fetus. At this point it is half the size of a mouse but all its major body organs have formed. It can move but can't yet hear or see. It will stay in the uterus for another 6 months.

7 Birth

After about 38 weeks, the baby is ready to be born. The entrance to the uterus widens, and muscles in the wall of the uterus begin contracting (squeezing). The mother feels these contractions, so she knows she's about to give birth. The bag of fluid around the baby (the amniotic sac) bursts, and the muscles in the uterus push the baby out, usually headfirst. The baby's lungs start working and it takes its first breath of air.

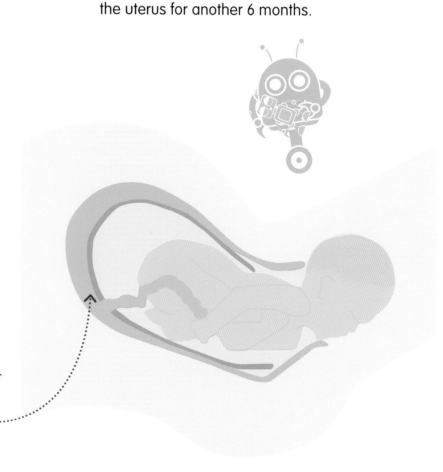

Muscles in the wall of the uterus squeeze to push the baby out. ....

Growth and development

As you get older, your body changes from a small baby into a full-grown adult. The most dramatic changes happen during childhood and adolescence, but you continue changing throughout your life.

The growing body

The processes of growth and development begin when an embryo first forms inside the mother's body and continue after birth. Growth is an increase in the body's size, while development involves changes in the way the body works.

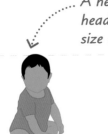

... A newborn baby's head is almost the size of an adult's.

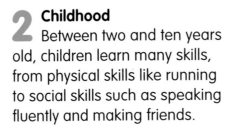

1 Infancy
Newborn babies are helpless, but they grow and become stronger in their first two years. By 12–18 months, they are able to walk.

2 Childhood
Between two and ten years old, children learn many skills, from physical skills like running to social skills such as speaking fluently and making friends.

3 Adolescence
Between 11 and 18 years old, teenagers go through adolescence—a period of physical changes that prepare the body to have babies.

Cell division

Your body grows and develops by producing more cells. Many kinds of cells can divide. Before they do so, each cell makes a copy of its genetic information.

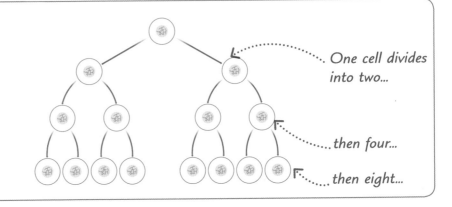

... One cell divides into two...

...then four...

...then eight...

Growth spurts

During adolescence, the body goes through a period of rapid growth (a growth spurt) as major bones in the skeleton lengthen. Girls reach adolescence before boys and grow taller around age 11, but by about age 14 boys catch up. Boys usually go on to reach a greater average adult height.

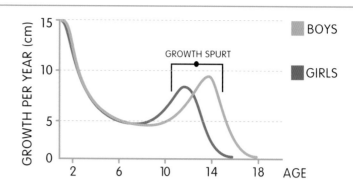

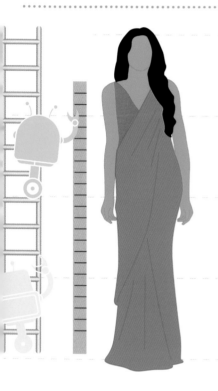

..Graying hair

. Height loss is caused by shrinking tissues.

4 Early adulthood
Early adulthood is when bones are strongest and full height is reached. Males and females can become parents.

5 Late adulthood
In late adulthood, skin loses its stretchiness and wrinkles appear. Hair begins to turn gray. In men, the hairline may recede.

6 Old age
Later in life, a person's bones, joints, and muscles become weaker, and their senses may deteriorate. The heart becomes less efficient.

REAL WORLD TECHNOLOGY

Stem cells

Most body cells have special roles and cannot change, but stem cells can develop into different body tissues. This makes stem cells important to science because they may one day be used to grow replacement organs to treat disease.

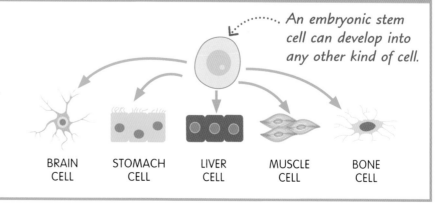

An embryonic stem cell can develop into any other kind of cell.

BRAIN CELL   STOMACH CELL   LIVER CELL   MUSCLE CELL   BONE CELL

Genes and DNA

The cells of all living things contain chemical instructions called genes, which are stored in a molecule called DNA. Genes are passed from parents to their offspring and control the way all organisms grow and develop.

Chromosomes are so tiny that 100,000 could fit inside a period.

1 Body
How an organism's body forms, works, and looks depends mainly on its genes. The human body is controlled by about 20,000 different genes.

2 Cell
All organisms are made of tiny units called cells. Each cell carries a complete set of all the organism's genes, usually stored in the cell nucleus.

3 Chromosome
Inside the nucleus, genes are carried by structures called chromosomes. A human cell has 46 chromosomes, but dog cells have 78 and pea plants have 14.

Making copies

DNA has the remarkable ability to make copies of itself. This allows genes to be copied when cells divide or when organisms reproduce.

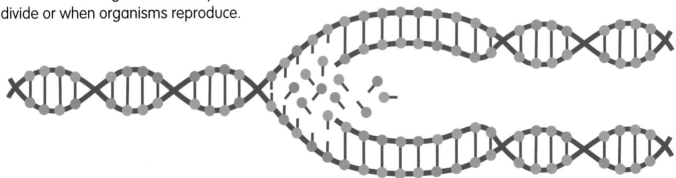

1 The DNA molecule unzips into two strands. Each has a sequence of bases carrying genetic information.

2 Bases always pair with certain partners, so the single strands serve as templates for new strands.

3 Two identical DNA molecules are produced, each with the same genetic information.

Four different bases (shown by the letters A, C, T, and G) form a sequence running along both sides of the DNA molecule.

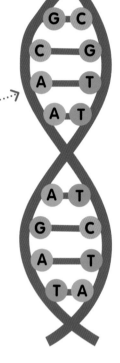

A protein molecule is a chain of small units called amino acids.

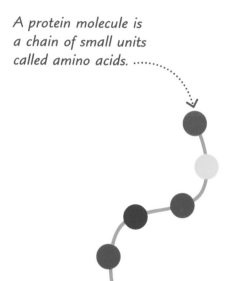

4 DNA
A chromosome contains a single, extremely long molecule of DNA (deoxyribonucleic acid). The DNA molecule resembles a ladder but is twisted into a shape called a double helix.

5 Gene
Running along the DNA molecule are chemicals called bases. Their order forms a code, like letters forming words. A gene is a stretch of DNA with the code for a particular job.

6 Protein
Genes code for protein molecules: the order of bases in the gene spells out the order of amino acids in the protein. Proteins, in turn, control the way cells and bodies work and look.

REAL WORLD TECHNOLOGY

DNA fingerprinting
Because each person has a unique set of genes, DNA from a crime scene can be used to create a kind of fingerprint that might help identify a suspect.

An electric current makes the fragments move along the sheet.

The DNA fingerprint is unique to one person.

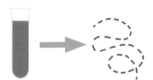

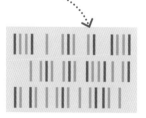

1 DNA from body fluids at a crime scene is cut into thousands of tiny fragments.

2 The fragments are placed in wells at the end of a sheet of gel and are left to seep through it.

3 A few hours later, the DNA fragments form a pattern of bands: a DNA fingerprint.

Variation

There are billions of organisms on Earth, but no two are exactly alike. This variation is caused partly by genetic differences and partly by the environment organisms live in.

Humans and chimps share about 96 percent of their DNA.

1 Variation between species

The natural world is full of variation. Scientists have identified around 2 million different species, and there may be millions more awaiting discovery. We use the word biodiversity to describe the great variety of organisms that live on Earth or that share a particular ecosystem.

2 Variation within species

Even within one species, no two individuals are identical. There may be obvious differences in appearance, as in these harlequin ladybugs, or more subtle variations in disease resistance, behavior, or any other characteristic. This variation makes the process of evolution (see page 82) possible.

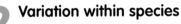

3 Continuous variation

Some characteristics, such as height in humans, show what's known as continuous variation. This means a person can be any height between the shortest and tallest. If you measured the height of lots of different people and plotted the results on a graph, they would form a shape called a bell curve. This shape is a typical feature of characteristics with continuous variation.

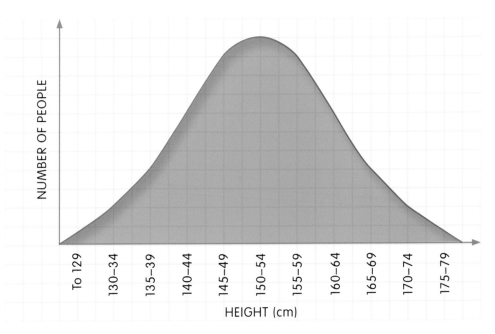

NUMBER OF PEOPLE

To 129 | 130–34 | 135–39 | 140–44 | 145–49 | 150–54 | 155–59 | 160–64 | 165–69 | 170–74 | 175–79

HEIGHT (cm)

4 Discontinuous variation
Other characteristics show what's known as discontinuous variation. This means there's a limited number of options, with nothing in between them. For example, there are only four blood groups in humans: A, B, AB, and O. Discontinuous variation is usually caused by one or just a few genes. In contrast, continuous variation is caused by multiple genes, by the environment, or by both.

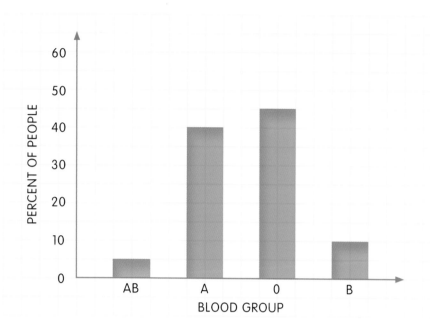

Sources of variation
Much of the variation within a species comes from genetic differences. Mutations create new genes, and sexual reproduction shuffles genes into new combinations. The environment also affects how organisms develop.

1 Errors called mutations can creep into the coded information stored in the DNA molecule that carries genes. As a result, new genes appear, creating variation. Mutations in the genes that control skin and fur color, for instance, can make animals albino.

2 Sexual reproduction gives each organism a unique blend of both parents' genes, which is why all the children in a family look different. Identical twins are an exception. They share identical genes, but differences in their environment as they grow up still make them unique.

3 The environment affects the way organisms develop. Plants that grow in the shade, for example, are taller and less bushy than plants that grow in full sun. The environment and genes can interact in complex ways. Some environmental factors can switch genes on or off, for instance.

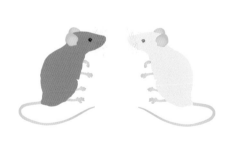

BROWN MOUSE   ALBINO MOUSE

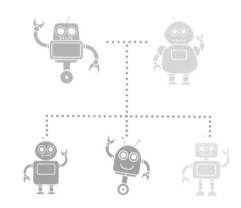

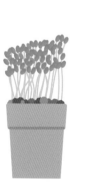

GROWN IN FULL SUN   GROWN IN THE SHADE

Inheritance

When organisms reproduce, their offspring usually look similar to the parents. This is because all organisms inherit genes from their parents, and genes control the way their bodies develop.

Identical twins share exactly the same set of genes.

Sexual reproduction

In sexual reproduction, organisms inherit genes from two parents. Each offspring usually gets a slightly different blend of both parents' genes, making every offspring unique.

1 Parents
Genes are stored on structures called chromosomes, which are found in the nuclei of nearly every type of cell. A human cell has 46 chromosomes. Together, these carry a complete set of all the body's genes.

2 Sex cells
In order to reproduce sexually, the bodies of men and women make sex cells—special cells with only 23 chromosomes each. Male sex cells are called sperm; female sex cells are called eggs. Each chromosome in a sex cell has a blend of genes from two of that parent's chromosomes.

3 Offspring
During sexual reproduction, a sperm cell and an egg cell join to form a new individual. The two sets of chromosomes combine, giving the child a full set of 46 chromosomes. Half the chromosomes come from the child's father and half come from the mother.

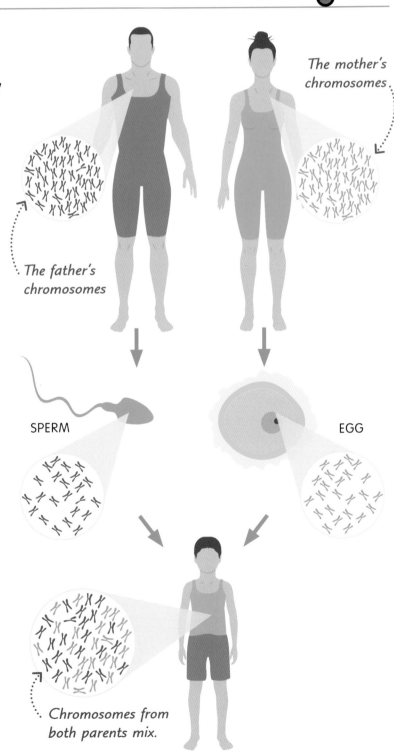

The mother's chromosomes

The father's chromosomes

SPERM

EGG

Chromosomes from both parents mix.

Gene pairs

Because sexually reproducing organisms inherit a set of chromosomes from both parents, they have two copies of every gene. Sometimes the two copies are slightly different. We call these different versions alleles. When an organism has two different alleles for a gene, one may overpower the other. The more powerful allele is described as dominant.

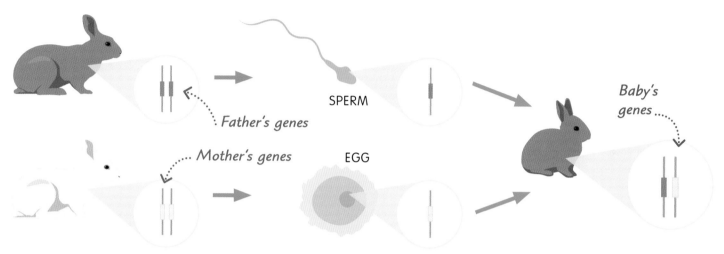

Father's genes

SPERM

Mother's genes

EGG

Baby's genes

1 Each of these adult rabbits has two genes for coat color. The brown father has two brown-coat genes, and the white mother has two white-coat genes.

2 All the father's sperm cells have a brown-coat gene, and all the mother's egg cells have a white-coat gene.

3 The offspring inherit both alleles, but the brown-coat allele is dominant—so the baby rabbits are all brown.

Sex chromosomes

In humans and other mammals, two special chromosomes—the sex chromosomes—control gender. Females have two X chromosomes and males have an X and a Y chromosome.

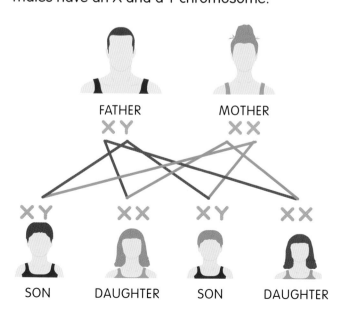

FATHER
X Y

MOTHER
X X

X Y
SON

X X
DAUGHTER

X Y
SON

X X
DAUGHTER

Genetic disorders

Some genetic disorders are caused by genes on the sex chromosomes. Color blindness, for instance, can be caused by a faulty gene on the X chromosome. It is less common in girls because their second X chromosome usually has a working copy of the same gene. In boys, however, the faulty gene takes effect as the Y chromosome lacks the matching allele.

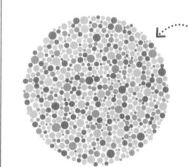

Color tests like this one are used to check for red–green color blindness.

Evolution

Over long periods of time, living things change as they adapt to the changing world around them. This change is called evolution and leads to the formation of new species (types of organisms). Evolution is driven by a process called natural selection.

The theory of evolution by natural selection was put forward in 1859 by English scientist Charles Darwin.

Natural selection

Life in the natural world is a competition, with winners and losers. Those that survive and breed pass on their winning genes to the next generation. But if conditions change, the winners may turn into losers.

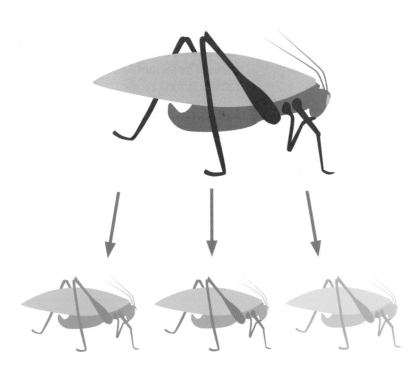

The bird sees orange and pink crickets more easily.

1 New genes create variation
When organisms reproduce, their genes are copied. Sometimes mistakes in the copying process create new genes, making the population more varied. For instance, mutations in genes that affect the skin color of crickets might result in a population of varying colors.

2 Survival of the fittest
Brown and pink crickets are easy for birds to see among leaves, so they get eaten more often. The green ones can hide more easily. They survive and pass on their genes, making green crickets more and more common. This process is called natural selection.

Evidence from the past

Evolution takes place over long periods, which makes it difficult to observe. However, fossils of prehistoric organisms provide a window into the past, allowing scientists to figure out the path that evolution has taken. For example, fossils of a creature called *Archaeopteryx* reveal that birds probably evolved from small dinosaurs. Unlike any living bird, *Archaeopteryx* had teeth, a bony tail, and large front claws. However, it also had feathered wings much like those of a modern bird.

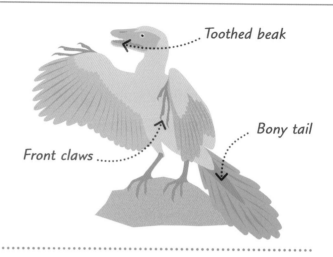

Toothed beak

Bony tail

Front claws

Now green crickets are easy to spot, so the population begins to change color.

3 The environment changes

Over time, environments change. For instance, a change in climate might turn a lush forest into a desert. In a sandy environment, brown crickets may be harder to see and stand a better chance of surviving. The cricket population would then change color, adapting to the new environment.

REAL WORLD TECHNOLOGY

Artificial selection

Humans can breed plants and animals and select offspring with features they like. Over time, this can change organisms dramatically, just as natural selection does in the wild. This process, called artificial selection, has created dog breeds that look and behave very differently from their wild ancestor, the gray wolf.

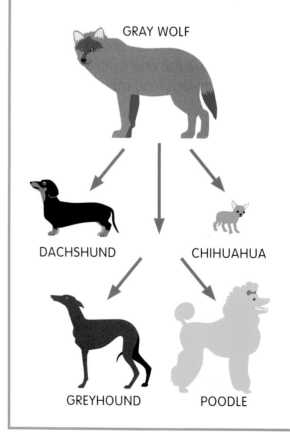

GRAY WOLF

DACHSHUND

CHIHUAHUA

GREYHOUND

POODLE

Plants

Plants are living things that grow on land or in water. Unlike animals, plants can't move from place to place. Nearly all plants make their own food, taking energy from sunlight.

Plants are green because they use a green chemical called chlorophyll to capture the Sun's energy.

Parts of a plant

Most plants have roots, a stem, and leaves. Many have flowers too. Each part of a plant has a special job to do.

1 Flowers
The flowers make seeds, which become new plants. The center of a flower is surrounded by petals.

2 Leaves
The leaves spread out to capture sunlight. They use the energy in light to create energy-rich food molecules.

3 Stem
The stem (stalk) holds the plant up toward the light. It carries water and nutrients from the roots to all parts of the plant. We call the stem of a tree a trunk and its side shoots branches.

4 Roots
The roots anchor the plant to the ground so it isn't washed away by the rain or blown away by the wind. They take in water and chemicals called minerals from the soil.

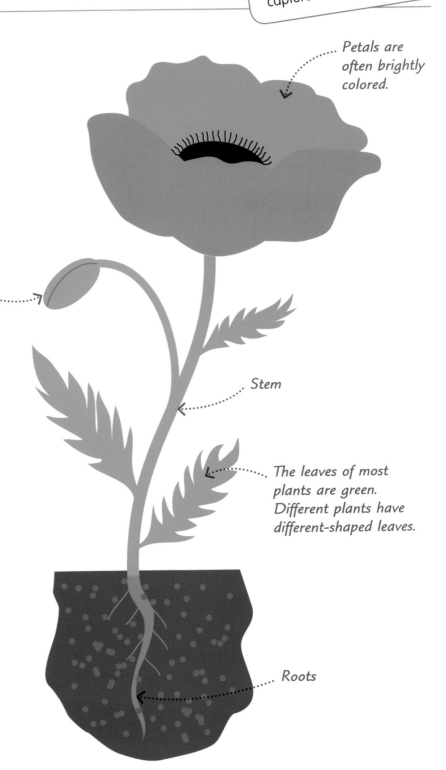

Petals are often brightly colored.

Flower bud (a flower that hasn't opened yet)

Stem

The leaves of most plants are green. Different plants have different-shaped leaves.

Roots

What plants need to grow

Plants need certain things to live, grow, and stay healthy. The most important of these are light and water. Plants also need a suitable temperature and chemicals called minerals.

3 Plants will grow best when the temperature is just right for them. Some plants like hot weather, while others prefer cooler conditions.

1 Plants use light to make their own food. If you leave a plant on a windowsill, it will bend and grow toward the light. It tries to get as much sunshine as possible.

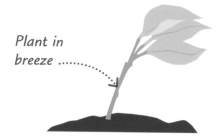

Plant in breeze ......

4 All plants need air. They use the gas carbon dioxide from air to make food, and they use oxygen from air to release energy from food.

2 Plants need water to survive and stay strong. When a plant does not get enough water, its stem wilts (gets floppy) and its leaves shrivel.

5 Minerals help a plant grow strongly. The roots of most plants absorb minerals from the soil. Floating plants get their minerals from water.

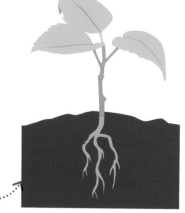

Soil contains nutrients. ......

REAL WORLD TECHNOLOGY

Greenhouses

Farmers grow some vegetables and fruit in greenhouses. The windows trap the Sun's heat, creating warmer conditions inside the greenhouse than outside. This makes it easier to grow plants from hot places, such as grapes and tomatoes.

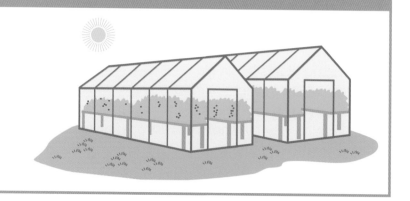

Types of plants

Plants vary from tiny specks of greenery that live in water to towering trees. The many types of plants are divided into two main groups: flowering plants and nonflowering plants.

Scientists have identified more than 400,000 different species (types) of plants.

Flowering plants

Most of the world's plants are flowering plants. All flowering plants share a similar life cycle, growing from seeds and producing flowers when they mature. Flowers allow plants to reproduce sexually by exchanging male and female sex cells with other plants.

Bright colors and sugar-rich nectar attract insects.

2

Feathery parachutes help dandelion seeds fly away.

3

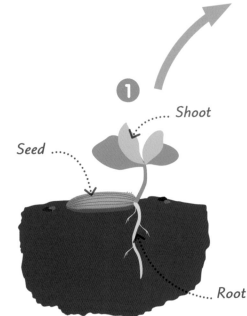

1

Shoot

Seed

Root

1 Seedling
Flowering plants begin life as seeds. When a seed absorbs water, it sprouts a root and a shoot, forming a baby plant called a seedling.

2 Flowers
Many flowers are brightly colored to attract insects or other animals, which carry sex cells from flower to flower. This process is called pollination.

3 New seeds
Pollinated flowers produce new seeds. To help them spread to new places, some seeds have wings or feathery parachutes that catch the wind.

Nonflowering plants

Not all plants reproduce by making flowers. Nonflowering plants include conifers, ferns, and mosses.

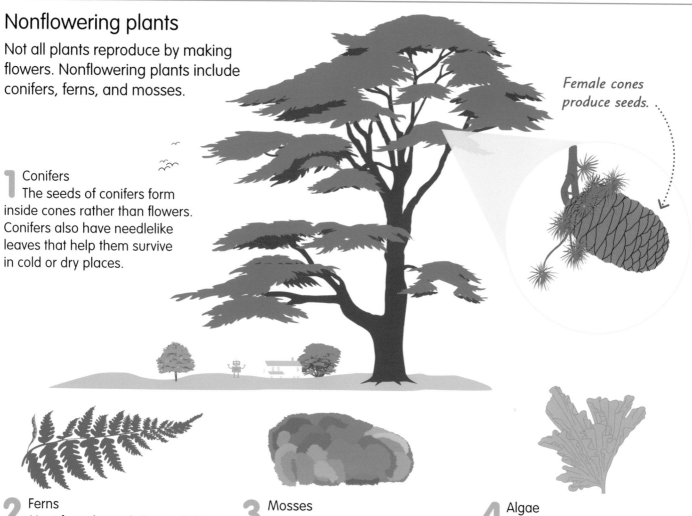

Female cones produce seeds.

1 Conifers
The seeds of conifers form inside cones rather than flowers. Conifers also have needlelike leaves that help them survive in cold or dry places.

2 Ferns
Most ferns have delicate, divided leaves and live in shady places. Ferns don't produce seeds. Instead, they grow from tiny single cells, called spores, that scatter on the wind.

3 Mosses
Most mosses are small plants that grow in damp places, often spreading like a cushion. They have no roots, flowers, or seeds. They reproduce by making spores.

4 Algae
Algae are simple, plantlike organisms that live in water and have no true stems, leaves, or roots. Many are microscopic. They reproduce by spreading spores in water.

Deciduous and evergreen

Some plants keep their leaves all year round and are called evergreen. Deciduous plants, however, survive winter by shedding their leaves and growing new ones in spring.

Leaves change color in fall.

Deciduous trees lose their leaves in winter.

SPRING   SUMMER   FALL   WINTER

Photosynthesis

Plants use the energy in sunlight to make the food they need to grow. This process of capturing the Sun's energy for food is known as photosynthesis.

Photosynthesis is vital to life on Earth because it provides food for nearly all living things.

How photosynthesis works

1 The plant's roots take in water and minerals from the soil. Veins transport water to the rest of the plant, including its leaves.

2 Carbon dioxide from air enters the leaves through tiny holes. These holes are called stomata.

3 The leaves contain a green substance called chlorophyll that absorbs energy from sunlight. Chlorophyll is also the substance that gives plants their color.

4 A series of chemical reactions takes place in the leaves. These reactions combine water from the soil with carbon dioxide from the air and energy from the Sun to produce glucose (a sugar) and oxygen.

5 The plant uses the glucose produced by photosynthesis to build new tissues or store energy. The oxygen is released into the air as a waste product.

SUNLIGHT

CARBON DIOXIDE

WATER

Making food

This chemical equation (see pages 140–41) shows what happens during photosynthesis. Water and carbon dioxide are combined to make glucose, and oxygen is produced as waste.

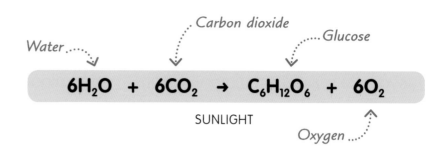

Water ......

Carbon dioxide

Glucose

$$6H_2O \; + \; 6CO_2 \; \rightarrow \; C_6H_{12}O_6 \; + \; 6O_2$$

SUNLIGHT

Oxygen ......

A waxy, waterproof layer protects the leaf's surface while letting in light. ......

A layer of loosely packed, "spongy cells" let gases move through the leaf. ......

Cells inside the leaf are packed with tiny green bodies called chloroplasts, where photosynthesis takes place.

Veins bring water into the leaf and take sugar to the rest of the plant.

The lower layer has tiny holes called stomata that open and close to let gases in and out.

INSIDE A LEAF

OXYGEN

5

Photosynthesis in action

Watch photosynthesis in action with this simple experiment. Place some pondweed inside a container full of water. Shine a light on the pondweed and you'll see it start to produce oxygen bubbles that float to the top. These oxygen bubbles are the waste product of photosynthesis. Try moving the light closer to or farther away from the pondweed—what happens to the number of bubbles?

Oxygen bubbles ......

Pondweed ......

Transport in plants

Just as we have a circulatory system to carry blood around our bodies, many plants have a transportation system to carry water and nutrients to wherever they are needed.

Tiny tubes inside plants move water and nutrients from place to place.

Transpiration

The movement of water through a plant is called transpiration. Leaves continually lose water to the air by evaporation, but this draws more water up through the plant from the ground. In a large tree, water may climb more than 160 ft (50 m) before it evaporates.

1 Tiny pores (holes) called stomata on the surface of the leaves allow water vapor inside leaves to escape into the air.

2 The loss of water from leaves causes more water to be pulled into them through tiny tubes called xylem (pronounced "zylem") vessels. Like a drink being sucked through a straw, water is pulled up through xylem vessels all the way from the roots.

3 Pressure inside the roots also helps push water upward into the trunk of the tree.

4 The roots continually absorb water from the soil to replace the water lost by the leaves. A large tree can absorb so much water that it makes the ground under it dry out.

Water flows up the trunk through the xylem vessels.

Water is absorbed by the roots.

Xylem and phloem

A plant's transportation system is made up of microscopic tubes called xylem vessels and phloem vessels. A liquid called sap flows through the tubes. It contains water and dissolved substances such as minerals and sugars.

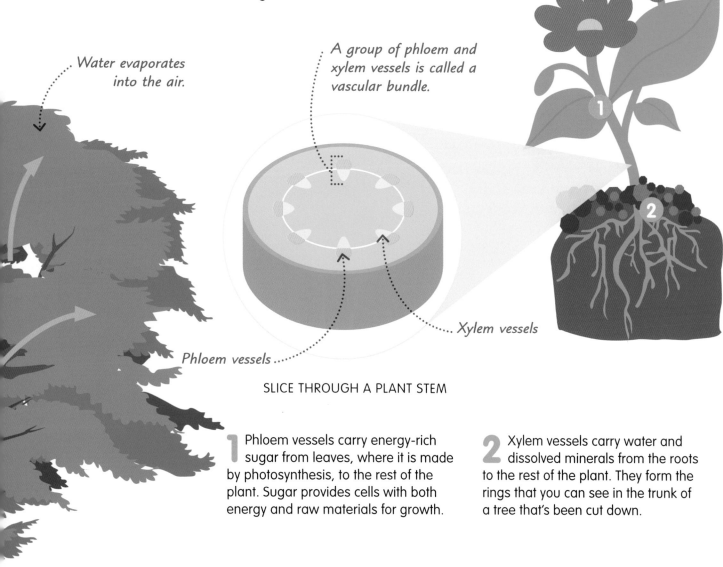

.... Water evaporates into the air.

A group of phloem and xylem vessels is called a vascular bundle.

Xylem vessels

Phloem vessels ....

SLICE THROUGH A PLANT STEM

1 Phloem vessels carry energy-rich sugar from leaves, where it is made by photosynthesis, to the rest of the plant. Sugar provides cells with both energy and raw materials for growth.

2 Xylem vessels carry water and dissolved minerals from the roots to the rest of the plant. They form the rings that you can see in the trunk of a tree that's been cut down.

TRY IT OUT

Changing colors

Perform some plant magic by changing the color of a flower. This experiment shows how water travels up the stem of a plant.

1 Fill a vase or beaker with water and add some food coloring. Any color will work.

2 Ask an adult to trim the stem of a white carnation at an angle. Then put the flower in the vase.

3 Leave it for a few hours. The flower will change color as the water moves up the stem.

Flowers

Whatever their size, shape, or color, all flowers do the same job: they produce the male and female cells that allow plants to reproduce sexually.

Plants that are pollinated by wind don't need colorful flowers to attract animals.

A typical flower

Many flowers rely on small animals such as bees to carry male cells from one flower to another. To attract them, a typical flower has colorful petals, a strong scent, and sugary nectar for the animals to eat.

1 Male parts
The male parts of flowers are called stamens. The top of a stamen makes a yellow powder called pollen, which sticks to visiting insects. Pollen grains contain male sex cells.

2 Female parts
The female parts of flowers are called carpels. Many flowers have only one carpel. At its base is an ovary (a chamber containing female sex cells). At the top of the carpel is a sticky pad called a stigma, which pollen sticks to.

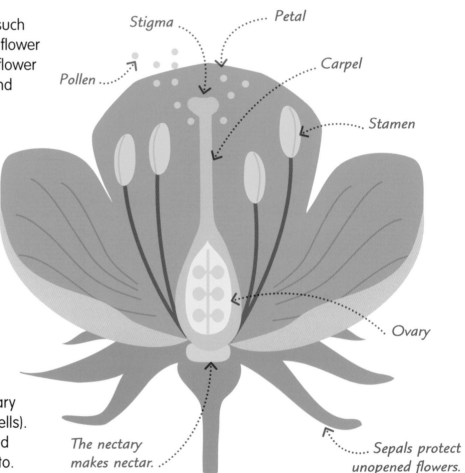

Stigma

Petal

Pollen

Carpel

Stamen

Ovary

The nectary makes nectar.

Sepals protect unopened flowers.

REAL WORLD TECHNOLOGY

Bees for hire

Farmers sometimes pay beekeepers to bring hives of honeybees or colonies of bumblebees into their fields and orchards to pollinate crop plants. This service helps more flowers to produce seeds and fruit, which improves the farmer's yield.

Pollination

A flower can only make seeds if pollen enters the ovary. This is called pollination. Some plants can pollinate themselves, but most need to receive pollen from another plant of the same species.

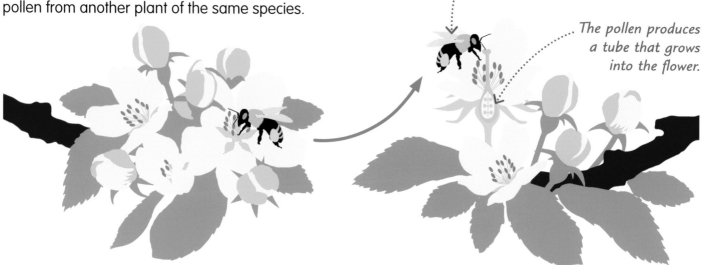

Pollen on the bee's body brushes off onto the carpel of a flower on another tree.

The pollen produces a tube that grows into the flower.

1 A honeybee visits flowers on an apple tree to feed on nectar and collect pollen to take back to the hive. As it feeds, pollen sticks to its body. The bee flies off to a different apple tree.

2 The bee lands on a flower on the next tree and pollen brushes onto the flower's stigma. The pollen grows a tube that burrows down to the ovary, carrying a male sex cell.

After pollination

When a flower has been pollinated, it produces seeds and fruit. Many kinds of fruit have sweet flesh so that animals will swallow them and carry the seeds to new homes.

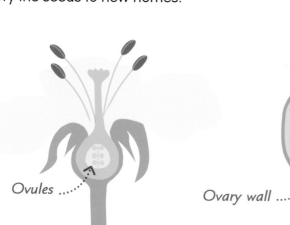

The flesh of an apple develops from the flower's base as well as from the ovary.

Remains of sepals

Dying petals

Ovules

Ovary wall

Seeds

1 After pollination, male and female cells join inside tiny round structures called ovules. These will become seeds.

2 The stamens fall off and the petals wither and die. The wall of the ovary swells up as it begins to form a fruit.

3 When the fruit is fully grown, it ripens, becoming sweet. Inside it, the seeds develop protective coats and harden.

Seed dispersal

Seeds must be dispersed (scattered) far from the parent plant if they are to find new habitats where they can thrive. Parent plants disperse their seeds in a variety of ways.

> The fruit of a dynamite tree explodes with a bang, firing seeds 100 ft (30 m) away.

Spread by animals

Many types of seeds are scattered by animals. Seeds transported in this way are released in smaller numbers and are often larger than seeds dispersed by the wind.

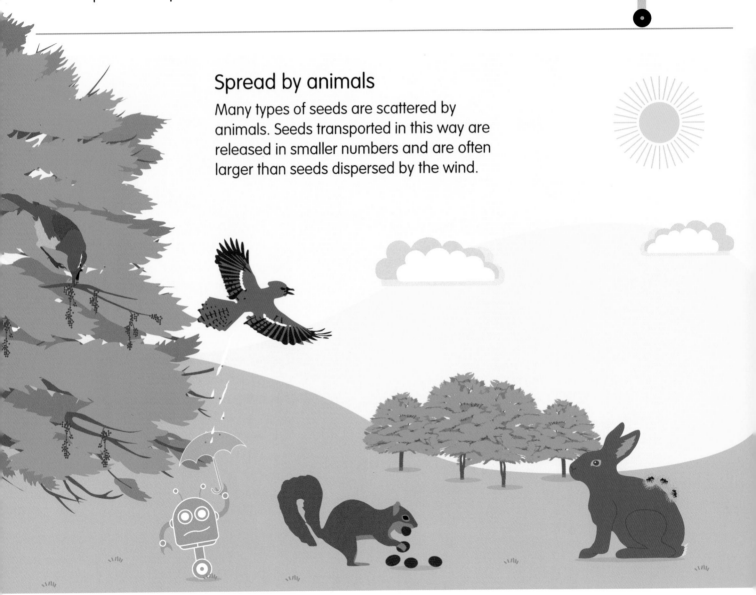

1 Edible fruit
Birds eat berries containing seeds that can pass unharmed through their intestines. The seeds are deposited in bird droppings, which fertilize the seedlings.

2 Hoarding
Squirrels carry away acorns to eat during winter and bury them in the ground. Some of the acorns are forgotten and grow into new oak trees.

3 Hitching a ride
The seeds of some plants, such as burdock, are covered in tiny hooks. They latch on to the fur of animals and are carried away to new habitats.

Spread by wind

Some plants produce seeds that are dispersed by wind. The seeds are usually very small and light, to help them travel as far as possible, and are produced in vast numbers.

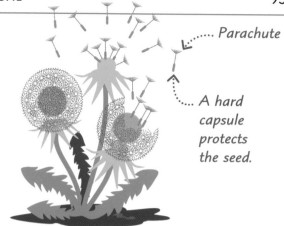

Parachute

A hard capsule protects the seed.

Winglike shape

1 Wings
Maple seeds are shaped like wings. The wing spins the seed, slowing it down as it falls from the tree and helping it to drift farther away.

2 Floating away
Dandelion flowers produce up to 150 seeds, each inside its own hard capsule. A parachute of feathery hairs lets the seed float in the wind.

Seeds are shaken out.

Seeds are thrown clear.

3 Shaken out
A poppy's seed head rattles in the wind. It shakes out its small, light seeds into the breeze.

4 Explosive fruits
The fruits of some plants burst open when their seeds are ready to be dispersed, and the seeds are thrown far from the parent.

Spread by water

Some plants growing near water produce seeds that float. These seeds are usually much larger than those spread by animals or wind. Coastal palm trees produce the biggest seeds of all—coconuts.

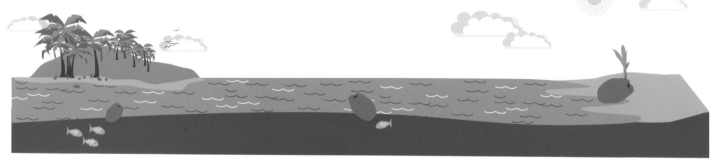

1 The coconut falls from the palm tree into the water and floats out into the ocean.

2 The coconut drifts in the water. Protected by a hard outer layer, it may survive for months.

3 The coconut washes up on a distant beach, where it sprouts and grows into a new palm tree.

How seeds grow

When conditions are right, seeds sprout and grow into new plants—a process called germination. Some seeds can survive for months, years, or even centuries before they germinate.

> Before a seed germinates, it is dormant (alive but inactive).

What is a seed?

A seed is the capsule from which a new plant grows. Protected by a tough outer coat, each seed contains a tiny baby plant, known as an embryo. The embryo has a root and shoot, including the first true leaves. Seeds also contain a store of food, often in the form of "seed leaves" that nearly fill the seed.

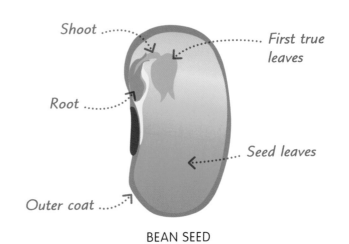

Shoot

First true leaves

Root

Seed leaves

Outer coat

BEAN SEED

Germination

Most seeds don't germinate until they absorb water, which causes dormant cells in the seed to spring to life. Before the seedling reaches the light, its growth is fuelled by its food store.

Seed leaves

True leaves

First root

1 Water in the ground makes the bean seed swell, causing the outer coat to crack.

2 The first root begins to grow downward. Tiny hairs on the root absorb water and minerals from the soil.

3 The first shoot breaks through the soil and into the light. The seed leaves supply the seedling with food.

The right conditions

To germinate, seeds need warmth, oxygen, and water. Plants usually produce lots of seeds because many will land on unsuitable ground and never grow at all. If the conditions are right, however, some of the scattered seeds will grow into young plants.

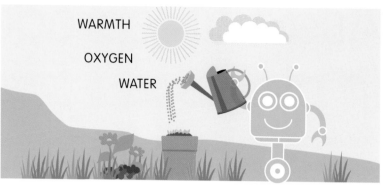

WARMTH

OXYGEN

WATER

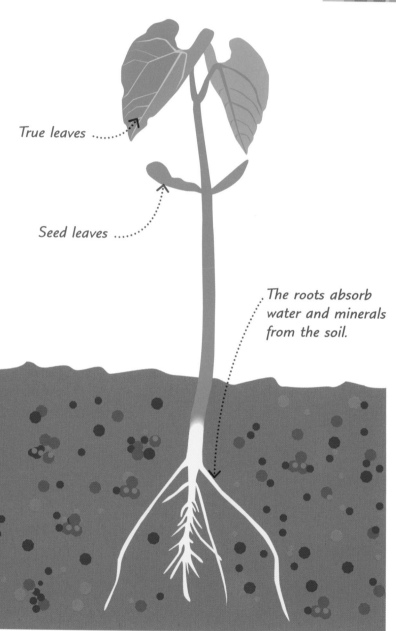

True leaves ....

Seed leaves ....

.. *The roots absorb water and minerals from the soil.*

4 The seedling grows its first true leaves. These true leaves will now make the seedling's food, allowing it to grow bigger.

TRY IT OUT

Germinating seeds

Seeds normally germinate in soil, making it difficult to see how they transform underground. In this simple activity, you can find out how a bean seed springs to life, using just a clear container and some damp cotton balls.

..... *Damp cotton balls*

1 Fill a clear container with damp cotton balls. Place a bean seed between the cotton balls and the container, then leave it in a warm, dark place. Every now and then, add some water to keep the cotton balls moist.

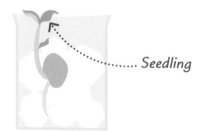

.... *Seedling*

2 It will take about a week for your bean seed to germinate. Watch for the first root and shoot, then when the first true leaves appear, move the container into the light.

Asexual reproduction in plants

In asexual reproduction, there is only one parent. Many plants reproduce asexually, which allows them to multiply in number and spread quickly.

Offspring produced asexually are clones—they are genetically identical to their parent.

How plants reproduce asexually

Almost any part of a plant can grow into a whole new plant, so plants have many ways of reproducing asexually.

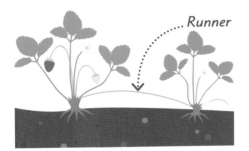

Runner

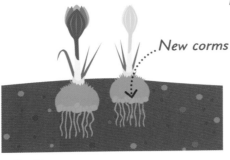

New shoot

Rhizome

Aspen trees produce of thousands of clones.

1 Runners
Plants such as strawberries create new plants from horizontal stems called runners. These take root to form new plants.

2 Rhizomes
Bamboos and many other plants produce new shoots from rhizomes—stems that grow horizontally underground.

3 Suckers
Some trees reproduce by sending out roots called suckers, which grow sideways. Buds on the suckers become new trees.

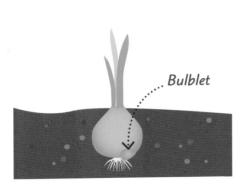

Bulblet

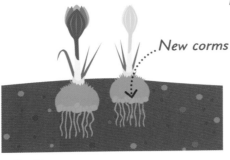

New corms

Plantlets

5 Bulbs
A bulb is an underground food store formed from layers of modified leaves. As well as storing nutrients, it produces new plants from bulblets around the base.

6 Corms
A corm looks like a bulb and does the same job, but it forms from a stem and is more solid. Buds on corms can develop into new corms.

7 Plantlets
This mother-of-thousands plant has the ability to produce tiny plantlets along the edge of its leaves. These drop off and grow into new plants.

Cuttings and grafting

The ability of plants to reproduce asexually makes it easy for gardeners and botanists to create new plants artificially. Taking cuttings and grafting plants are the most common methods.

Cutting......

Cutting is placed in soil, where it forms roots.

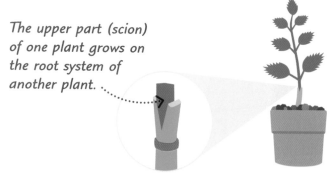

The upper part (scion) of one plant grows on the root system of another plant.

1 Cuttings are made by cutting a fragment off a plant and placing the cut stem in soil. Within a few weeks the stem grows roots, forming a whole new plant.

2 Grafting means joining a cutting to another plant so they grow together. Rose cuttings, for example, are often grafted onto a different kind of rose that has stronger, healthier roots.

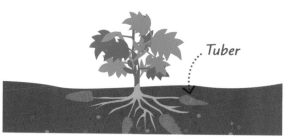

Tuber

4 Tubers
Some plants store nutrients in underground swellings called tubers. These also produce buds that grow into new plants.

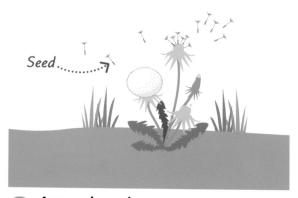

Seed......

8 Asexual seeds
Dandelion flowers produce unusual seeds that are clones of the parent plant, a type of asexual reproduction known as apomixis.

REAL WORLD TECHNOLOGY

Cultivated bananas

Most cultivated bananas are genetically identical descendants of a banana variety called the Cavendish banana. Cavendish bananas are seedless and cannot reproduce sexually, so new plants are grown from suckers. In the wild, bananas can reproduce sexually but their fruits have large seeds, which makes them difficult to eat.

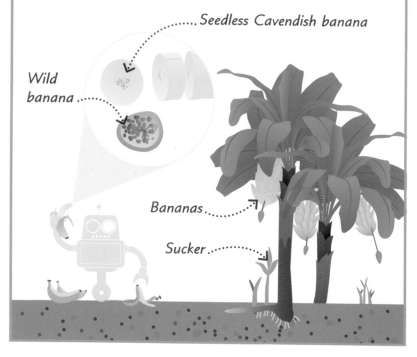

Seedless Cavendish banana

Wild banana

Bananas......

Sucker......

Single-celled organisms

Unlike animals and plants, whose bodies are made of billions of cells, single-celled organisms are made of just one cell each. The world is teeming with them, and they live everywhere—even on and inside your body.

Bacteria

Bacteria are the most common single-celled organisms and the smallest organisms known to science. A teaspoonful of soil contains more than 100 million bacteria, and your body is home to about 40 trillion. Some types are helpful. The bacteria that live inside the human gut, for instance, help you digest food. Other types are harmful and can cause diseases if they get into the body.

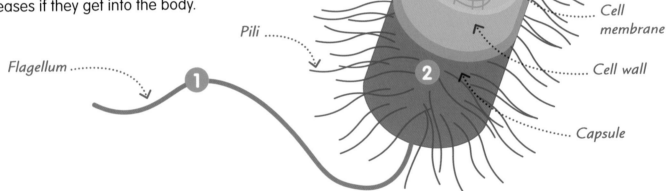

DNA · Cytoplasm

Cell membrane

Cell wall

Capsule

Pili · · · · · · · ·

Flagellum · · · · · · · ·

1 Flagellum
Some bacteria have a long whiplike fiber called a flagellum. This can rotate to make the bacteria move around.

2 Capsule
Many bacteria have a protective outer coat, or capsule. This may have hairs, called pili, to help the cell attach to things.

3 DNA
Bacteria don't have a cell nucleus to store genes. Their genes are carried by a tangled loop of DNA in the cytoplasm.

Bacteria shapes

Many bacteria are named after their distinctive shapes. The most common shapes are round (coccus), rod-shaped (bacillus), and spiral. Some bacteria join to form chains, clusters, or mats.

BACILLUS

STREPTOCOCCUS

VIBRIO

SPIRILLUM

SPIROCHAETA

Algae

Algae are plantlike organisms that live in water and use sunlight to make food. Vast numbers float in the surface of lakes and seas, where they form a food source for aquatic animals. Just a few of the many types of algae are shown here.

Some algae have flagella that flick back and forth like whips.

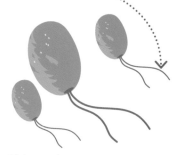

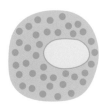

Many algae make protective shells from minerals such as chalk or silica.

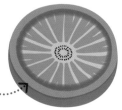

1 Chlorella
This alga lives in rivers and lakes. It sometimes multiplies in aquariums, giving the water a greenish haze.

2 Diatom
About a third of the oxygen in Earth's air comes from diatoms, which live in lakes and oceans. They have shells of silica, the mineral in sand.

3 Chlamydomonas
This alga can survive in soil and snow as well as lakes and oceans. It has a simple eyespot that allows it to swim toward or away from light.

Protozoa

The protozoa are a diverse group of single-celled organisms that mostly feed by hunting other single-celled organisms. Some of the largest are amoebas, which move and hunt by changing shape.

Pseudopod

Cell vacuole

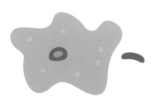

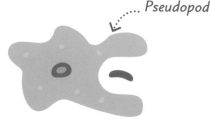

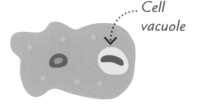

1 Amoebas don't have a mouth to swallow food. Instead, they react to prey such as bacteria by slowly flowing around it.

2 The amoeba's cell contents flow into extensions called pseudopods, which reach around the prey and trap it.

3 The pseudopods join to enclose the prey in a bubble of fluid— a cell vacuole. Digestive juices are secreted into this to digest the cell.

REAL WORLD TECHNOLOGY

Cleaning dirty water

Sewage plants use tanks of bacteria and other microorganisms to clean dirty water. One common design is the "trickling bed." Rotating arms trickle dirty water onto ponds full of gravel. Organic matter in the water feeds bacteria growing as a slimy film on the gravel particles. The bacteria kill and digest harmful germs, and clean water flows out from the bottom.

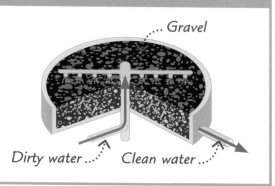

Gravel

Dirty water *Clean water*

Ecology

Ecology is the study of ecosystems. An ecosystem is a community of living organisms and the physical environment they inhabit and interact with.

Ecosystems include nonliving elements of the environment, such as soil, rocks, and water.

Ecosystems

An ecosystem may be as small as a puddle or as large as a rainforest. Every ecosystem includes populations of different species that interact with each other to form a community.

Every ecosystem needs an energy source.

The different species in a community depend on one another for their survival.

This population is made up of gazelles.

1 Population
A population is a group of organisms that belong to the same species and live in the same area. Animal populations usually include a mixture of breeding adults and their offspring.

2 Community
A community is made up of all the different populations that share an environment. It includes plants, herbivores (plant eaters), carnivores (meat eaters), and decomposers (organisms that break down dead matter).

3 Ecosystem
An ecosystem is made up of a community of organisms and its nonliving environment. Most ecosystems use the Sun as an energy source. Plants absorb the Sun's energy, then pass it on to the organisms that eat them.

Environmental factors

Environmental factors such as rainfall and temperature affect which species can live in an ecosystem.

1 Rainfall
Some parts of the world are always dry, while others get lots of rainfall throughout the year. A desert has just a few specialized plants, but a wet, rainy environment allows lush forests to grow.

Wetter conditions

DESERT   GRASSLAND   RAINFOREST

2 Temperature
As you travel from Earth's poles to the equator, the temperature rises and the type of vegetation changes. Coniferous forests flourish where the summers are cool and the winters are harsh, while rainforests grow at the equator where it is warm all year.

Warmer conditions

CONIFEROUS FOREST   DECIDUOUS FOREST   RAINFOREST

Relationships in ecosystems

A healthy ecosystem usually has many species that interact with each other in a variety of different ways, forming a web of relationships.

1 Competition
Members of the same population have to compete for a limited supply of food. This competition prevents that population from growing too big.

2 Predation
Predators hunt other animals for food. They allow plants to thrive, by preventing herbivores from becoming too numerous.

3 Parasitism
Parasites are animals that live on or inside other animals' bodies. They cause disease, which slows how quickly or how large a population can grow.

4 Mutualism
Mutualistic relationships benefit both partners. For example, insects help plants to reproduce by collecting pollen, which also provides food for the insects.

Food chains and recycling

A food chain shows how energy flows through an ecosystem as it passes from one organism to another in the form of food. Matter also flows through ecosystems, but unlike energy it is continually recycled.

Food chains

All living things need food to survive. Some animals eat plants, and in turn those animals are preyed on by other animals. In this way, the energy in the food is passed along a food chain, from one organism to the next.

> Marine food chains depend on tiny floating organisms called plankton.

1 Energy source
The Sun is the source of the energy that flows through nearly all food chains. Its energy travels to Earth as light.

2 Producers
Organisms that create food are called producers. Plants use the energy in sunlight to produce energy-rich food molecules.

3 Primary consumers
Primary consumers are animals that eat producers. Plant-eating snails are primary consumers.

Fungi and earthworms are decomposers.

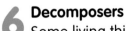

6 Decomposers
Some living things get food by digesting dead organisms and their wastes. These are called decomposers.

5 Tertiary consumers
Animals that prey on secondary consumers are called tertiary consumers. Weasels hunt birds and other small animals.

4 Secondary consumers
Secondary consumers eat plant eaters. Thrushes, for example, feed on snails and other invertebrates.

Pyramid of biomass

As energy passes through a food chain, most of it escapes as heat or other forms of energy. As a result, the amount of energy available as food gets smaller and smaller along the chain. This is why meat eaters are less common than plant eaters. A pyramid of biomass shows that the total weight of all organisms at each level gets smaller toward the top.

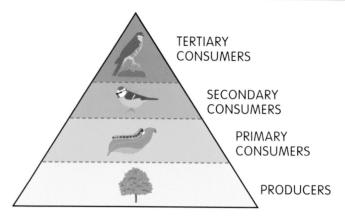

TERTIARY CONSUMERS

SECONDARY CONSUMERS

PRIMARY CONSUMERS

PRODUCERS

Recycling

The atoms that make up all living things are continually recycled, passing between living tissues and the nonliving environment over and over. Plants, for instance, take in carbon atoms from carbon dioxide in the air and use them to make food during photosynthesis. Animals take in the carbon when they eat plants, but animals and plants release it back to the air by the process of respiration. Plants take in nitrogen atoms from the ground through their roots and use nitrogen to make food molecules called proteins. Animals use these to build their body tissues, but the nitrogen returns to the soil as waste or dead matter.

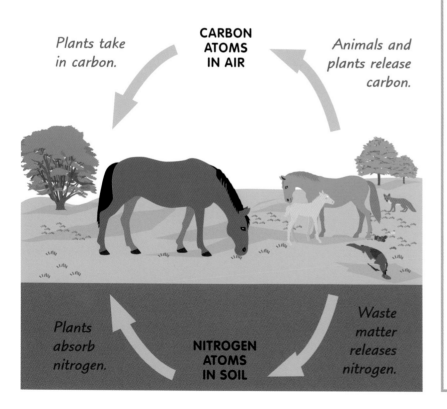

Plants take in carbon.

CARBON ATOMS IN AIR

Animals and plants release carbon.

Plants absorb nitrogen.

NITROGEN ATOMS IN SOIL

Waste matter releases nitrogen.

Biomass energy

Biomass energy is a renewable source of energy made from waste plant matter such as wood, crop waste, paper, and sawdust. Unlike fossil fuels, such as coil and oil, biomass energy doesn't pollute the atmosphere with carbon dioxide (CO_2). This is because the CO_2 released by burning the fuel is balanced by CO_2 absorbed as new crops and forests are grown.

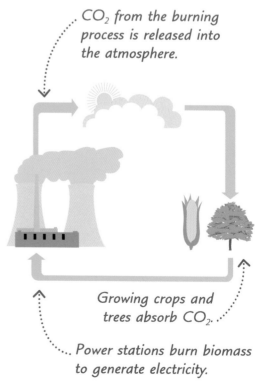

CO_2 from the burning process is released into the atmosphere.

Growing crops and trees absorb CO_2.

Power stations burn biomass to generate electricity.

Humans and the environment

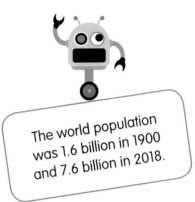

Earth's human population has quadrupled in the last 100 years, and the number of people continues to rise steeply. Supplying the growing population with energy, food, water, and other resources can harm the natural environment in many ways.

The world population was 1.6 billion in 1900 and 7.6 billion in 2018.

Trees are felled for lumber and to make room for farming.

1 Habitat loss
Wildlife is threatened by the loss of natural habitats such as forests. These habitats are cleared and their resources harvested to meet human demands for land, food, drinking water, energy, and other resources.

Smoke pollutes the air.

Waste chemicals pollute water.

2 Pollution
Waste chemicals from human activities can harm the environment. Some chemicals are poisonous to wildlife or build up to toxic levels in the food chain. Others, such as carbon dioxide gas, can change Earth's climate.

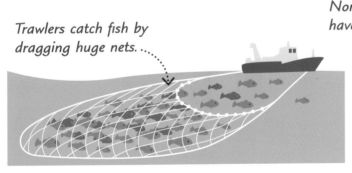

Trawlers catch fish by dragging huge nets.

3 Overexploitation
Some types of food, such as fish, are gathered from the wild. If animals are hunted faster than they can reproduce, their numbers decline and they may disappear altogether.

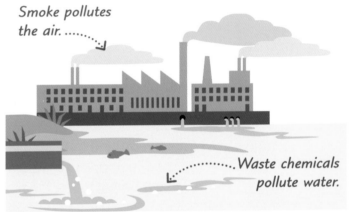

North American gray squirrels have spread to Europe.

4 Invasive species
When people introduce species to new parts of the world, they can harm the local wildlife. If the newcomers have no natural predators, they can multiply so quickly that they replace native species.

Biodiversity

If an ecosystem contains a wide variety of different species, we say it has high biodiversity. Protecting areas of high biodiversity is important because they benefit humans in many ways.

Just three plant species provide 60 percent of the world's food.

WHEAT   RICE   CORN

1 Food supply
The wild relatives of plants we grow as crops can be used to develop new varieties that can withstand disease or other problems, ensuring our future food supply.

2 Water supply
Plant-rich ecosystems such as forests can reduce floods by absorbing rain and releasing it slowly. They also filter water, helping prevent diseases caused by sewage.

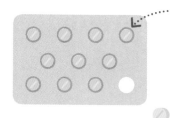

The malaria drug artemisinin is made from an herb called sweet wormwood.

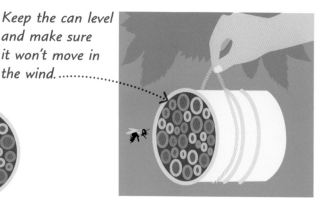

Bees carry pollen between plants, helping plants reproduce.

3 Medicines
Many medicines, such as aspirin, originally came from plants. Ecosystems such as rainforests could be a source of new drugs to help fight disease.

4 Insect helpers
Insects such as bees pollinate many food crops, including apples and peaches. Other insects, such as lady beetles, prey on the pests that can damage crops.

TRY IT OUT

Build a bee hotel

Not all bees live in hives! Help solitary bees by building a bee hotel, which gives them a safe nest to rear their young.

Keep the can level and make sure it won't move in the wind.

1 Collect hollow stems and let them dry out, or ask an adult to cut bamboo into short lengths.

2 Fill an empty container, such as a soup can, with the stems until they are tightly packed together.

3 Tie some string around the can and hang it next to a sunny wall, near grass or flowers.

From the air you breathe and the food you eat to the ground you walk on, everything is made of matter. All matter consists of particles called atoms. These are so amazingly tiny that it takes 300 billion billion to form just one raindrop. There are only 118 different kinds of atoms, but they can join together in endless combinations to create every kind of matter in the universe.

Atoms and molecules

All the things in the universe—from raindrops and specks of dust to plants, rocks, stars, planets, and the air we breathe—are forms of matter. Animals and people are matter too. All matter is made up of tiny particles called atoms and molecules.

1 Atoms
Atoms are the building blocks from which everything is made. They are so small that the human body contains about 7 billion billion billion of them. There are 118 different types of atoms.

2 Elements
A pure substance made of only one type of atom is known as an element. Copper, gold, silver, iron, and oxygen are examples of elements. Since there are 118 different types of atoms, there are also 118 different elements.

Gold is an element. Pure gold contains only gold atoms.

3 Molecules
The atoms of some elements, such as hydrogen, oxygen, and nitrogen, join to form groups called molecules. Forces called chemical bonds "glue" the atoms together. Some molecules have just a few atoms; others have thousands.

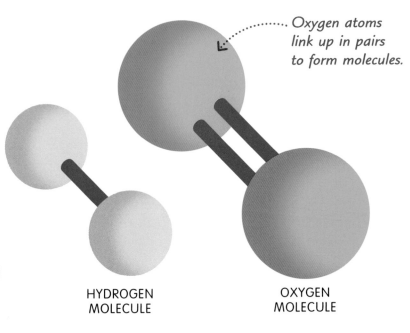

Oxygen atoms link up in pairs to form molecules.

Helium atoms don't join together.

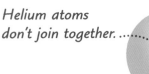

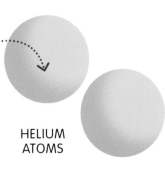

HELIUM
ATOMS

HYDROGEN
MOLECULE

OXYGEN
MOLECULE

4 Compounds

Molecules containing more than one type of atom are called compounds. Water, for example, is a compound of the elements hydrogen and oxygen. Carbon dioxide, which we breathe out from our lungs, is a compound of oxygen and the element carbon.

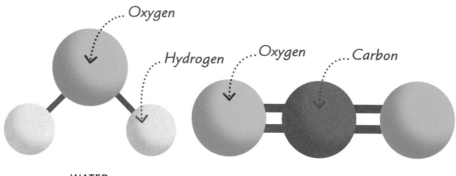

Oxygen

Hydrogen

Oxygen

Carbon

WATER
MOLECULE

CARBON DIOXIDE
MOLECULE

5 Chemical symbols

Each element has its own unique symbol, made up of one or two letters. For example, C stands for carbon, H for hydrogen, He for helium, N for nitrogen, and O for oxygen.

Chemical symbols always start with a capital.

If there's a second letter, it's written in lower case.

He = helium

Pb = lead

Pb comes from plumbum, the Latin word for lead.

6 Chemical formulas

Scientists use chemical symbols and numbers to show how elements combine together in a compound. This is called a chemical formula. The formula for water is H_2O, while carbon dioxide is CO_2.

Two hydrogen atoms

One oxygen atom

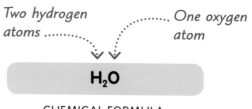

H_2O

CHEMICAL FORMULA
FOR WATER

One carbon atom

Two oxygen atoms

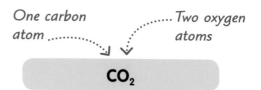

CO_2

CHEMICAL FORMULA
FOR CARBON DIOXIDE

TRY IT OUT

Make your own molecules

You can make your own molecules by connecting small balls of modeling clay with cocktail sticks. Try making water (H_2O) and carbon dioxide (CO_2). Use a different color for each element: white for hydrogen, red for oxygen, and black for carbon.

States of matter

Most substances can exist in three different forms: solid, liquid, or gas. These are called the three states of matter, and they exist because molecules can pack together in different ways.

Only two of the 118 known chemical elements are liquid at room temperature. All the rest are solids or gases.

1 Solids

The molecules in a solid are packed together tightly and held in place by bonds; this gives solids a fixed shape and makes them strong. Solids don't flow or change shape as liquids and gases do.

2 Liquids

The molecules in a liquid can slip and slide around each other, which allows liquids to change shape quickly. Liquids can be poured and will take the shape of any container.

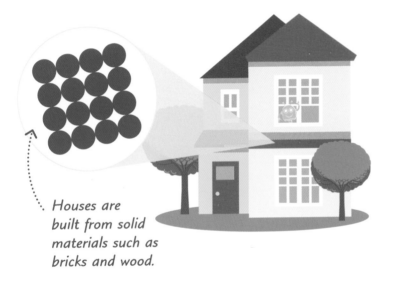

Houses are built from solid materials such as bricks and wood.

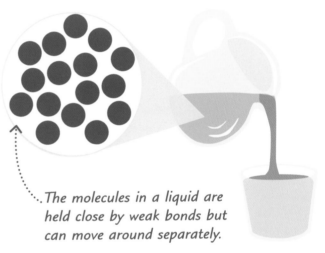

The molecules in a liquid are held close by weak bonds but can move around separately.

TOOTHBRUSH

PAINT   VEGETABLE OIL

SILVERWARE

WOOD

HONEY

TRY IT OUT

Squeeze test

Screw the cap on an empty plastic bottle and squeeze it with your hand. Then fill it with water and try again—you won't be able to squeeze. This is because the molecules in a liquid are packed together and can't be pushed any closer, but the molecules in a gas are much farther apart.

Easy to squeeze

Impossible to squeeze

3 Gases

There are no bonds between gas molecules, so they move around freely and spread out to fill any container. Air is made of gases. You can't see them, but you can trap them in bubbles or balloons.

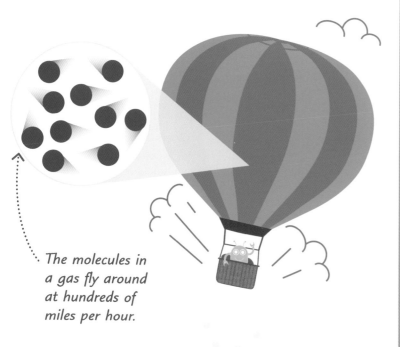

The molecules in a gas fly around at hundreds of miles per hour.

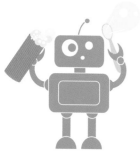

SOAP BUBBLES

GAS BUBBLES

REAL WORLD TECHNOLOGY

Aerosol cans

An aerosol can contains substances in all three states of matter. The can is solid metal; the spray inside is a liquid; and the top of the can contains a gas called a propellant, which is squeezed into a tight space under high pressure. When you press the button, it releases pressure, and the propellant pushes the liquid out as a mist of tiny droplets.

The propellant pushes down on the liquid.

The liquid is pushed through a tube running up to the cap.

Changing state

When solids melt or liquids freeze, we say they've changed state. Each time a substance changes state, it loses or gains energy.

> When a substance changes state, it is still the same chemical. Ice, liquid water, and steam are all forms of water.

Reversible changes

Adding heat energy to a substance can make it change from a solid to a liquid or from a liquid to a gas. When the substance loses energy, the reverse happens. All substances can change state if they lose or gain enough energy. Even air can turn to liquid or freeze and metals can melt and then turn into gas.

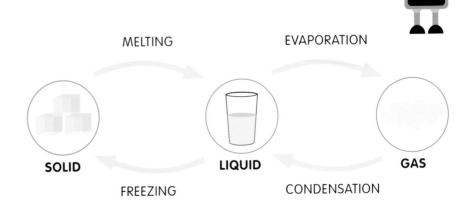

MELTING   EVAPORATION

SOLID   **LIQUID**   **GAS**

FREEZING   CONDENSATION

1 Freezing
When a liquid gets sufficiently cold, it freezes and becomes a solid. Water, for example, freezes at 32°F (0°C) and turns to ice. The molecules that make up the liquid water lose energy and become tightly bonded (fixed) together.

2 Melting
When you heat a solid, it melts and becomes liquid. The energy breaks the bonds between the molecules and allows them to move past each other. As a result, the liquid can flow. The temperature at which a solid becomes a liquid is called its melting point.

REAL WORLD TECHNOLOGY

Casting metal

Even substances like metal and glass can melt if they get hot enough. Some objects are made using molten metal. This process is called casting and involves pouring molten metal into a mold. When the molten metal cools and solidifies, it takes the shape of the mold.

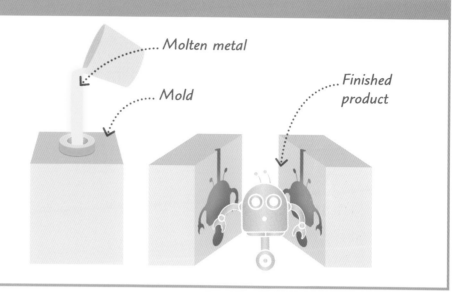

Molten metal

Mold

Finished product

3 Evaporation

When a liquid is heated, the molecules move faster and start to break free, escaping as a gas. This is called evaporation. If water is heated to 212°F (100°C), the water molecules change into a gas so quickly that the water boils.

4 Condensation

When a gas cools, the molecules lose energy and stick together, turning the gas into a liquid. This is called condensation. Condensation causes rain, fog, mist, or dew. It also causes clouds to form and makes your breath misty in cold weather.

Properties of matter

To make sure they pick the right material for the job, engineers have to consider the material's properties. A bridge made of jelly is useless—it can't support a car's weight—but a bridge of stone can.

The hardest substance in the human body is the enamel that protects your teeth.

Describing materials

Depending on the arrangement of its molecules, a solid material may be hard or soft, brittle or stretchy. Scientists use special terms to describe these properties.

1 Elasticity
Elasticity is a solid's ability to go back to its original shape and size after it has been stretched or squeezed. If you let go of a stretched rubber band, it returns to its original shape immediately.

2 Strength
The strength of a material tells you how well it resists a force that pushes or pulls on it. Bricks are strong enough to hold up the weight of a whole building.

3 Malleability
A malleable material can be beaten or pressed into shape. Modeling clay is malleable. Metals are also malleable—aluminum is rolled into thin sheets to make kitchen foil.

4 Ductility
A material that can be drawn out into a thin wire is said to be ductile. Gold and copper are very ductile. They can be stretched to make wire that's finer than a human hair.

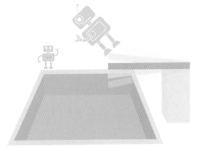

5 Flexibility
Some objects are flexible—for example, a diving board bends a little so you can bounce on it. The flexibility of an object depends on both its material and its shape.

6 Brittleness
A brittle material doesn't bend, stretch, or change shape. When the forces acting on it are great enough, it simply breaks. Ceramics and many glass products are brittle.

7 Hardness

Hard materials are difficult to scratch, but soft materials scratch easily. The hardness of a substance is measured on the Mohs scale. This scale compares materials to the hardness of ten common minerals rated from 1 (softest) to 10 (hardest).

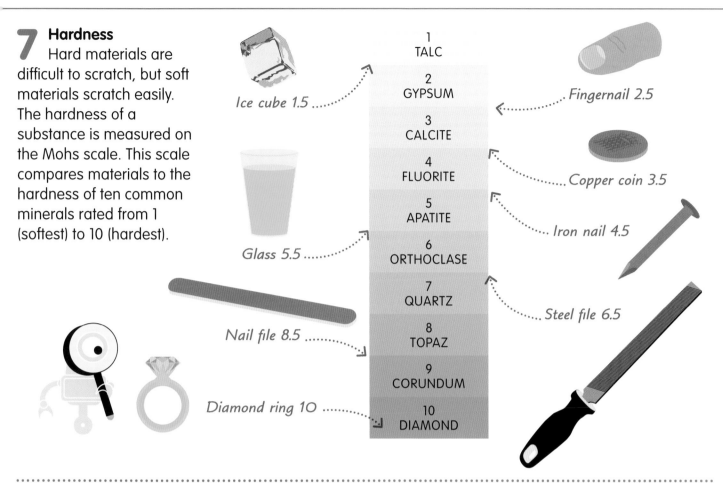

Ice cube 1.5

1 TALC
2 GYPSUM
3 CALCITE
4 FLUORITE
5 APATITE
6 ORTHOCLASE
7 QUARTZ
8 TOPAZ
9 CORUNDUM
10 DIAMOND

Fingernail 2.5

Copper coin 3.5

Iron nail 4.5

Glass 5.5

Steel file 6.5

Nail file 8.5

Diamond ring 10

Changing properties

Heat and cold can change a material's properties. Certain metals, for example, are only malleable when heated. Clay, on the other hand, is normally very easy to shape. However, it becomes hard and brittle after it's baked in a kiln (oven).

TRY IT OUT

Viscosity race

Liquids vary in how easily they flow—a property known as viscosity. Thin and runny liquids have low viscosity, while viscous liquids are thick and sticky. Compare the viscosity of different liquids by setting up a viscosity race. Put a spoonful of the following liquids along one side of a tray: water, peanut butter, honey, ketchup, vegetable oil, and cream. Tilt the tray and see how fast each liquid flows. Which is the most viscous?

Starting line

Finish line

Expanding gases

Gases are made up of billions of atoms or molecules that move around freely. The hotter a gas gets, the faster these particles move and the farther they spread out, making the gas expand.

Hot-air balloons

The first-ever aircraft—a hot-air balloon—was launched in 1783. The hot-air balloon is one of the simplest forms of transportation and is still in use today. It uses hot air trapped inside a huge balloon to lift passengers high into the sky.

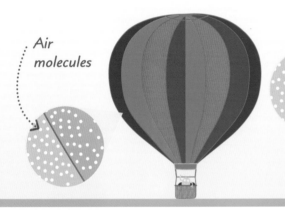

Air molecules

Air in the balloon becomes less dense as it heats up.

The hot air keeps expanding.

Burner

1 The balloon is on the ground because the air inside it is not much warmer than the air outside. Air molecules inside and out are equally spaced—we say they have the same density.

2 When the pilot heats the air inside the balloon, the molecules spread out. The air in the balloon becomes less dense, which makes it lighter. As a result, the balloon rises.

3 The warmer the air in the balloon gets, the less dense and lighter it gets compared to the heavier, cooler air outside. The balloon rises higher and higher.

REAL WORLD TECHNOLOGY

Lighter than air

Soon after the first hot-air balloon was flown, people began experimenting with giant balloons that could carry passengers long distances. Called airships, some of these used hydrogen gas instead of hot air because hydrogen has a much lower density than air. However, hydrogen burns, and it caused disastrous explosions. Today, airships are filled with the gas helium, which has a low density but doesn't burn.

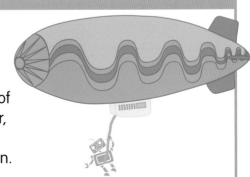

Hot air in nature

Rising hot air can be found in nature, too. The Sun acts as the perfect heating system, creating thermal columns that can lift soaring birds and gliders high into the sky.

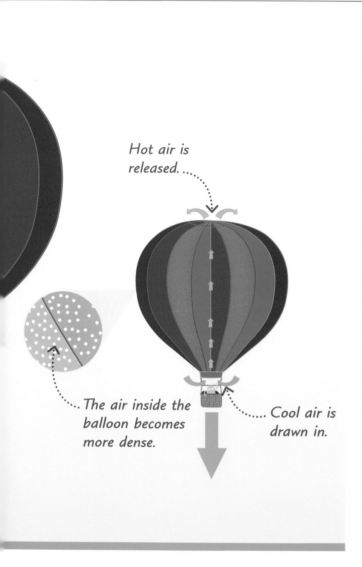

Hot air is released.

The air inside the balloon becomes more dense.

Cool air is drawn in.

4 To bring the balloon back down, the pilot needs to cool the air inside it. He releases some of the hot air through a vent at the top. Cool air is drawn in at the bottom to replace it, and the balloon sinks.

Hot air rises above cold air because it is less dense. Cold air sinks below hot air because it is more dense.

The Sun warms the ground.

1 The Sun transfers heat into the ground, so the ground warms up.

The ground warms the air above it.

2 The warm ground transfers heat into the air that sits above it.

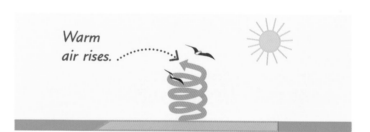

Warm air rises.

3 This warmed air rises above the cooler air because it is less dense. Birds use the rising air to lift them into the sky.

Cool air sinks back to the ground.

4 The air cools back down when it gets high in the sky, so it sinks back toward the ground, where the cycle begins again.

Density

A pebble is smaller than a bathroom sponge but it's also heavier. Small objects can be heavier than larger ones if they have more matter packed into them. We say they're more dense.

Objects less dense than water float, and objects more dense than water sink.

Comparing mass, volume, and density

Mass is how much matter there is in an object, while volume is how much space it takes up. Density is the amount of mass per unit of volume.

1 Equal mass
These two robots are made of the same material and so have equal density. They are also the same volume, so they have equal mass and balance on the seesaw.

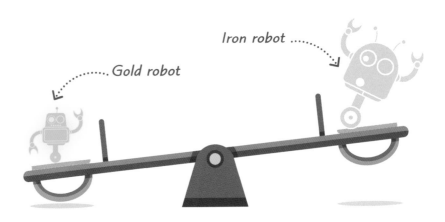

2 Different volume
These robots are made of the same material and have equal density, but the robot on the right has a greater volume and so has more mass. As a result, it tips the seesaw.

3 Different density
These robots are made of different materials with different densities. The gold robot is smaller than the iron robot but has more mass because gold is about 2½ times denser than iron.

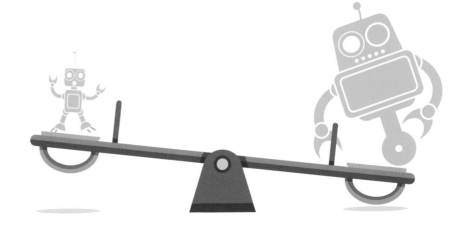

Iron robot

Gold robot

Density in different states

Most solids are denser than liquids because their molecules are more tightly packed. Gases are much less dense than solids or liquids because the molecules spread out, with empty spaces between them.

Solid molecules are tightly packed.

Liquid molecules are less tightly packed.

Gas molecules are far apart.

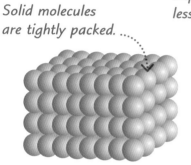
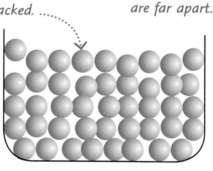
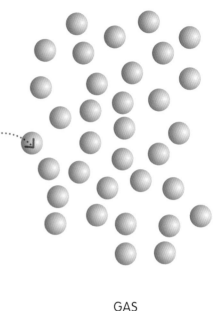

SOLID

LIQUID

GAS

Density of metals

You can calculate density by dividing an object's mass by its volume. These blocks of aluminum, iron, and gold all have a volume of 1 cubic centimeter (1 cm³). However, they have different masses because these metals have different densities. Aluminum has the lowest density, at 2.7 grams per cubic centimeter (g/cm³). Gold is more than seven times denser, at 19.3 g/cm³.

ALUMINUM
MASS = 2.7 grams
DENSITY = 2.7 g/cm³

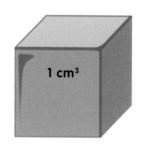

IRON
MASS = 7.9 grams
DENSITY = 7.9 g/cm³

GOLD
MASS = 19.3 grams
DENSITY = 19.3 g/cm³

REAL WORLD TECHNOLOGY

Polystyrene foam

A piece of polystyrene foam is more than 95 per cent air, giving it a very low density and making it incredibly light. It is also good at absorbing shocks. As a result, it makes an ideal packaging material. Fragile objects are often packed in boxes filled with foam peanuts—small pieces of polystyrene about the size and shape of unshelled peanuts.

Foam peanuts

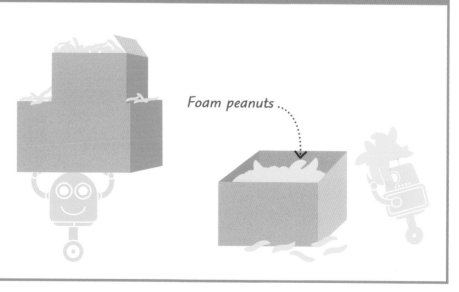

Mixtures

Unlike a pure chemical, a mixture contains different chemicals jumbled together, without being chemically bonded. Solids, liquids, and gases can mix together in lots of different ways.

Air is a mixture of gases, while rocks are mixtures of solids.

Types of mixtures

In a mixture, one substance disperses (spreads) to form particles in another. Depending on the size of the particles, the mixture may be called a solution, a colloid, or a suspension.

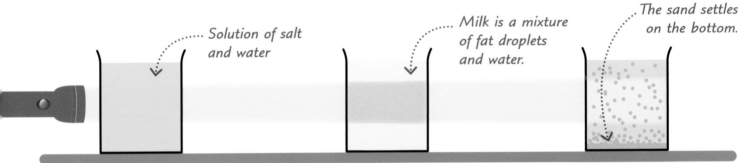

Solution of salt and water

Milk is a mixture of fat droplets and water.

The sand settles on the bottom.

1 Solution
In a solution, such as salt and water, the salt particles are so small that you can't see them. The solution is clear and light passes straight through it.

2 Colloid
In a colloid, such as milk, the particles are bigger than those in a solution. They are often large enough to scatter light, making a flashlight beam visible.

3 Suspension
A suspension, such as sandy water, has very large particles. They are clearly visible and settle on the bottom if the mixture is left to stand.

Types of colloids

Colloids can be made from different combinations of solids, liquids, and gas. Each combination has a particular name.

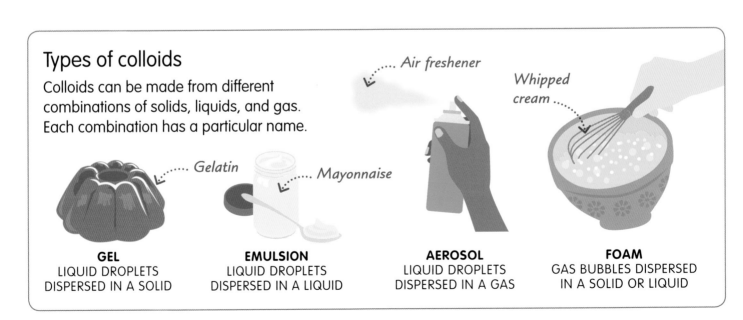

Air freshener

Whipped cream

Gelatin

Mayonnaise

GEL
LIQUID DROPLETS DISPERSED IN A SOLID

EMULSION
LIQUID DROPLETS DISPERSED IN A LIQUID

AEROSOL
LIQUID DROPLETS DISPERSED IN A GAS

FOAM
GAS BUBBLES DISPERSED IN A SOLID OR LIQUID

Mixtures and compounds

Unlike a mixture, a compound is a substance that forms when the atoms of two or more chemicals become chemically bonded together. A mixture is easy to separate, but a compound isn't.

SULFUR + IRON FILINGS → MIXTURE

Mixture of iron filings and sulfur

1 Iron and sulfur mixture
A mixture of iron filings and powdered sulfur is easy to separate with a magnet. The magnet pulls the iron filings out of the mixture and leaves the sulfur behind.

Iron sulfide

2 Iron sulfide compound
If you heat iron and sulfur, a chemical reaction occurs, producing a black compound called iron sulfide. The iron and sulfur atoms are now chemically bonded and can't be separated with a magnet.

Pure chemicals

A pure chemical contains only one type of atom or molecule. Compounds may be pure, but mixtures aren't. Tap water isn't pure—its a mixture of water and dissolved minerals. Completely pure water, called distilled water, contains water molecules and nothing else.

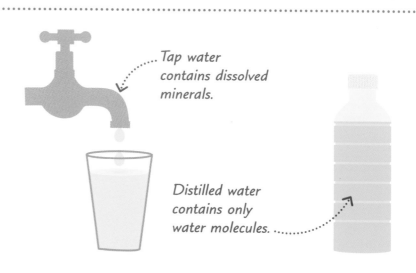

Tap water contains dissolved minerals.

Distilled water contains only water molecules.

Alloys

An alloy is a mixture of different metals or a mixture of a metal and a nonmetal, such as carbon. Alloys tend to be harder than the pure metals they're made from, which makes them more useful.

BRONZE
COPPER + TIN

BRASS
COPPER + ZINC

DENTAL AMALGAM
MERCURY + SILVER + TIN + COPPER

Solutions

When you stir sugar into water, it appears to vanish. When a substance mixes evenly with a liquid in this way, we say it dissolves. The resulting mixture is called a solution.

> You can't see sugar after it dissolves in water, but you can still taste it.

Dissolving

A substance that dissolves in a liquid is called a solute, and the liquid that dissolves it is called a solvent. Water is a good solvent because it can dissolve lots of different things, such as sugar and salt.

1 When a solid such as sugar dissolves in water, its molecules spread out and fit between the water molecules. No large pieces of sugar remain, so the sugar becomes invisible.

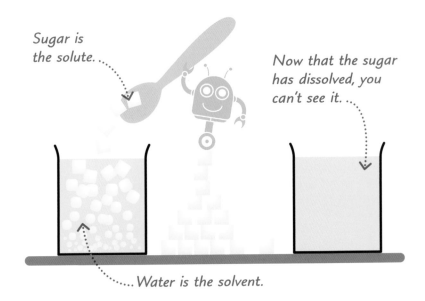

Sugar is the solute. ⋯

Now that the sugar has dissolved, you can't see it. ⋯

⋯ Water is the solvent.

2 Not everything will dissolve in water—otherwise you'd vanish when you take a shower. If you stir soil into water, it won't dissolve. Instead, it will settle in a pile at the bottom.

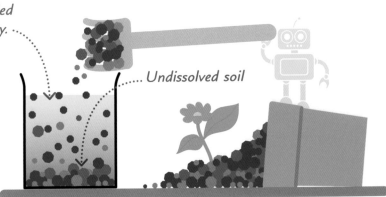

Some soil will stay suspended in the water, making it dirty. ⋯

⋯ Undissolved soil

REAL WORLD TECHNOLOGY

Putting the fizz into water!

Gases can dissolve as well as solids. Sparkling water is carbonated, which means the gas carbon dioxide is dissolved in the water. If you open a bottle, you release the pressure that keeps the gas dissolved. As a result, it leaves the solution as bubbles, making the water fizzy.

TRY IT OUT

Soluble or insoluble?

Which foods in your kitchen cupboards dissolve and which ones don't? Experiment with coffee, jelly, pepper, cooking oil, flour … or whatever else your parents let you try!

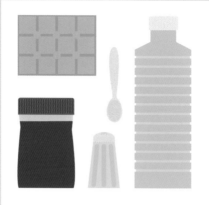

1 Put a teaspoon of your chosen food into a cup of cold water.

2 Stir it in. Does it dissolve or does it eventually settle on the bottom?

3 Try the experiment again with warm water. Is the result the same?

4 Do the same for other foods. Which food is the easiest to dissolve?

---

3 Stirring makes solutes dissolve more quickly in water. It moves the solute molecules around, helping them spread out between the water molecules. That's why people stir sugar into their coffee or tea with a spoon.

4 Solutes dissolve more quickly in hot water. When you heat water, its molecules move faster. They bump into the solute molecules more often, so the water and the solute rapidly mix. Detergents such as soap and shampoo clean better in hot water because they dissolve more easily.

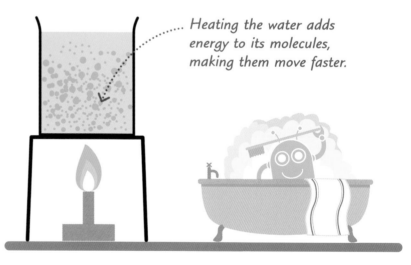

Heating the water adds energy to its molecules, making them move faster.

5 A solution with a small amount of solute in it is described as dilute (weak). If there's a lot of solute, the solution is concentrated (strong). If you keep adding solute, eventually no more will dissolve and the solution is saturated.

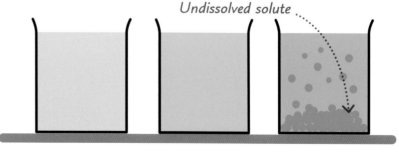

Undissolved solute

DILUTE   CONCENTRATED   SATURATED

Separating mixtures 1

The chemicals in a mixture are not chemically bonded and can be separated. Sifting, decanting, and filtering are simple ways of separating mixtures.

> An easy way to separate a solid substance from water is to let the solid dry.

Sifting

You can use a sieve to separate a mixture of two solids with different-sized particles. A sieve is like a basket with small holes in the bottom. Small particles fit through the holes, but big ones don't.

1 If you try to separate a mixture of sand and stones by picking out the stones one by one, it will be a long job. Using a sieve will make the task easier.

Mixture of sand and stones

2 The holes in the sieve let the small sand grains fall through but not the larger stones. The stones stay in the sieve and the sand piles up underneath.

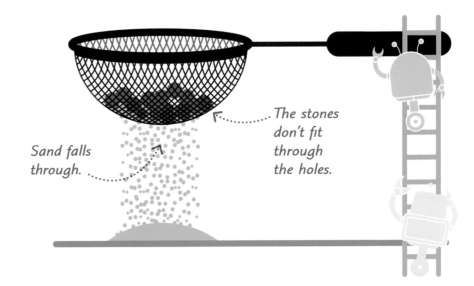

Sand falls through.

The stones don't fit through the holes.

REAL WORLD TECHNOLOGY

Water filtration

Dirty water can be cleaned by passing it through filter beds, which have layers of sand and stones that trap dirt but let water through. Clear water runs out and is then returned to the river or cleaned by another filter bed to remove germs.

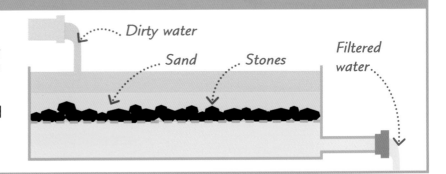

Dirty water

Sand   *Stones*

Filtered water.

Decanting

When insoluble solid particles mix with a liquid and settle on the bottom, they can be separated by pouring off the liquid. This is called decanting.

1 To separate a mixture of sand and water, you first need to wait and let the sand settle on the bottom.

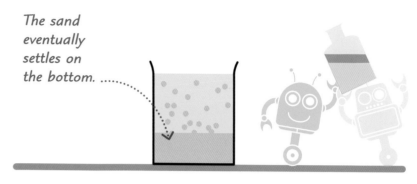

The sand eventually settles on the bottom. ......

2 If you carefully tip the beaker, you can now pour off the water without disturbing the layer of sand at the bottom.

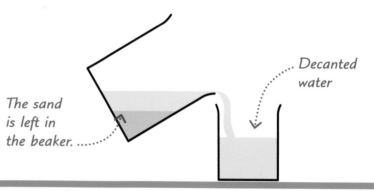

The sand is left in the beaker. ......

Decanted water

Filtering

Another way of separating insoluble solid particles from a liquid is to use a filter. This is a material with tiny holes in it. The filter lets the liquid through but not the solid particles.

1 When we drink ground coffee, we need to filter it so we don't get bits of ground coffee beans in our drink.

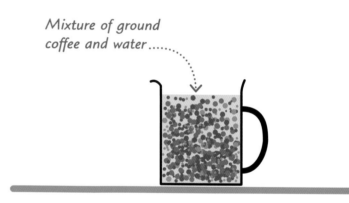

Mixture of ground coffee and water ......

2 To filter coffee, line a funnel with a filter paper and pour in the coffee. The coffee liquid soaks through tiny holes in the paper, leaving the ground coffee behind.

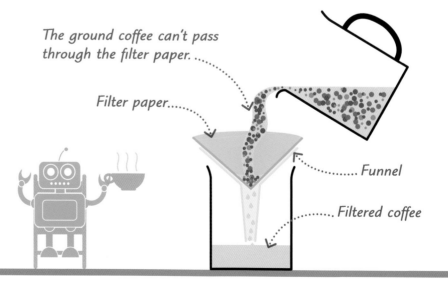

The ground coffee can't pass through the filter paper. ......

Filter paper ......

Funnel

Filtered coffee

Separating mixtures 2

Like other mixtures, solutions can be separated because the chemicals in them aren't bonded. Three ways of separating solutions are evaporation, distillation, and chromatography.

When paint dries, evaporation separates the solvent from the color, or pigment.

Evaporation

We can separate a soluble solid from a solution by heating the solution until the liquid part of it turns to gas, leaving the solid behind. We call this evaporation.

...Copper sulfate solution

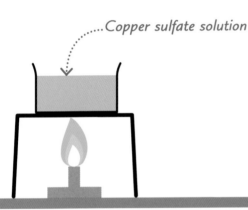

The water escapes as gas.

Only solid copper sulfate is left. ...

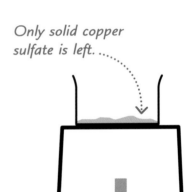

1 Heating
A bright blue solution of copper sulfate dissolved in water is heated so that it will start to boil and evaporate.

2 Evaporation
The water escapes as gas and the solution becomes more concentrated (stronger). Solid particles start to form.

3 Solid residue
When all the water has evaporated, only solid copper sulfate crystals remain. This leftover solid is called residue.

REAL WORLD TECHNOLOGY

Water for drinking

In countries where there isn't much fresh water on land, desalination plants are built on the coast. They separate salt from sea water, providing pure water for people to drink. Most desalination plants work by evaporating and then collecting the fresh drinking water.

Distillation

This separation method is similar to evaporation, but this time the vapor (gas) from the boiling solution is collected and cooled until it condenses (becomes liquid). Simple distillation can separate water from a salt solution.

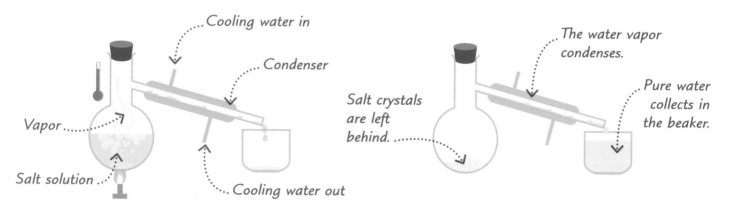

Cooling water in

Condenser

Vapor

Salt solution

Cooling water out

The water vapor condenses.

Salt crystals are left behind.

Pure water collects in the beaker.

1 Heating and evaporation
A salt solution is heated until the water in the solution boils. The water vapor passes through a cooling chamber called a condenser.

2 Condensing and collection
The cooled vapor condenses back into liquid water and drips into a beaker. It's now pure and salt-free. The salt is left in the flask.

Chromatography

Colored chemicals can be separated by a technique called chromatography. This involves dissolving the chemicals in water and then making them spread through an absorbent material, such as paper.

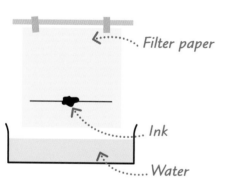

Filter paper

Ink

Water

1 To separate the different dyes in black ink, a spot of ink is put on a sheet of filter paper, and the end of the paper is lowered into water.

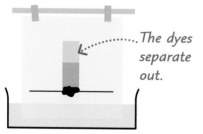

The dyes separate out.

2 As the paper soaks up the water, the ink dissolves and travels with it. Different dye molecules travel at different speeds, so the colors separate out into horizontal bands.

TRY IT OUT

Chromatography flowers

Use chromatography to make colorful paper flowers. All you need is filter paper, water, and a black marker pen.

1 Draw a circle in the middle of the filter paper.

2 Fold the paper in half twice to make a cone.

3 Place the tip of the cone in water. Make sure you keep your ink circle above the water line.

4 Watch as the different colors in the ink travel up the paper and separate.

Moving molecules

Molecules are always moving around, which is why smells can travel easily through air. When molecules gradually spread out through gases or liquids, it's called diffusion.

The molecules in a solid vibrate but can't move from place to place, so diffusion doesn't happen in solids.

How diffusion works

Diffusion happens because the molecules in a liquid or a gas all move around randomly. As a result, when different liquids or gases are put together, their molecules gradually mix, spreading from areas of high concentration to areas of low concentration. Over time, the different molecules become evenly mixed.

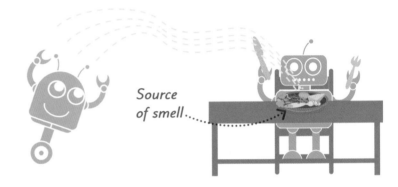

Source of smell

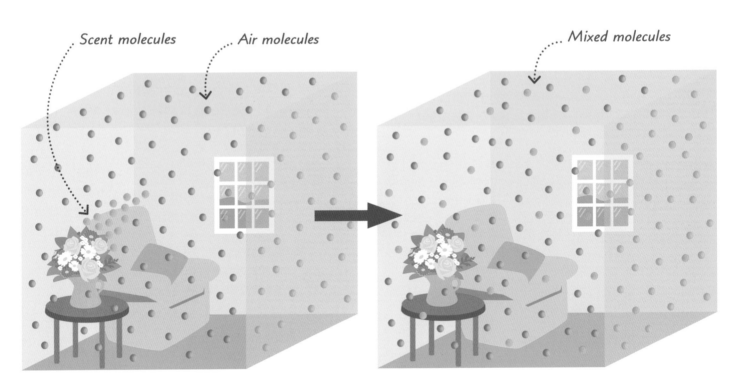

Scent molecules   Air molecules   Mixed molecules

1 Spreading out
When you first put flowers in a room, the scent molecules that give flowers their smell are concentrated around the vase. But they soon start to spread out and mix with air molecules.

2 Evenly mixed
Because the scent molecules move randomly, they eventually spread out until they're evenly mixed with the air. The smell of the flowers then fills the room.

Diffusion in solutions

Substances that dissolve in liquids can move by diffusion. When you put salt or sugar in water, for instance, it will eventually dissolve and spread out even if you don't stir the water.

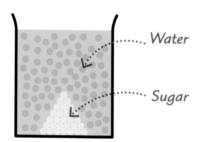

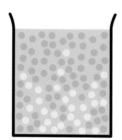

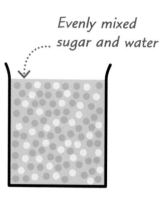

Evenly mixed sugar and water

Water

Sugar

1 When sugar is first added to water, the crystals make a pile at the bottom of the glass.

2 The sugar gradually dissolves, but at first the molecules are more concentrated at the bottom.

3 The sugar molecules move around randomly until they are evenly spread.

Brownian motion

In 1827 a Scottish scientist named Robert Brown was looking through his microscope when he noticed specks of dust jiggling around oddly in water. This mysterious movement, now called Brownian motion, was later explained by German scientist Albert Einstein. Einstein realized the dust particles were being struck repeatedly by water molecules as they moved around randomly. This random movement of molecules in liquids and gases also causes diffusion.

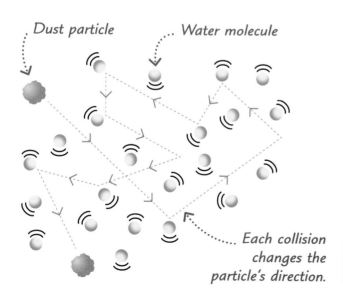

Dust particle   *Water molecule*

Each collision changes the particle's direction.

Osmosis

When one substance can diffuse through a barrier but others can't, a process called osmosis can happen. Osmosis is important in living cells, which have an outer membrane that lets water through but blocks other substances. For example, if the inside of a cell has a more concentrated sugar solution than the outside, water diffuses across the barrier until both sides are equally concentrated. As a result, the cell absorbs extra water and expands.

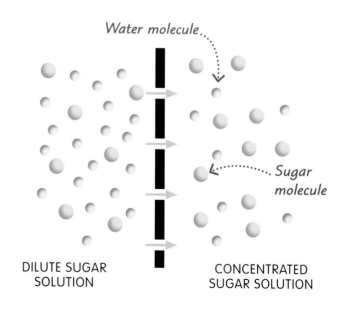

Water molecule

Sugar molecule

DILUTE SUGAR SOLUTION

CONCENTRATED SUGAR SOLUTION

Atomic structure

All matter is made of particles called atoms. Each atom has a nucleus (center) made up of tiny particles called protons and neutrons. Surrounding this are even tinier particles called electrons.

The number of electrons in an atom is usually equal to the number of protons.

Carbon atom

Each element has a different number and arrangement of particles in its atoms. Inside this carbon atom, for example, there are six protons, six neutrons, and six electrons.

1 Protons
Protons have positive electrical charges that attract the negatively charged electrons, holding them in place around the nucleus.

2 Neutrons
These particles have no charge.

3 Electrons
Electrons are outside the nucleus. Their negative charges balance the positive charges of the protons, so the whole atom is electrically neutral.

4 Nucleus
The atom's center, or nucleus, is made up of protons and neutrons.

5 Electron shell
The electrons form groups called shells at different distances from the nucleus. An atom can have up to seven shells.

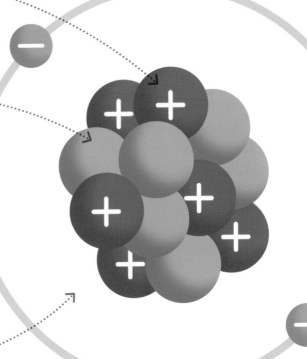

Inner shell

Outer shell

Mass number and atomic number

Electrons have almost no mass, so nearly all the mass of an atom is in the nucleus. Protons have the same mass as neutrons, so you can work out an atom's mass just by counting both. The total is called the mass number. The number of protons in an atom is called the atomic number.

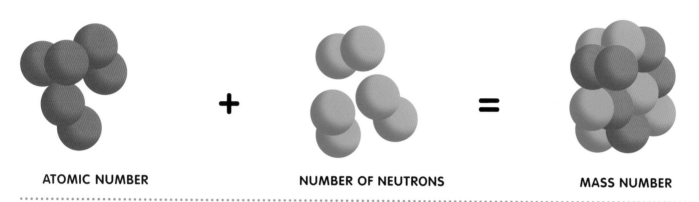

ATOMIC NUMBER   **+**   **NUMBER OF NEUTRONS**   **=**   **MASS NUMBER**

Atoms and elements

Every chemical element has a unique atomic number (number of protons), so the number of protons in an atom tells you what element the atom belongs to. Hydrogen atoms, for instance, always have one proton (an atomic number of 1).

Lithium has three protons and four neutrons.

Hydrogen has a single proton and no neutrons.

Helium has two protons and two neutrons.

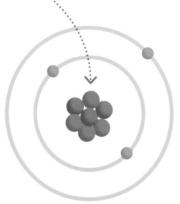

HYDROGEN
ATOMIC NUMBER = 1
MASS NUMBER = 1

HELIUM
ATOMIC NUMBER = 2
MASS NUMBER = 4

LITHIUM
ATOMIC NUMBER = 3
MASS NUMBER = 7

REAL WORLD TECHNOLOGY

Atom smashing

Scientists study the particles inside atoms in machines called particle accelerators. At the Large Hadron Collider in Switzerland, they use electromagnets to make these particles fly through long tunnels at incredible speeds and then smash together, producing even smaller fragments. In this way, new particles have been discovered.

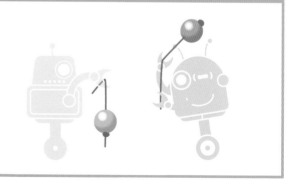

Ionic bonds

An ionic bond forms when one atom gives electrons to another atom, causing the two to become firmly attached. Atoms that have gained or lost electrons this way are called ions.

Ionic bonds often form between a metal element and a nonmetal.

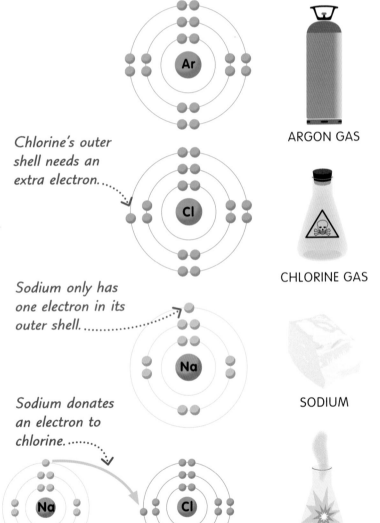

1 The electrons in an atom are arranged in shells (see pages 132–33). The inner shell can hold two electrons, and the other shells can usually hold eight. This atom of the gas argon has three full shells.

ARGON GAS

2 To be stable, most atoms "want" a full outer shell of eight electrons. However, many elements have an incomplete outer shell. The poisonous gas chlorine, for instance, has only seven electrons in its outer shell. It needs an extra electron to become stable.

Chlorine's outer shell needs an extra electron.

CHLORINE GAS

3 Sodium—a soft, silvery metal—only has one electron in its outer shell. If it can get rid of that electron, the full shell underneath will become its outer shell, making it stable.

Sodium only has one electron in its outer shell.

SODIUM

4 When sodium and chlorine mix, the sodium atoms give their spare outer electrons to the chlorine atoms, so both atoms have a complete outer shell. The result is a powerful chemical reaction that produces lots of heat and light.

Sodium donates an electron to chlorine.

SODIUM AND CHLORINE REACTING

5 Electrons are negatively charged, so chlorine's extra electron gives it a negative charge. It is now called a chloride ion. Sodium loses an electron and becomes a positive ion. Because opposite charges attract, the two ions join to create an ionic bond. They have formed salt.

Ionic bond

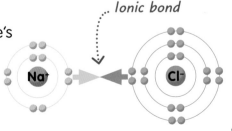

SALT (SODIUM CHLORIDE)

6 Ionic bonds often hold ions together in a regular structure called a lattice. In salt, each negatively charged chloride ion is surrounded by positively charged sodium ions, and vice versa.

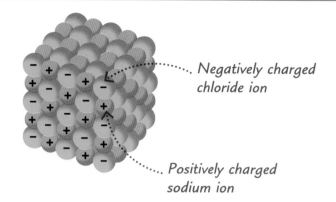

Negatively charged chloride ion

Positively charged sodium ion

7 Ionic bonds are strong and difficult to break, so ionic compounds are usually very hard, brittle solids that don't melt easily. Because their ions are arranged in a regular shape, many ionic compounds form crystals. The shape of the lattice gives the crystals a distinctive shape.

Natural salt crystals are square.

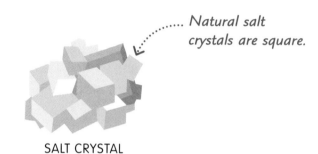

SALT CRYSTAL

Dissolving in water

Although ionic compounds are hard and don't melt easily, many of them dissolve easily in water. This is because water molecules have positively and negatively charged ends that attract the ions and make them separate.

1 When salt is solid, ionic bonds hold its positively charged sodium ions and negatively charged chloride ions tightly together.

SALT

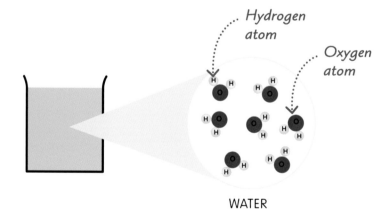

Hydrogen atom

Oxygen atom

WATER

DISSOLVED SALT

2 Water molecules have one oxygen atom and two hydrogen atoms. The oxygen atom has a slight negative charge, and the hydrogen atoms have a slight positive charge.

3 When you put salt in water, the positive ends of the water molecules attract the negative chloride ions, and the negative ends of the water molecules attract the positive sodium ions. The ionic bonds in the salt break, and the salt dissolves completely as the ions disperse.

Covalent bonds

Some atoms link together in molecules by sharing their electrons. This makes a very strong type of bond called a covalent bond.

> Most covalent bonds are single, double, or triple bonds.

1 A hydrogen atom has only one electron in its outer shell, but it needs two in this shell to become stable. A chlorine atom has seven electrons in its outer shell, but it needs eight to fill the shell and make it stable.

One electron in outer shell

Inner shell

Innermost shell

Seven electrons in outer shell

HYDROGEN ATOM   CHLORINE ATOM

2 The hydrogen atom shares its electron with the chlorine atom, and the chlorine atom shares one of its electrons with the hydrogen atom. Both atoms now have a full outer shell, forming a covalent bond that holds them together as a molecule of hydrogen chloride.

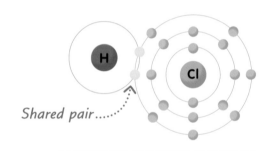

Shared pair

HYDROGEN CHLORIDE MOLECULE

3 An atom can form covalent bonds with several atoms, creating larger molecules. In water molecules, for example, two hydrogen atoms are linked to one oxygen atom, each by a separate covalent bond.

Covalent bond

WATER MOLECULE

A double bond has four shared electrons.

4 Sometimes the atoms in a molecule share two pairs of electrons. We call this a double bond. In a carbon dioxide molecule, for example, double bonds link two oxygen atoms to a carbon atom.

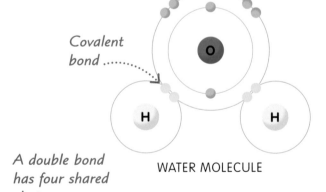

CARBON DIOXIDE MOLECULE

5 Three shared pairs of electrons form a triple bond. The nitrogen molecules in air (see page 170) consist of two nitrogen atoms linked by a triple bond.

Six shared electrons form a triple bond.

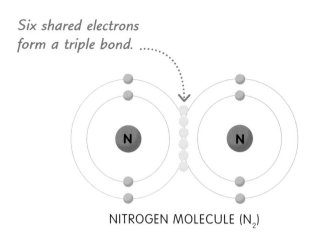

NITROGEN MOLECULE (N_2)

Forces between molecules

The molecules formed by covalent bonds are attracted to each other by weaker bonds called intermolecular forces.

1 Intermolecular forces make gases become liquid as they cool and make liquids become solid as they freeze. It doesn't take much energy to break these weak forces, so unlike ionic compounds, covalent compounds have low melting or boiling points.

2 The intermolecular forces between water molecules make them pull together into droplets and form a kind of surface. The force that forms the surface is called surface tension. Although it's easy for us to break this surface, small insects are light enough to stand on it.

Float a paper clip

The molecules at the surface of water are pulled together and down by intermolecular forces. This makes the surface behave like a stretchy elastic skin. Scientists call this force surface tension. Try this experiment to see surface tension in action.

1 Fill a dish with water.

2 Place a paper clip on a square of tissue.

3 Gently lower the tissue into the water so it rests on the surface.

4 The paper will absorb the water and eventually sink, but the paper clip will float, held up by surface tension.

5 If you add a drop of dishwashing liquid to the water, it weakens the surface tension and the paper clip will drop.

Chemical reactions

A chemical reaction breaks chemicals apart and forms new ones from the pieces. All chemical reactions involve the breaking or making of chemical bonds.

Iron objects rust because of a chemical reaction between iron and oxygen.

Physical and chemical changes

In a physical change, such as when butter melts, a substance has the same chemical makeup after the change as before it. But in a chemical change, such as when bread turns into toast, new chemicals are formed.

Melted butter is still butter.

Burned toast is mainly carbon.

Untoasted bread

Solid butter

1 Bread
Bread contains starch, a compound made of the elements carbon, hydrogen, and oxygen. When you heat bread to make toast, a chemical reaction changes the starch molecules.

2 Toast
Heat burns the surface of the bread, turning starch into carbon, which is black, and water, which escapes into the air as a gas.

How reactions work

During a chemical reaction, the atoms in the reacting chemicals rearrange to form new molecules or ions. As a result, reactions produce new chemicals with properties very different from the original ones.

Reactant 1

Reactant 2

Product

1 The chemicals that take part in a reaction are called reactants. The reaction shown here has two different reactants.

2 When the reactants mix, their molecules break apart and the atoms rearrange. Many reactions release energy as heat or light.

3 The chemicals produced by a reaction are called products. In this reaction, the reactants have combined to form a single product.

Conservation of mass

The products of a chemical reaction always have the same total mass as the reactants. The same atoms are present at the start and end, so their total mass can't change. We say that mass is conserved.

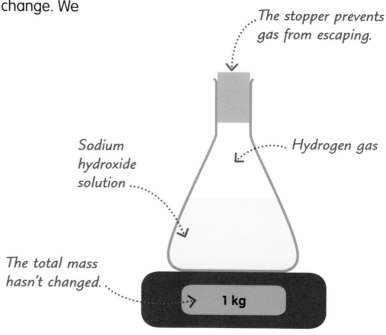

The stopper prevents gas from escaping.

Water

Sodium

Hydrogen gas

Sodium hydroxide solution

The total mass hasn't changed.

1 kg

1 kg

1 When the element sodium (a kind of metal) is dropped in water, it reacts violently to produce hydrogen gas (which may catch fire) and a chemical called sodium hydroxide.

2 After the reaction there's no sodium left, but the total mass of the equipment and the products hasn't changed. The mass has been conserved.

Crazy foam

When you add baking soda (sodium bicarbonate) to vinegar (ethanoic acid), a chemical reaction occurs. One of the products of this reaction is carbon dioxide gas (CO_2). This experiment shows how you can make crazy amounts of foam with the carbon dioxide bubbles.

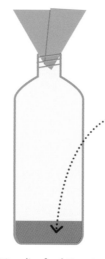

White vinegar mixed with food coloring and dishwashing liquid

1 Mix 2 fl oz (60 ml) of white vinegar with a few drops of food coloring and ten drops of dishwashing liquid in an empty plastic bottle. Make a funnel from a cone of paper.

2 Place the bottle in a large bowl and add two tablespoons of baking soda through the funnel. Swirl the bottle and stand back.

Chemical equations

Chemical equations show what happens to the atoms involved in a chemical reaction. The left side of an equation shows the reactants. The right side shows the products.

Chemical equations are written the same way in all languages.

1 Word equations

A simple way to write a chemical equation is in words. For instance, when powdered iron and sulfur are heated, they react to make the compound iron sulfide. The words to the left of the arrow show the reactants, and the words on the right show the product.

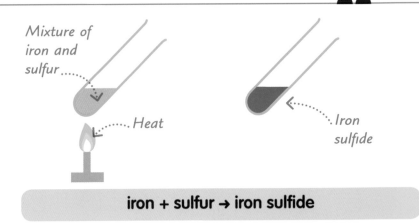

Mixture of iron and sulfur

Heat

Iron sulfide

iron + sulfur → iron sulfide

2 Symbol equations

You can also write equations using chemical symbols. The chemical symbol for iron is Fe and the chemical symbol for sulfur is S, so the reaction between iron and sulfur can be written as shown here. Unlike a word equation, a symbol equation shows the number of atoms involved in the reaction. In this example, each iron atom reacts with one sulfur atom.

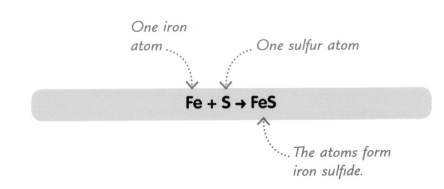

One iron atom

One sulfur atom

Fe + S → FeS

The atoms form iron sulfide.

Balanced equations

Chemical equations must be balanced, with as many atoms on one side as there are on the other. In other words, the total number of each type of atom must be the same in the products as in the reactants. This equation, showing how water forms when hydrogen reacts with oxygen, is balanced.

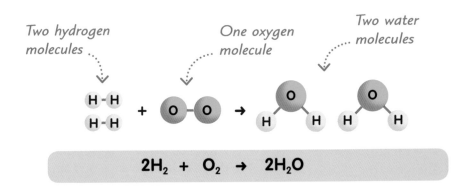

Two hydrogen molecules

One oxygen molecule

Two water molecules

$$2H_2 + O_2 \rightarrow 2H_2O$$

Reversible reactions

Some reactions are reversible, which means they can happen in both directions. For example, when the brown gas nitrogen dioxide is heated, it breaks down into the colorless gases nitrogen monoxide and oxygen. When these cool, they react to form nitrogen dioxide again. The equation has a special two-way arrow to show the reaction is reversible.

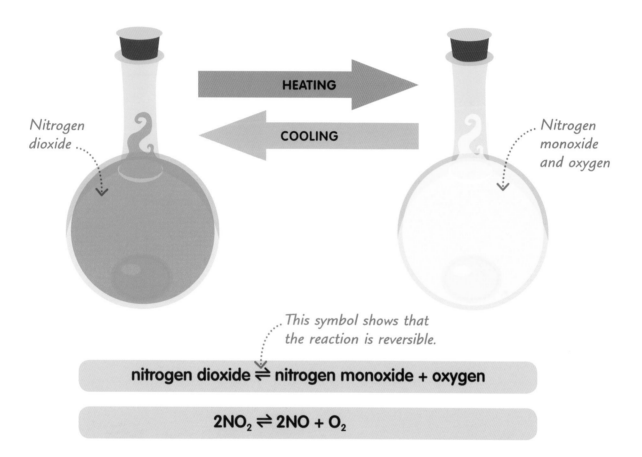

Nitrogen dioxide

HEATING

COOLING

Nitrogen monoxide and oxygen

..This symbol shows that the reaction is reversible.

nitrogen dioxide $\rightleftharpoons$ nitrogen monoxide + oxygen

$2NO_2 \rightleftharpoons 2NO + O_2$

TRY IT OUT

Work it out

Try to complete this equation for the reaction (shown on page 139) between sodium and water to form sodium hydroxide (NaOH) and hydrogen (H_2) using chemical symbols and formulas. The first part has been done for you. Remember—equations must balance!

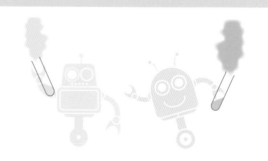

sodium + water → sodium hydroxide + hydrogen

$2Na + 2H_2O$ → ??? + ???

Answer: $2Na + 2H_2O \rightarrow 2NaOH + H_2$

Types of reactions

There are many different types of chemical reactions, but most of them fall into one of three main types: synthesis reactions, decomposition reactions, and displacement reactions.

The human body uses decomposition reactions to break down food.

Synthesis

1 In a synthesis reaction, two or more simple reactants join together to make a more complex product.

2 For example, the metal sodium (Na) and the gas chlorine (Cl) react together to make sodium chloride (NaCl)— the salt we put on food.

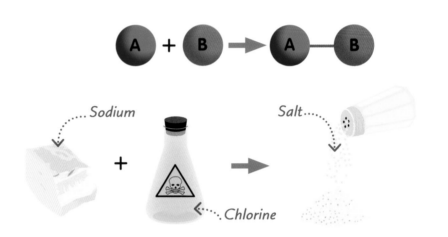

sodium + chlorine → sodium chloride (salt)

$$2Na + Cl_2 \rightarrow 2NaCl$$

Decomposition

1 In a decomposition reaction, a reactant breaks down into smaller and simpler products.

2 For example, the blue-green salt copper carbonate ($CuCO_3$) decomposes when it's heated to make black copper oxide (CuO) and carbon dioxide (CO_2) gas.

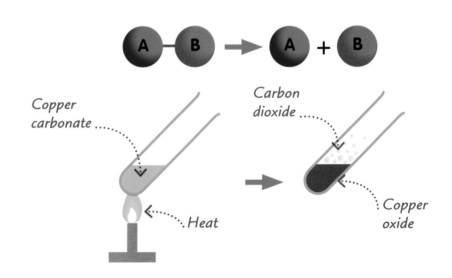

copper carbonate → copper oxide + carbon dioxide

$$CuCO_3 \rightarrow CuO + CO_2$$

Displacement

1 In a displacement reaction, one element takes the place of another in a compound. The more reactive element forces the other element out of the compound.

2 For example, if you put a copper strip into a solution of silver nitrate, copper atoms displace the silver atoms. The copper dissolves, turning the solution blue-green, and the silver comes out of the solution, forming a coating on the strip.

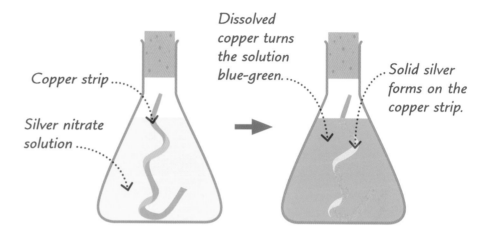

Copper strip

Silver nitrate solution

Dissolved copper turns the solution blue-green.

Solid silver forms on the copper strip.

copper + silver nitrate → copper nitrate + silver

$$Cu + 2AgNO_3 \rightarrow Cu(NO_3)_2 + 2Ag$$

Double displacement

1 In this kind of reaction, two ionic compounds react and their positive and negative ions switch places, forming two new compounds.

2 For instance, if you mix a solution of silver nitrate with a solution of sodium chloride, the positive and negative ions swap and form sodium nitrate, which is soluble, and silver chloride, which isn't. The silver chloride comes out of the solution as a white solid, making the liquid cloudy.

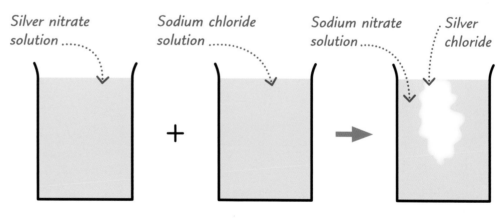

Silver nitrate solution

Sodium chloride solution

Sodium nitrate solution

Silver chloride

silver nitrate + sodium chloride → silver chloride + sodium nitrate

$$AgNO_3 + NaCl \rightarrow AgCl + NaNO_3$$

Energy and reactions

A chemical reaction involves a transfer of energy. Some reactions release energy—for instance, as heat or light— but others absorb it from their surroundings.

Reactions that suddenly release lots of energy cause explosions.

Activation energy

All chemical reactions need to be kick-started by energy because energy is needed to break the bonds between atoms before new molecules can form. That's why a match won't light until you strike it, and a candle won't burn unless you hold a flame to it. The energy needed to set off a reaction is called the activation energy and is like a hill that the reactants have to get over.

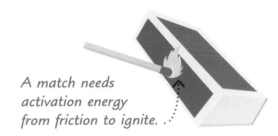

A match needs activation energy from friction to ignite.

Exothermic reactions

It takes energy to break chemical bonds, but when new bonds form, energy is released again. If more energy is released than is taken in, a reaction releases energy to its surroundings, usually as heat and light. We call these reactions exothermic.

$$CH_4 + 2O_2 \rightarrow CO_2 + 2H_2O$$

methane + oxygen → carbon dioxide + water

1 Methane (CH_4) is the gas used for cooking food on gas stoves. When you set light to it, it reacts with oxygen (O_2) in the air and burns.

2 The chemical equation for the reaction of methane with oxygen shows that the atoms are rearranged to make carbon dioxide (CO_2) and water (H_2O).

TRY IT OUT

Feel the heat

Here's a simple exothermic reaction you can try out. Put some laundry detergent powder in a plastic bag and add water to make a paste. Hold the bag in your hand—you'll feel heat given off as the chemicals react with water.

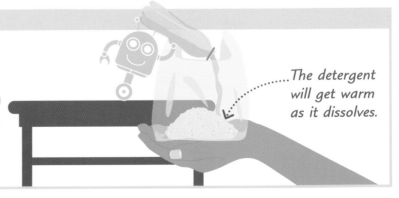

The detergent will get warm as it dissolves.

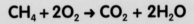

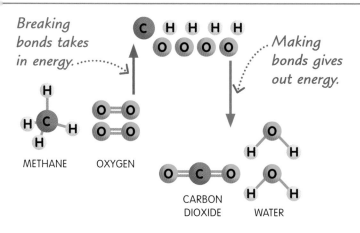

Breaking bonds takes in energy.

Making bonds gives out energy.

METHANE   OXYGEN

CARBON DIOXIDE   WATER

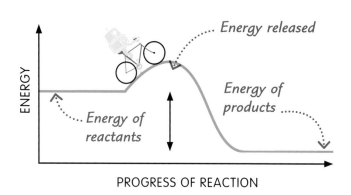

Energy released

Energy of reactants

Energy of products

PROGRESS OF REACTION

3 During the reaction, the bonds in the methane and oxygen molecules break, and new bonds form to make carbon dioxide and water molecules. Heat is given off because the new bonds store less energy than the bonds in the reactants.

4 This graph shows the energy changes during an exothermic reaction. At the end of the reaction, the energy in the products is lower than the energy in the reactants.

Endothermic reactions

In some reactions, the energy needed to break the existing bonds is more than the energy given out by making the new bonds. The extra energy is taken in from the surroundings. We call this an endothermic reaction.

1 Plants use an endothermic reaction called photosynthesis (see pages 88–89) to absorb energy from sunlight and store it in sugars.

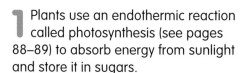
carbon dioxide + water → sugar + oxygen

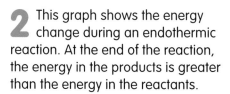
$6CO_2 + 6H_2O \rightarrow C_6H_{12}O_6 + 6O_2$

2 This graph shows the energy change during an endothermic reaction. At the end of the reaction, the energy in the products is greater than the energy in the reactants.

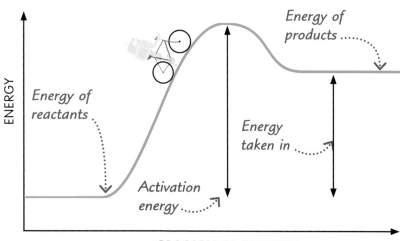

Energy of reactants

Energy of products

Energy taken in

Activation energy

PROGRESS OF REACTION

Catalysts

A catalyst is a chemical that makes a reaction go faster. Your body uses biological catalysts called enzymes for many things, including digesting food.

Saliva (spit) contains a catalyst that digests the starch in food.

Energy barrier

Some chemical reactions are slow or won't start unless you put extra energy in. For instance, the reaction that makes wood burn doesn't start unless you heat wood with a flame. This extra energy is called activation energy. Catalysts make reactions happen more easily by providing a kind of shortcut that reduces how much activation energy is needed.

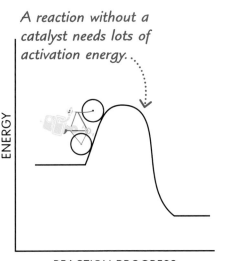

A reaction without a catalyst needs lots of activation energy.

ENERGY

REACTION PROGRESS

A reaction with a catalyst needs less activation energy.

ENERGY

REACTION PROGRESS

How catalysts work

Catalysts combine with the molecules in a chemical reaction and bring them close together. This makes the reaction take place more quickly and easily.

Catalyst

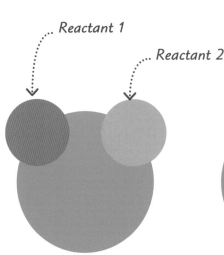

Reactant 1

Reactant 2

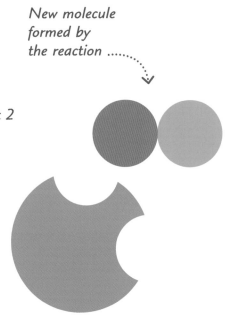

New molecule formed by the reaction

1 A catalyst molecule has a shape that enables it to bond temporarily with the molecules it will help to react (the reactants).

2 The two reactant molecules stick to the catalyst and react with each other, bonding to form a new molecule.

3 The new molecule separates from the catalyst. The catalyst is unchanged after the reaction and can be used again.

Solid catalysts

Some catalysts are solids that provide a physical surface to which other molecules can attach. Plant fertilizers for farms and gardens contain the chemical ammonia. Ammonia is made from the gases nitrogen (N_2) and hydrogen (H_2), which react with the aid of a catalyst made of powdered iron. This reaction is called the Haber process.

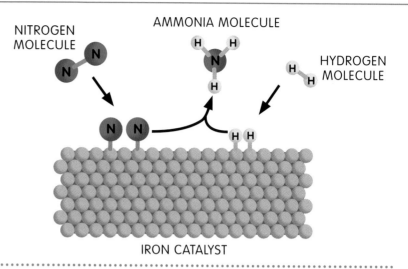

NITROGEN MOLECULE

AMMONIA MOLECULE

HYDROGEN MOLECULE

IRON CATALYST

Enzymes

Your body uses biological catalysts called enzymes for many things, including breaking down large food molecules into smaller molecules that your blood can absorb. Food molecules fit into specially shaped "active sites" on digestive enzymes. This causes the food molecules to react with water and split.

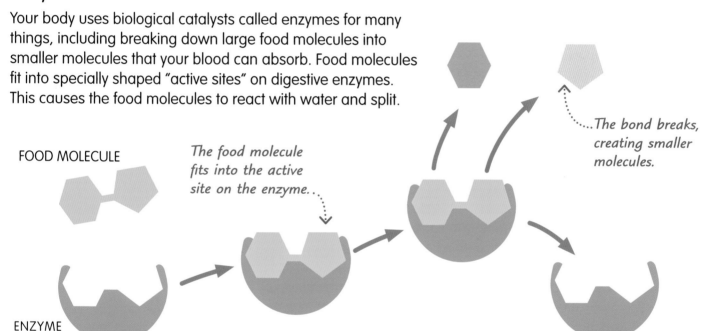

FOOD MOLECULE

The food molecule fits into the active site on the enzyme...

...The bond breaks, creating smaller molecules.

ENZYME

REAL WORLD TECHNOLOGY

Catalytic converter

The catalytic converter in a car exhaust contains a honeycomb structure coated in a thin layer of the precious metals platinum and rhodium. The surface area of this coating is huge—about the area of two football fields. As exhaust gases from the engine pass through, the metals catalyze the conversion of unburned fuel and toxic nitrogen oxide and carbon monoxide into less harmful carbon dioxide, water, and nitrogen.

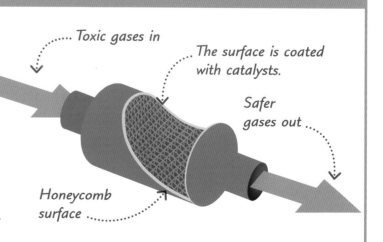

Toxic gases in

The surface is coated with catalysts.

Safer gases out

Honeycomb surface

Acids and bases

Powerful acids can attack metal and burn flesh, but weak acids are safe to eat—the sharp taste of lemon juice comes from an acid. Bases are chemicals that neutralize acids.

> Strong acids are corrosive, which means they react so strongly with some substances that they destroy them.

What are acids?

Acids are compounds that split in water to release highly reactive hydrogen ions (protons). The more hydrogen ions an acid releases in water, the stronger it is.

Hydrogen ion

Hydrogen ion

1 Strong acids
Strong acids break up completely in water, producing large numbers of hydrogen ions. They must be handled with great care because they can attack your skin and eyes. Your stomach produces the strong acid hydrochloric acid, which attacks germs and kills them.

2 Weak acids
Weak acids only partly break up in water. They taste sour because the surface of your tongue has taste buds to detect acids. They can irritate your eyes but they won't harm your skin. Vinegar, orange juice, lemon juice, coffee, and yogurt all contain weak acids.

What are bases?

Bases are metal compounds that react with acids and cancel out their acidity. We say they neutralize acids. Bases that can dissolve in water are called alkalis. Strong alkalis can be just as corrosive and dangerous as acids.

Baking powder
Cooks add baking powder to cake batter to help it rise. Baking powder is a mixture of a weak acid and a base called sodium bicarbonate. When these dissolve in the water in cake batter, they react and release carbon dioxide bubbles, making the batter light and fluffy.

Measuring acidity

You can measure how acidic a substance is by using strips of indicator paper—a special kind of paper that changes color with acidity. The color tells you the solution's pH, which stands for "potential of hydrogen." Acids have a pH under 7; alkalis have a pH over 7. A pH of 7 means a substance is neutral (neither acidic nor alkaline).

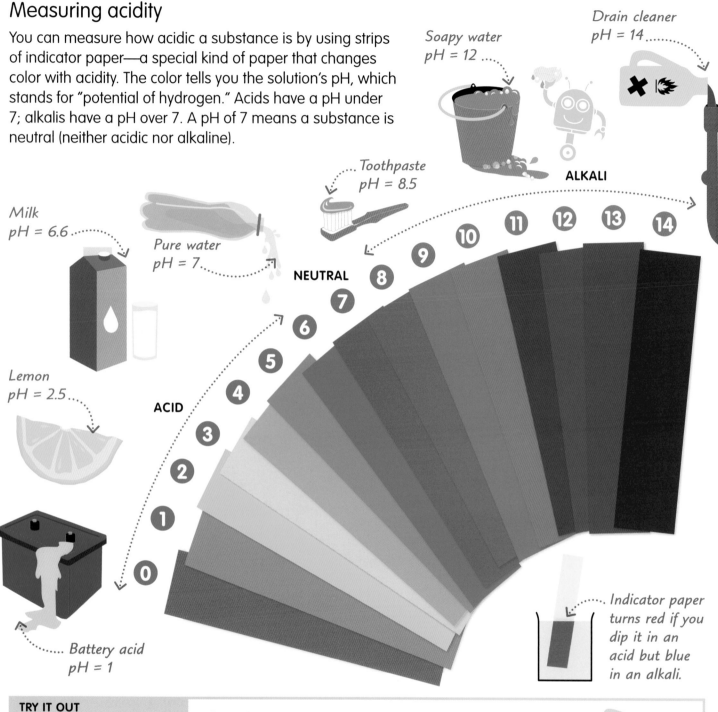

Soapy water
pH = 12

Drain cleaner
pH = 14

ALKALI

Toothpaste
pH = 8.5

Milk
pH = 6.6

Pure water
pH = 7

NEUTRAL

Lemon
pH = 2.5

ACID

Battery acid
pH = 1

Indicator paper turns red if you dip it in an acid but blue in an alkali.

TRY IT OUT

Red cabbage indicator

You can see how acidic something is by making your own indicator liquid from red cabbage.

① Ask an adult to chop a red cabbage, boil it in water, and strain off the purple liquid. Let it get cold. Pour the cabbage water into a series of glasses.

② Add white vinegar to a glass. The water will become acidic and turn bright pink.

③ Add baking soda to another glass. It will become alkaline and turn blue-green.

How acids and bases react

The reaction between an acid and a base is called a neutralization reaction. The three types of bases—alkalis, metal oxides, and metal carbonates—all neutralize acids to form salts and water.

> Indigestion tablets work by neutralizing the natural acid in your stomach.

1 Acids and alkalis

Alkalis are bases that release hydroxide ions (OH⁻) in water. When acids and alkalis mix, hydrogen ions from the acid react with hydroxide ions to form water. The remaining ions form a salt. Some acids and alkalis react so powerfully that they release enough heat to make the water boil.

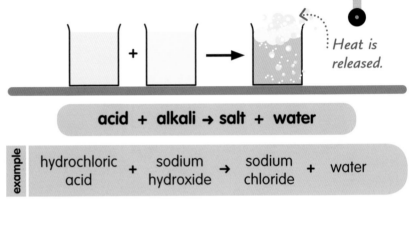

Heat is released.

acid + alkali → salt + water

example

| hydrochloric acid | + | sodium hydroxide | → | sodium chloride | + | water |

2 Acids and metal oxides

Metal oxides are compounds formed from a metal and oxygen. When an acid reacts with a metal oxide, it forms a salt and water. For instance, copper oxide (a black powder) reacts with sulfuric acid (a clear liquid) to form the salt copper sulfate and water. Copper sulfate is bright blue, so this reaction creates a dramatic change in color.

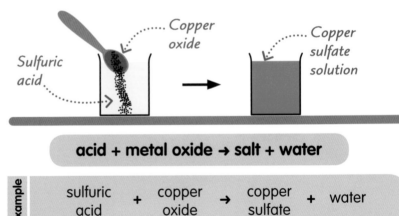

Sulfuric acid ·····*Copper oxide* ·····*Copper sulfate solution*

acid + metal oxide → salt + water

example

| sulfuric acid | + | copper oxide | → | copper sulfate | + | water |

3 Acids and metal carbonates

Metal carbonates are compounds formed from metals and carbonate ions or bicarbonate ions. They react with acids to form a salt, water, and carbon dioxide gas. The carbon dioxide makes bubbles in the water.

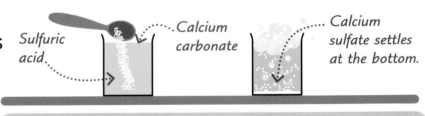

Sulfuric acid ·····*Calcium carbonate* ·····*Calcium sulfate settles at the bottom.*

acid + metal carbonate → salt + water + carbon dioxide

example

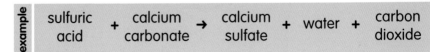

| sulfuric acid | + | calcium carbonate | → | calcium sulfate | + | water | + | carbon dioxide |

Acids and metals

Acids don't just react with bases—they also react with metals. When a metal object has been damaged by acid, we say it's corroded. The reaction between an acid and a metal produces a salt and hydrogen gas. Some metals, such as iron or zinc, react quickly with acids, but others, such as silver and gold, don't react at all.

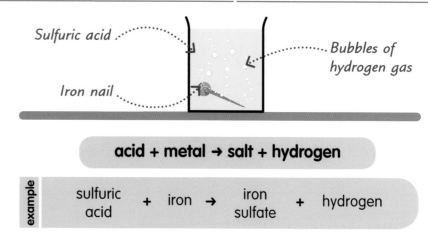

Sulfuric acid

Iron nail

Bubbles of hydrogen gas

acid + metal → salt + hydrogen

example

| sulfuric acid | + | iron | → | iron sulfate | + | hydrogen |

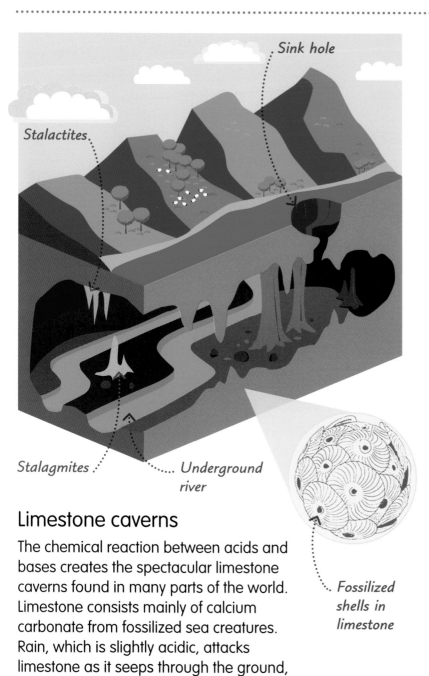

Sink hole

Stalactites

Stalagmites

Underground river

Fossilized shells in limestone

Limestone caverns

The chemical reaction between acids and bases creates the spectacular limestone caverns found in many parts of the world. Limestone consists mainly of calcium carbonate from fossilized sea creatures. Rain, which is slightly acidic, attacks limestone as it seeps through the ground, forming hollows that slowly grow into caverns.

TRY IT OUT

Polish your coins

Use the reaction between an acid and a metal oxide to polish old brown coins and make them shine like new. The acid strips dark copper oxide from the surface, revealing pure copper below.

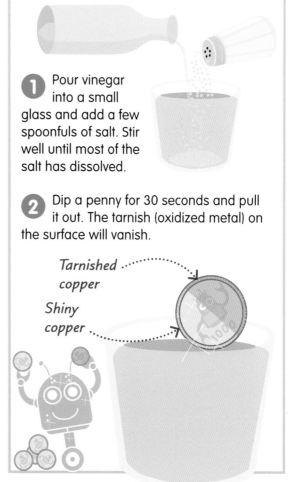

1 Pour vinegar into a small glass and add a few spoonfuls of salt. Stir well until most of the salt has dissolved.

2 Dip a penny for 30 seconds and pull it out. The tarnish (oxidized metal) on the surface will vanish.

Tarnished copper

Shiny copper

Electrolysis

Compounds made of ions (charged particles) can be split into chemical elements by passing an electric current through them. We call this electrolysis.

In pure water, one in every 600 million water molecules is split into ions.

How electrolysis works

Electrolysis only works when ions (see page 134) are free to move around in a liquid and so can conduct electricity. Water conducts electricity because a small number of water molecules split into positively charged hydrogen ions (H^+) and negatively charged hydroxide ions (OH^-). When a current passes through water, these ions turn into oxygen and hydrogen gas bubbles.

1 Electrodes
Two metal or carbon rods called electrodes are placed in the compound to be split (the electrolyte). One electrode (the anode) has a positive charge; the other (the cathode) has a negative charge. When the electrodes are connected to a battery, electricity flows through the water.

2 Moving ions
Negative hydroxide ions (OH^-) are attracted by the positive anode, so they move toward it. Positive hydrogen ions (H^+) move toward the negative cathode, attracted by its opposite charge.

3 At the anode
Negative hydroxide (OH^-) ions arriving at the anode lose electrons. The oxygen is freed, forming atoms that pair up to make oxygen molecules. Bubbles of oxygen gas appear.

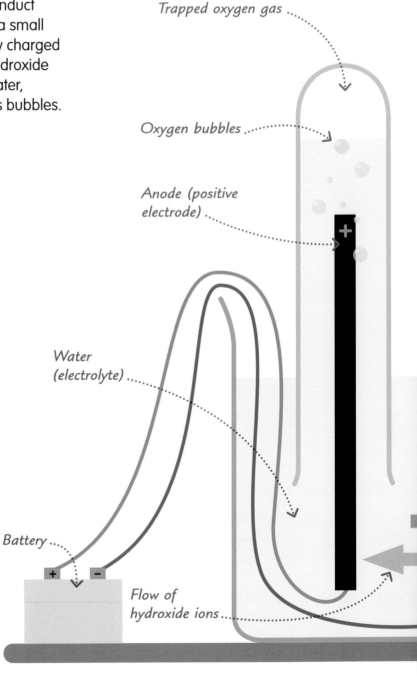

Trapped oxygen gas

Oxygen bubbles

Anode (positive electrode)

Water (electrolyte)

Battery

Flow of hydroxide ions

Split water!

You can carry out electrolysis yourself, using the equipment shown here. Make sure the pencils are sharpened at both ends, and each wire touches the lead of one of the pencils. The pencil connected to the battery's negative terminal is the cathode, and the pencil wired to the positive terminal is the anode.

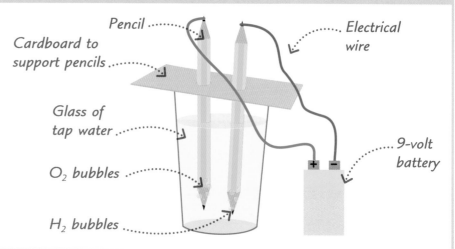

Pencil

Cardboard to support pencils

Electrical wire

Glass of tap water

O_2 bubbles

9-volt battery

H_2 bubbles

Trapped hydrogen gas

Test tube to collect gas

Hydrogen bubbles

Cathode (negative electrode)

4 At the cathode
Positive hydrogen ions arriving at the cathode gain electrons and become atoms. The hydrogen atoms pair up to make molecules of hydrogen gas, forming bubbles.

5 Collecting the gases
The hydrogen gas is collected by a test tube over the cathode. Another tube over the anode collects the oxygen gas. Water contains two hydrogen atoms for every oxygen atom, so twice as much hydrogen as oxygen is produced.

Flow of hydrogen ions

Electroplating

Using electrolysis to coat objects with a thin layer of metal is called electroplating. Spoons, for example, can be plated with silver. The spoon forms the cathode. The anode is a piece of pure silver. The electrolyte solution contains a silver compound. During electrolysis, silver ions move through the solution from the anode to the cathode, coating the spoon.

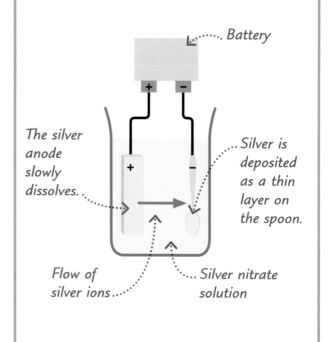

Battery

The silver anode slowly dissolves.

Silver is deposited as a thin layer on the spoon.

Flow of silver ions

Silver nitrate solution

The periodic table

The periodic table is a chart of all the chemical elements known to science. They are arranged in order of their atomic number—the number of protons in their atoms.

> Most chemical elements formed inside exploding stars called supernovas.

Organizing the elements

The chart arranges elements into horizontal rows called periods and vertical columns called groups. Each element is unique, but those that share similar physical and chemical properties are grouped together.

1 Element
Each box gives information about an element, including its name, chemical symbol, and atomic number (see pages 132–33).

Atomic number

1
H
HYDROGEN

Symbol

Element name

2 Period
The atomic number increases as you go along a row. This means that each element has one more proton in the nucleus of its atoms than the element to its left.

3 Group
If you know what one element in a group is like, you can make predictions about the other elements in the group. For example, all the metals in group 1 react strongly with water.

4 Extra rows
These two sections, made up of the rare earth metals, are too long to fit the shape of the table. They are usually shown on their own at the bottom.

1							
H HYDROGEN							

3	4
Li LITHIUM	**Be** BERYLLIUM

11	12
Na SODIUM	**Mg** MAGNESIUM

PERIOD

19	20	21	22	23	24	25	26
K POTASSIUM	**Ca** CALCIUM	**Sc** SCANDIUM	**Ti** TITANIUM	**V** VANADIUM	**Cr** CHROMIUM	**Mn** MANGANESE	**Fe** IRON
37	38	39	40	41	42	43	44
Rb RUBIDIUM	**Sr** STRONTIUM	**Y** YTTRIUM	**Zr** ZIRCONIUM	**Nb** NIOBIUM	**Mo** MOLYBDENUM	**Tc** TECHNETIUM	**Ru** RUTHENIUM
55	56	57–71	72	73	74	75	76
Cs CAESIUM	**Ba** BARIUM	**La–Lu** LANTHANIDE	**Hf** HAFNIUM	**Ta** TANTALUM	**W** TUNGSTEN	**Re** RHENIUM	**Os** OSMIUM
87	88	89–103	104	105	106	107	108
Fr FRANCIUM	**Ra** RADIUM	**Ac–Lr** ACTINIDE	**Rf** RUTHERFORDIUM	**Db** DUBNIUM	**Sg** SEABORGIUM	**Bh** BOHRIUM	**Hs** HASSIUM

GROUP

57	58	59	60	61
La LANTHANUM	**Ce** CERIUM	**Pr** PRASEODYMIUM	**Nd** NEODYMIUM	**Pm** PROMETHIUM
89	90	91	92	93
Ac ACTINIUM	**Th** THORIUM	**Pa** PROTACTINIUM	**U** URANIUM	**Np** NEPTUNIUM

Dmitri Mendeleev

The modern periodic table was devised by Russian chemist Dmitri Mendeleev in 1869. At the time, only 63 elements were known. Mendeleev is said to have written each element's name and symbol on a card and arranged the cards according to how heavy the element was. He left gaps in his table for elements that he predicted would be found—he was later proved right.

DMITRI MENDELEEV
1834–1907

Discovering new elements

New elements are still being predicted and discovered, but it gets harder and harder because the new ones are so unstable they only exist in labs for a fraction of a second before the atoms split and turn into other elements.

Boron is a gray shiny metalloid found in meteorites (lumps of rocks from space).

Lighter than air, the gas helium is used in balloons and airships.

Aluminum is a soft, light metal that doesn't rust and is used to make items such as foil and cans.

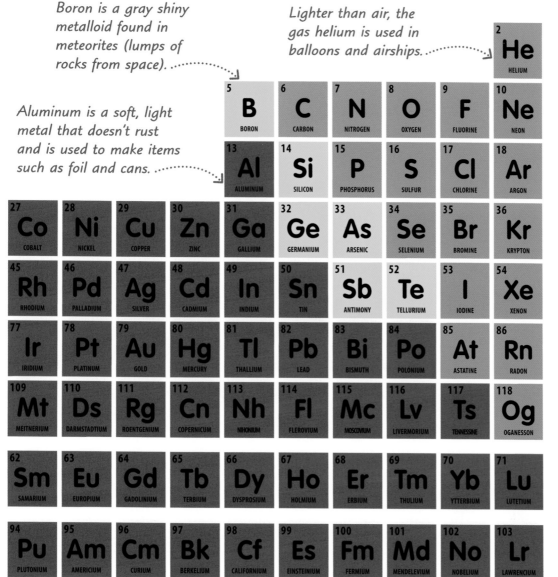

KEY

METALS

Most elements are metals. Generally, they share similar properties—they are strong, have a shiny appearance, conduct heat and electricity, and can be shaped without breaking.

METALLOIDS

Metalloids, which we also call semimetals, have properties of both metals and nonmetals. Some metalloids partially conduct electricity, and are used in calculators and computers.

NONMETALS

Most nonmetals are solid and share similar properties—they are dull, conduct heat and electricity poorly, and are brittle when solid. Some of them are very reactive, such as fluorine (F) and oxygen (O). Eleven of the nonmetals are gases. The gases in the group that starts with helium (He) are the least reactive of all the elements.

Metals

Typically hard and shiny and cold to the touch, metals are easy to recognize. Iron, silver, and gold are among the best known metals, but there are many more. In fact, metals make up more than three-fourths of all the elements in the periodic table.

Iron is the most common metal in the universe.

Properties of metals

There are over 90 known metals and they are all unique. Most metals, however, tend to have the same physical properties.

Objects made of hard metals ring like a bell when they're struck.

1 Most metals have a shiny, silvery surface because of the way they reflect light. However, not all metals are silver-colored. Gold is yellow, and copper is reddish-brown.

2 Most metals are hard solids at room temperature, but there are some exceptions. You can scratch gold with a fingernail, and mercury is a liquid.

3 Metals are usually malleable, which means we can hammer them into thin sheets of foil or stretch them out to make wires.

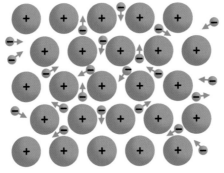

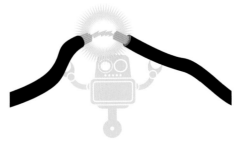

4 Metals are good at conducting heat, which makes them ideal for making pans. When you touch a metal object, it conducts heat away from your skin, which is why metals feel cold.

5 Pure metals don't form molecules. Instead, their atoms knit together into a lattice, held together by special bonds called metallic bonds. The electrons can move around between the atoms.

6 Many metals are good at conducting electricity because their electrons can move freely. Copper is one of the best conductors. It's used to make the wires that carry power around our homes.

Groups of metals

There are so many metals that chemists divide them into different groups, each of which has distinct chemical properties.

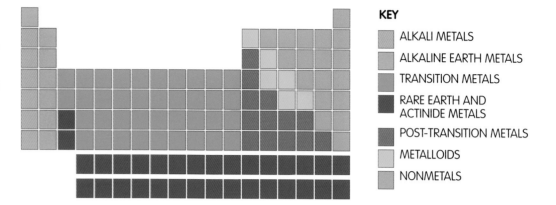

KEY

▢	ALKALI METALS
▢	ALKALINE EARTH METALS
▢	TRANSITION METALS
▢	RARE EARTH AND ACTINIDE METALS
▢	POST-TRANSITION METALS
▢	METALLOIDS
▢	NONMETALS

1 Alkali metals are highly reactive. They form chemicals called alkalis (see page 148) when they react with water. They are soft enough to cut with a knife, and they melt at low temperatures.

2 Alkaline earth metals are harder than alkali metals and melt at higher temperatures. They include calcium, which is found in teeth and bones.

3 Transition metals are hard, shiny, and strong, with high melting points. They are useful for making tools, bridges, ships, and cars.

4 Rare earth and actinide metals are only found in small quantities, but some are very useful. For example, neodymium is used to make magnets and headphones.

5 Post-transition metals are generally quite soft, but some, such as aluminum and lead, are still very useful. Lead protects against radiation such as X-rays.

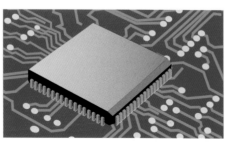

6 Metalloids have properties of both metals and nonmetals. Some metalloids, such as silicon, partially conduct electricity and are used in computer chips.

REAL WORLD TECHNOLOGY

Flame tests

Many metal elements burn with a flame of a distinctive color. This means we can identify which metals are present in a solution or a compound containing an unknown metal element. A sample of the chemical is picked up with a loop of wire and then held in a hot flame to see what color flame it produces.

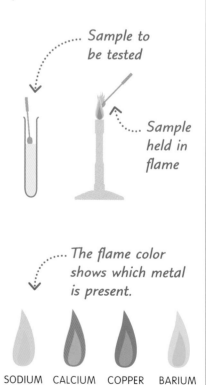

.... *Sample to be tested*

.... *Sample held in flame*

.... *The flame color shows which metal is present.*

SODIUM   CALCIUM   COPPER   BARIUM

The reactivity series

The reactivity series is a list of common metals in order of how reactive they are. The higher in the list a metal appears, the more easily it reacts with other chemicals.

If you touched potassium, it would react instantly with moisture in your skin.

1 Some metal elements are highly reactive, but others aren't. The metal potassium, for instance, reacts explosively with water.

Potassium reacts violently with water.

2 You can tell how chemically reactive a metal is from its position in the periodic table (see pages 154–55). Metals closer to the left or bottom of the table are more reactive. That's because their atoms can lose electrons easily and form chemical bonds with other elements.

MORE REACTIVE

MORE REACTIVE

KEY

METALS

METALLOIDS AND NONMETALS

3 When metals are arranged in a list with more reactive ones at the top, they form what is known as the reactivity series. This list (which includes the nonmetal carbon for reference) helps us predict which other chemicals a metal will react with and how quickly it will react.

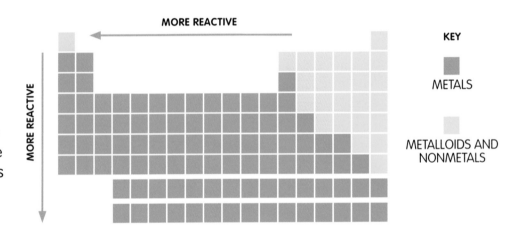

METAL	REACTS WITH WATER	REACTS WITH ACIDS	REACTS WITH OXYGEN
POTASSIUM SODIUM CALCIUM	●●●	●●●	●●●
MAGNESIUM ALUMINUM		●●	●●
(CARBON)			
ZINC IRON TIN LEAD		●●●●	●●●●
COPPER SILVER			●●
GOLD			

MORE REACTIVE

LESS REACTIVE

4 A more reactive metal will take the place of a less reactive metal in a compound. This is called a displacement reaction. For instance, if you put an iron nail in a copper sulfate solution, iron displaces copper because it is more reactive. The solution turns to iron sulfate and changes color, and copper atoms come out of the solution and form a thin coat of metal on the nail.

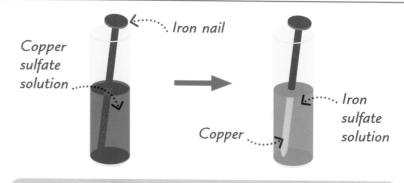

Copper sulfate solution ....
Iron nail
Copper ....
Iron sulfate solution

copper sulfate + iron → iron sulfate + copper

Extracting metals

1 Only a few metals, such as gold, are found in their pure form in nature. Most occur as chemical compounds in rocks called ores. The higher a metal is in the reactivity series, the harder it is to extract from its ore. The most reactive metals can only be extracted by an expensive technique called electrolysis. Less reactive metals, such as iron, can be extracted by heating the ore with carbon.

METAL	EXTRACTION
POTASSIUM SODIUM CALCIUM MAGNESIUM ALUMINUM	THROUGH ELECTROLYSIS
(CARBON)	
ZINC IRON TIN LEAD	BY BURNING WITH CARBON
COPPER MERCURY	BY BURNING DIRECTLY IN AIR
SILVER GOLD	NO EXTRACTION NEEDED, FOUND PURE

2 Carbon is a nonmetal but is included in the reactivity series because it can displace metals lower down the series from their compounds. Iron, for instance, is extracted from its ore by burning the rock with carbon. The carbon displaces the iron from iron oxide, releasing the pure metal.

iron oxide + carbon → carbon dioxide + iron

REAL WORLD TECHNOLOGY

Blast furnace

Iron is extracted from rock by heating iron ore (a rock rich in iron oxide) with carbon in a huge fire called a blast furnace, which is kept alight for many years. Carbon is added as coke (a fuel made from coal), and hot air is blasted in to keep the fire burning. The carbon displaces iron from its oxide, and the molten iron flows out at the bottom.

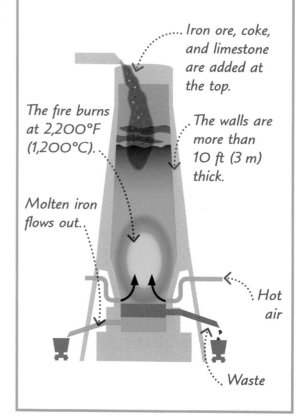

Iron ore, coke, and limestone are added at the top.

The fire burns at 2,200°F (1,200°C)..

The walls are more than 10 ft (3 m) thick.

Molten iron flows out..

Hot air

Waste

Iron

Iron is one of the most common and useful of all metals. People have used iron for thousands of years and still use it today to make everything from cars and ships to skyscrapers.

The average adult has about 4 g of iron in their body.

1 Iron Age
Iron is the only element that has an era of history named after it—the Iron Age. This began around 1,000 BC after people discovered how to extract iron from rocks. Soon, iron was used to make farming tools, weapons, and armor.

Red iron oxides

2 Earth's iron
Iron is the most common metal on Earth. Much is locked up in Earth's core, which gives Earth its magnetic field. However, iron is also the second most plentiful metal in Earth's crust. Its oxides color the ground red in many parts of the world.

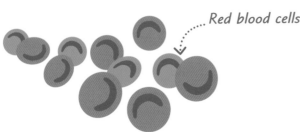

Red blood cells

3 Iron for life
We need iron in our diet to stay healthy. Our bodies use iron to make hemoglobin, the substance in red blood cells that carries oxygen from the lungs to our cells. Iron-rich foods include meat, seafood, beans, and leafy green vegetables.

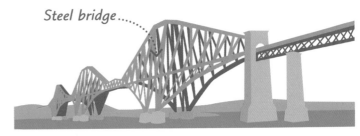

Steel bridge

4 Steel
Pure iron is quite soft compared to other metals. However, iron can be made a lot stronger by mixing it with a small amount of carbon to form steel. The carbon atoms stop the iron atoms from slipping past each other, making steel more rigid.

REAL WORLD TECHNOLOGY

Stainless steel

Adding the metal chromium to steel creates stainless steel. This type of steel is more hard-wearing, rust-resistant, and less likely to stain than normal steel. Kitchen cutlery and surgical instruments used by doctors are usually made of stainless steel.

Aluminum

Aluminum is the most common metal in Earth's crust. It is lightweight, easy to shape, and can be alloyed (mixed) with other metals to make it stronger.

Aluminum is the second most widely used metal after iron.

1 On the move
Aluminum weighs less than steel. Aluminum alloys are used to make parts for bikes, cars, trucks, trains, ships, and planes. This keeps the vehicles' weight down so they use less fuel.

2 Rust beater
When aluminum is exposed to air, a very hard coating of aluminum oxide forms on its surface, sealing the metal from the air so it doesn't rust. That's why aluminum is great for making bikes.

Foil keeps food fresh.

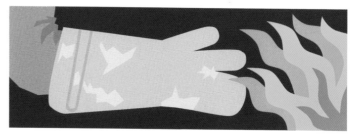

3 Aluminum foil
When rolled out thin, aluminum makes a strong, shiny foil that's ideal for packaging. The foil keeps out water, light, germs, and harmful chemicals. It doesn't smell and is nontoxic.

4 Fire suit
Aluminum is good at reflecting heat, so it's often used as a thermal insulator. A fire protection suit made from materials containing aluminum protects a firefighter from the heat of flames.

REAL WORLD TECHNOLOGY

Recycling aluminum

Aluminum can be recycled by melting it and rolling it into sheets. This uses a fraction of the energy it takes to extract new aluminum from rock, so recycling aluminum is much cheaper than producing it from scratch.

Crushed into blocks

Shredded

Rolled into sheets

Silver

People have used silver to make coins and jewelry for thousands of years. Silver also forms light-sensitive compounds that are used in photography and X-rays.

Pure silver is found in Earth's crust.

1 Excellent conductor
Of all the metals, silver is the best conductor of electricity. Some circuit board parts have a silver coating, but copper is more widely used in circuits because silver is expensive.

2 Sterling silver
Pure silver is a soft metal that can easily be cut into various shapes. In coins and jewelry, silver is mixed with a small amount of copper to make it harder. We call this sterling silver.

The dark parts of an X-ray are made of tiny grains of silver.

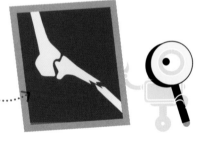

3 Light-sensitive compounds
Silver forms light-sensitive compounds with chlorine, bromine, and iodine. These are used in photographic film and X-rays. When light hits them, they turn to pure silver and become dark.

4 Kills bacteria
Because silver is deadly to bacteria, silver nitrate—a compound of silver, nitrogen, and oxygen—is mixed with water and used to clean cuts and grazes.

REAL WORLD TECHNOLOGY

Making clouds

If there isn't enough rain for crops, a plane releases silver iodide powder, and ice and water droplets cling to the powder to form a cloud. When the water droplets become heavy enough, rain falls.

Gold

Gold was one of the first metals to be discovered and used by people. Its beauty and rarity make it the most prized metal of all.

The largest piece of natural gold ever found contained more than 198 lb (90 kg) of pure gold.

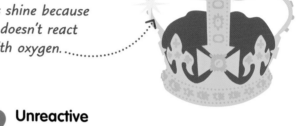

The gold on this crown won't lose its shine because it doesn't react with oxygen.

1 Gold in nature
In nature, gold is usually found as tiny specks or particles in rocks. Gold miners crush the rocks and use water or strong acid to wash out the gold dust.

2 Unreactive
Gold is one of the most unreactive elements. It doesn't react with oxygen at normal temperatures, which means it never rusts or loses its shine.

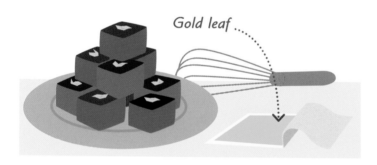

Gold leaf

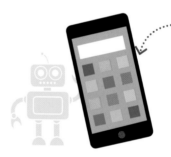

A typical cell phone contains around 0.034 g of gold.

3 Edible gold
Pure gold isn't toxic, and you can even eat it. Gold can be rolled into extremely thin sheets called gold leaf, which chefs sometimes use to decorate expensive cakes and desserts.

4 Gold in electronics
Unlike most other metals, gold doesn't react with oxygen in air, so it makes very reliable tiny connections in electronic components. There's a small amount of gold in every cell phone.

REAL WORLD TECHNOLOGY

Astronaut's visor

The visor in an astronaut's helmet is coated with a very thin layer of gold—so thin that the astronaut can still see through it. Gold is very good at reflecting light and heat, so the gold protects the astronaut from the Sun's rays.

Gold reflects harmful rays and protects the astronaut's eyes.

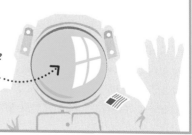

Hydrogen

Most of the universe is made of hydrogen. It's the simplest of the chemical elements and the first element in the periodic table. Pure hydrogen is a transparent gas.

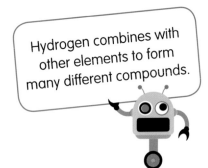

Hydrogen combines with other elements to form many different compounds.

1 Hydrogen atoms

Hydrogen has the simplest atom of any element, consisting of just one proton in the nucleus and one electron outside it. Hydrogen atoms pair up to make molecules of hydrogen gas (H_2).

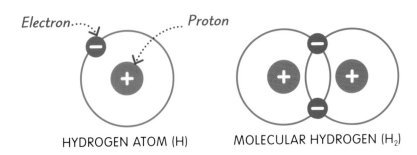

Electron

Proton

HYDROGEN ATOM (H)   MOLECULAR HYDROGEN (H_2)

2 Water

Water is a transparent and nearly colorless chemical substance. It is the main constituent of Earth's oceans and of most living organisms. Its chemical formula is H_2O (one oxygen and two hydrogen atoms that are connected).

hydrogen ($2H_2$) + oxygen (O_2) → water ($2H_2O$)

3 Hydrogen everywhere

You can't get away from hydrogen. It's a key part of all organic compounds (the chemicals that make up living things) and forms water with oxygen. Most of the atoms in your body are hydrogen atoms.

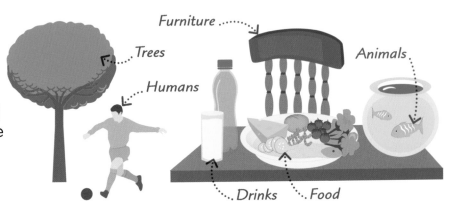

Furniture

Trees

Humans

Animals

Drinks   Food

4 Lost in space

Hydrogen molecules have so little mass that they float up through Earth's atmosphere and escape into space. The Sun, however, is much more massive than Earth and has enough gravity to hold on to hydrogen.

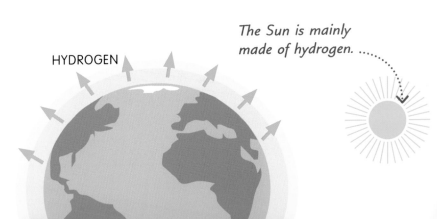

HYDROGEN

The Sun is mainly made of hydrogen.

REAL WORLD TECHNOLOGY

Hydrogen fuel cell

Hydrogen makes a great fuel because it creates no pollution—only water is produced as a waste product. Future cars may be powered by hydrogen fuel cells. These use a supply of hydrogen from a tank and oxygen from the air to generate clean electricity and so power motors that drive the wheels.

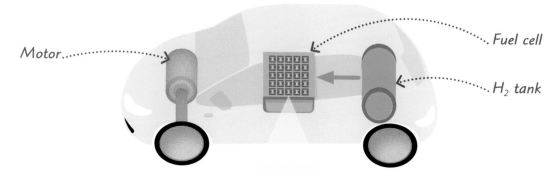

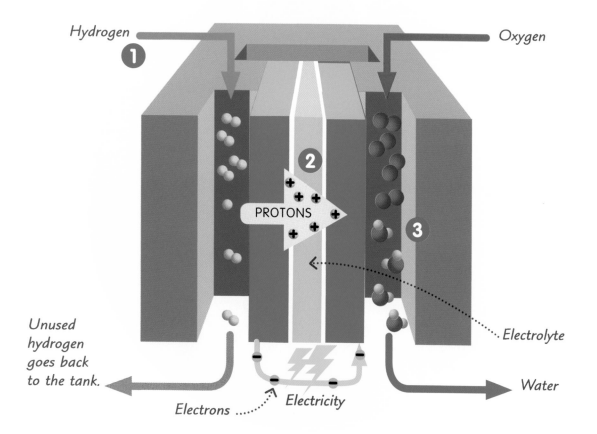

1 Hydrogen and oxygen enter the fuel cell. A chemical reaction takes place, and the hydrogen atoms split into protons and electrons.

2 The protons pass across a chemical called an electrolyte, and the electrons flow through a wire, creating the electricity that powers the motor.

3 The protons, electrons (from hydrogen), and oxygen react to form water. Water then leaves the car's exhaust as steam.

Carbon

All life on Earth is based on the element carbon, thanks to the remarkable ability of its atoms to link together in chains and form millions of different chemicals, called organic compounds.

Carbon forms at least 10 million known compounds—more than any other element.

Forms of carbon

Pure carbon comes in several different forms, called allotropes of carbon.

1 Diamond is the hardest naturally occurring substance on Earth. Its strength comes from the way the atoms bond in a repeating pyramid pattern. Diamonds form at high temperature and pressure hundreds of miles underground and take billions of years to grow. Although strong, they aren't indestructible—diamond can burn.

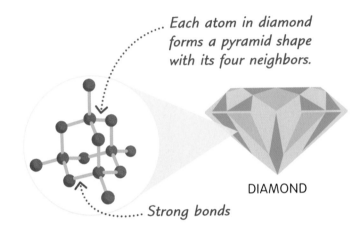

Each atom in diamond forms a pyramid shape with its four neighbors.

DIAMOND

Strong bonds

2 The "lead" in pencils isn't lead at all but graphite—a soft, crumbly allotrope of carbon. It's soft because the carbon atoms are linked to form sheets that can slide over one another easily. That's why it is used both for pencils and as a lubricant.

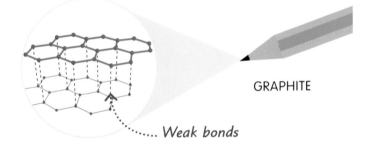

GRAPHITE

Weak bonds

3 Coal and soot contain graphite particles mixed with a glasslike form of carbon called amorphous carbon. Amorphous carbon doesn't have a regular crystalline structure and consists of a random jumble of molecules of different shapes.

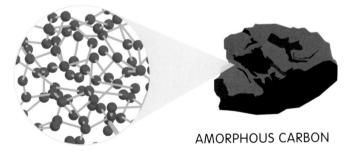

AMORPHOUS CARBON

4 Fullerenes are carbon molecules with 60 or more atoms linked in a regular geometric shape, such as a sphere. The first to be discovered was buckminsterfullerene, which is made of 20 hexagons and 12 pentagons—like a soccer ball.

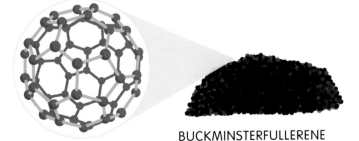

BUCKMINSTERFULLERENE

Carbon capture

Carbon dioxide (CO_2) released from fossil fuels is the main cause of global warming. One idea being tested by power stations to reduce emissions is carbon capture. CO_2 is removed from smoke by reaction with chemicals called amines, and the waste is pumped underground. Power stations can cut emissions by 90 percent this way, but the extra energy needed makes them much less efficient.

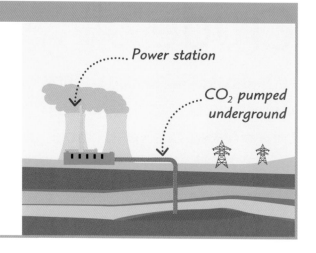

Power station

CO_2 pumped underground

Useful carbon

Carbon compounds are incredibly useful. Natural carbon compounds form our food, clothes, and materials such as paper and wood. Carbon compounds derived from crude oil are used as fuels or made into plastics.

1 Many of the fuels we use are hydrocarbons— compounds made only of carbon and hydrogen atoms, often arranged in chains. One of the simplest hydrocarbons is propane, which is used as a fuel for barbecue grills.

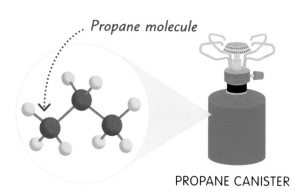

Propane molecule

PROPANE CANISTER

2 Diamond's strength makes it useful for cutting hard materials. Diamond blade saws have rotating metal blades embedded with small synthetic diamonds. They can saw through glass, brick, concrete, and solid rock.

DIAMOND BLADE SAW

3 Carbon fiber is an artificial material made of very fine carbon threads that are woven into a fabric and then set in plastic by heating. The resulting material is strong enough to make cars, bikes, and planes, but much lighter than steel or aluminum.

CARBON FIBER BIKE

4 Nearly all of our clothes are made from carbon compounds. Natural fabrics like cotton and wool are made of carbon compounds from plants and animals. Nylon and polyester are synthetic fabrics made from fine plastic threads woven together.

CARBON COMPOUNDS

Crude oil

From plastics to gasoline, many useful products come from crude oil. Crude oil is a mixture of hydrocarbons—chains of hydrogen and carbon atoms. The hydrocarbons are separated by a process called fractional distillation.

1 Extracting and transporting
Crude oil is pumped out of the ground by oil wells. It is then carried by trucks or ships to a refinery to be turned into useful products like gasoline, diesel, and jet fuel.

2 Heating
The crude oil is heated until it boils and forms a mixture of hot gases. These gases enter a tall tower equipped with trays and outlet pipes at different heights. The trays catch the liquids that form as the gases cool down.

3 Largest molecules
The hydrocarbons with the largest molecules have high boiling points. As a result, they cool and turn back to liquid as soon as they enter the tower. This liquid is collected by a pipe at the bottom.

4 Smaller molecules
Hydrocarbons with smaller molecules rise higher in the tower and turn back to liquid at lower temperatures. Pipes at different levels collect different kinds of hydrocarbon.

4
70°F (20°C)

The lightest gases rise to the top.

160°F (70°C)

250°F (120°C)

Crude oil formed over millions of years from the remains of dead sea organisms.

390°F (200°C)

570°F (300°C)

The temperature inside the tower is higher near the bottom.

700°F (375°C)

Hot gases enter the tower.

3
750°F (400°C)

Crude oil in

❶   ❷

OIL WELL   TRANSPORTING   HEATING CRUDE OIL   FRACTIONATING TOWER

The smallest molecules are collected at the top.

REFINERY GASES

1 Refinery gases
The smallest hydrocarbons are gases such as methane and ethane. They are bottled and used as fuels for heating and cooking.

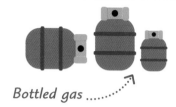

Bottled gas

GASOLINE

2 Gasoline
Gasoline compounds have larger molecules. We use them as fuel for cars and other vehicles.

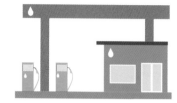

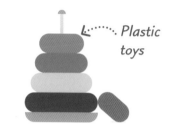

NAPHTHA

3 Naphtha
Naphtha is a yellow liquid with 8–12 carbon atoms in its chains. It's used to make plastics, drugs, pesticides, and fertilizers.

Plastic toys

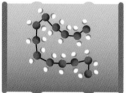

KEROSENE

4 Kerosene
Kerosene is a light, oily liquid used as fuel in jet engines. It can also be burned in camping stoves and lanterns.

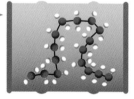

DIESEL

5 Diesel
Diesel has longer hydrocarbon chains and a higher boiling point than gasoline. We use it as fuel for trucks, buses, and some cars.

FUEL OIL

6 Fuel oil
Lighter fuel oils are used as fuel for ships and tractors or as heating oil. Heavier fuel oils are used in factories and industrial boilers.

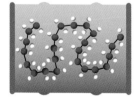

BITUMEN

7 Bitumen
The largest molecules form a sticky, semisolid substance called bitumen. This is used as tar for roads and roof surfaces.

HYDROCARBONS   **PRODUCTS AND USES**

Nitrogen

The gas nitrogen makes up 78 percent of the air in Earth's atmosphere and you breathe it every day without noticing.

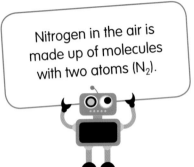

Nitrogen in the air is made up of molecules with two atoms (N_2).

The nitrogen cycle

Nitrogen is essential to life because it's a crucial ingredient in nutrients called proteins, which all organisms need. However, plants and animals can't get nitrogen straight from the air. Instead, they rely on the nitrogen cycle.

1 Nitrogen gas enters the soil from the air. Nitrogen-fixing bacteria living in soil and in the roots of plants turn the nitrogen into nitrates—salts that dissolve in water in the ground.

2 Plants obtain nitrates from the water their roots absorb. They use it to make the amino acids and proteins that help them grow.

3 Animals eat the plants, digest the proteins, and use the resulting amino acids to build the proteins their own bodies need.

The nitrogen in the air is nitrogen gas (N_2).

The sky is blue on sunny days because nitrogen and oxygen molecules scatter blue light.

Lightning can change nitrogen gas into nitrates.

Bacteria

Fungi

4 Waste materials—such as dung, urine, and dead plants and animals—return nitrogen to the soil.

5 Bacteria and fungi in the soil feed on waste material, releasing nitrates that plants can then absorb.

Oxygen

Oxygen is a transparent gas and makes up just over 20 percent of the air in Earth's atmosphere. It is a very reactive element and vital for life.

Oxygen in water molecules makes up most of the mass in the human body.

1 Essential gas
We need a continual supply of oxygen to stay alive. We get it by breathing air.

A diver can only stay underwater by taking in air from an oxygen tank.

2 Oxygen supply
The oxygen in Earth's atmosphere is continually replenished by plants, which produce oxygen as a by-product of photosynthesis.

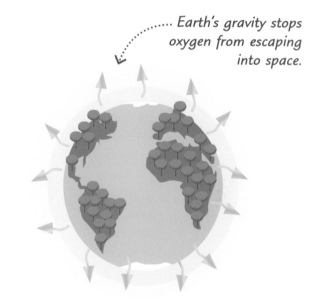

Earth's gravity stops oxygen from escaping into space.

How oxygen reacts

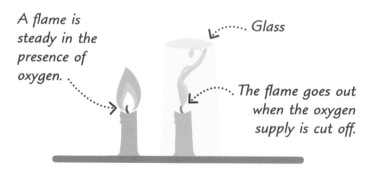

A flame is steady in the presence of oxygen.

Glass

The flame goes out when the oxygen supply is cut off.

1 Oxygen and fire
Fire is a chemical reaction between oxygen in the air and a fuel. Without a supply of oxygen, a flame will go out.

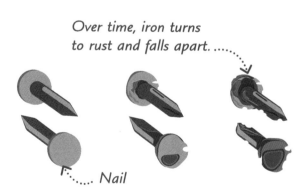

Over time, iron turns to rust and falls apart.

Nail

2 Rusting
Oxygen can react with many chemicals without causing fire. For example, iron and steel left in the air slowly react with oxygen to form iron oxide (rust).

Phosphorus

Phosphorus is highly reactive and so is never found as a pure element in nature. Pure phosphorus can be made in a lab, however, and has several different coloured forms.

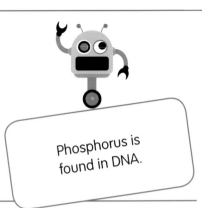

Phosphorus is found in DNA.

Types of phosphorus

1 Red phosphorus is a dark red powder and is used to make the striking surface of matchboxes.

2 White phosphorus glows in the dark if it is exposed to air. When it comes in contact with oxygen, it catches fire.

3 Black phosphorus is a flaky substance that looks like graphite (the material used to make pencils).

Discovering phosphorus

In 1669 the German alchemist Hennig Brand carried out a strange experiment. He boiled urine and kept it for many weeks. When he heated it up and added sand, the urine formed a glowing, waxy white solid lump—he had discovered phosphorus.

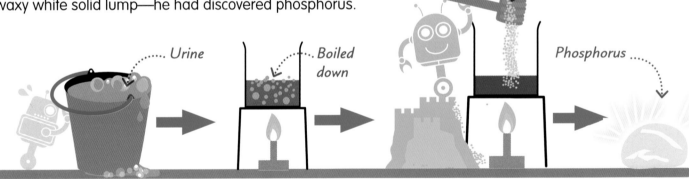

Urine

Boiled down

Sand

Phosphorus

Strong teeth and bones

Teeth and bones get their strength from the very hard mineral calcium phosphate, which contains phosphorus. For centuries, the bones

of cattle have been ground into dust to make bone china, a strong, durable porcelain used to make cups, plates, and bowls.

REAL WORLD TECHNOLOGY

Matchbox

The pattern printed on the side of a box of matches is made of ground glass and red phosphorus. When a match is scraped against the surface, friction with the glass heats the phosphorus, which ignites. The phosphorus then sets fire to flammable compounds in the match's head.

Sulfur

In its pure form, sulfur consists of crystals and usually appears as a bright yellow, crumbly solid. It is found in nature near volcanoes, where it is deposited by hot gases.

Chopped onions release sulfur compounds that make your eyes water.

1 Types of sulfur
There are two types of sulfur: one has wide crystals while the other has needle-shaped crystals.

WIDE CRYSTALS   NEEDLE-SHAPED CRYSTALS

2 Explosive sulfur
Gunpowder is a mix of charcoal and potassium nitrate, used in fireworks and weapons. It also contains sulfur, which makes the gunpowder burn more easily.

3 Smelly sulfur
Many sulfur compounds, such as hydrogen sulfide, have very strong, unpleasant odors. They create the strong smells in a skunk's spray, blocked drains, and garlic.

4 Acid rain
Fossil fuels, such as oil and coal, produce sulfur fumes when they burn. These fumes mix with water in the air, forming sulfuric acid. This acid falls to the ground as acid rain, which damages buildings and can kill trees.

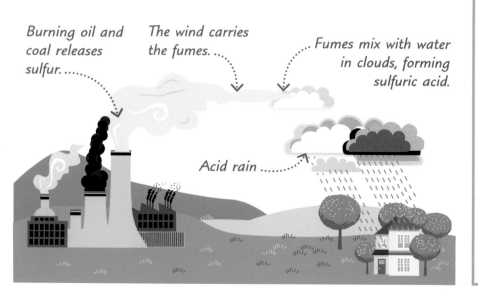

Burning oil and coal releases sulfur.

The wind carries the fumes.

Fumes mix with water in clouds, forming sulfuric acid.

Acid rain

REAL WORLD TECHNOLOGY

Sulfuric acid
Although sulfuric acid can be harmful when it falls as acid rain, it is also one of the most useful sulfur compounds. The chemical industry uses sulfuric acid to make paints, detergents, inks, plant fertilizers, and many other products.

Halogens

The halogens are a group of highly reactive elements. They are too reactive to exist in their pure forms in nature, but halogens form many different compounds.

Earth's oceans contain 39 million billion tons of sodium chloride (salt).

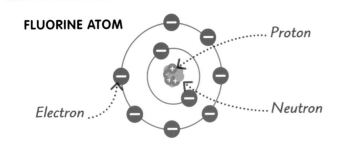

FLUORINE ATOM

Proton

Electron

Neutron

Reactive atoms

Halogen atoms have seven electrons in their outer shells but need eight to become stable. As a result, they react easily with elements that can share or donate an electron, giving the halogen atom a full shell of eight without any gaps.

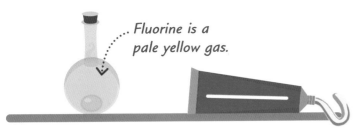

Fluorine is a pale yellow gas.

1 Fluorine
The most reactive of all halogens, fluorine is a deadly yellow gas that can burn through brick, glass, and steel. Fluorides (salts containing fluorine) are put in toothpaste as they strengthen teeth.

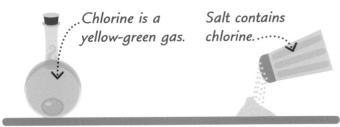

Chlorine is a yellow-green gas.

Salt contains chlorine.

2 Chlorine
This poisonous gas was used as a weapon during World War I. However, it is part of sodium chloride (salt), which the human body needs.

Bromine is a brown liquid.

3 Bromine
The fire-retardant chemicals found in fire extinguishers are made with bromine. Bromine is also used to clean water in swimming pools.

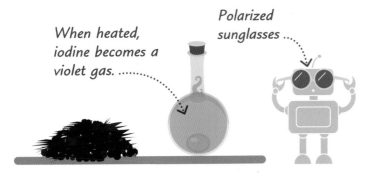

When heated, iodine becomes a violet gas.

Polarized sunglasses

4 Iodine
The only halogen that is solid at room temperature, iodine is a purple-black color. It is used to make polarized sunglasses and to disinfect wounds.

Noble gases

Unlike the highly reactive halogens, the noble gases are very unreactive. They are all colorless and have no smell.

After hydrogen, helium is the most abundant element in the universe.

Unreactive atoms

Noble gas atoms have a full set of eight electrons in their outer shells. This full set means that they are very unreactive, because they don't need to gain or lose any electrons. They rarely form compounds.

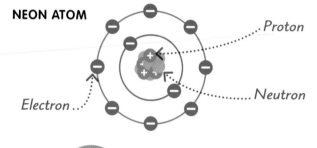

NEON ATOM

Proton

Neutron

Electron

1 Helium
The atoms of this colorless, odorless gas weigh very little, which explains why helium-filled balloons float upward.

2 Neon
When electricity passes through a noble gas, the gas glows brightly. Neon is widely used in brightly colored neon signs and for making lasers.

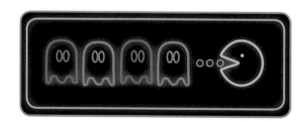

3 Argon
Argon is an excellent insulator, so it is used between the glass panes of thermal windows and in scuba diving suits to keep divers warm in cold water. Low-energy light bulbs contain argon.

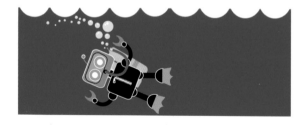

4 Xenon
Xenon glows bright blue when electricity passes through it. Searchlights and camera flashbulbs are made with xenon.

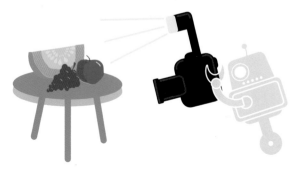

Materials science

Materials science combines the skills of chemists, physicists, and engineers to create new materials with special properties, such as strength, flexibility, or lightness. Some of the most important of these materials are composites, ceramics, and polymers.

Composites

Composites are made by weaving together or layering multiple materials in a way that makes them incredibly strong. Many consist of fibers of a flexible material embedded in a "matrix" of something else, such as plastic, metal, or even concrete. The fibers stiffen the matrix so it can resist fractures.

1 A windshield consists of two layers of glass with a layer of plastic sandwiched between them to stop the glass from shattering.

2 The bodies of many high-performance cars are made of carbon fiber, which consists of fine carbon threads woven into a fabric and set in plastic. This is lighter than steel but just as strong.

3 Tires are made of tough polyester fabrics coated in rubber and layered together, with steel cords giving extra strength.

Ceramics

Ceramics are hard, brittle materials such as porcelain. People have been making them for thousands of years by baking clay to make bricks, tiles, and pottery. Scientists can now engineer more advanced ceramics designed for specific jobs, such as filtering pollutants from a car's exhaust.

4 Ceramic engine parts include insulators for the spark plugs that set light to gasoline in the engine and ceramic coatings that help piston heads withstand heat.

5 Catalytic converters absorb harmful gases from a car's exhaust fumes. They're made of lightweight but strong ceramics that can withstand high temperatures.

REAL WORLD TECHNOLOGY

Breathable fabrics

Waterproof but "breathable" hiking jackets are made with a clever polymer called PTFE (polytetrafluoroethylene)—the same material used to make nonstick pans. It has billions of tiny holes that let water vapor from sweat get out but are too small to let rain get in.

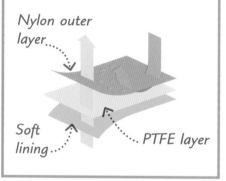

Nylon outer layer

Soft lining

PTFE layer

Polymers

Polymers are long, chainlike molecules based on the element carbon. Plastics are artificial polymers made in labs or factories. Most polymers are waterproof and chemically unreactive, which makes them very long-lasting. Many can be easily molded into almost any shape.

9 Bumpers are made of plastics such as polypropylene, which is rugged and easy to mold. Plastics are used for many other parts, from door linings to the dashboard and even headlight lenses.

8 The waterproof trim used to make door seals and window seals for cars is made of EDPM, a synthetic rubber that is very hard-wearing.

7 Polyurethane makes a strong, lightweight foam for car seats that is both stiff enough to provide support and soft enough to provide comfort.

6 Ceramics can be used to make tire pressure sensors that generate an electric signal when they bend. The sensors tell the driver to reinflate the tires.

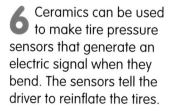

Polymers

Polymers are compounds with long, chainlike molecules made of repeating parts. Many natural materials, like wood and wool, are made of polymers. Plastics are artificial polymers.

Most polymers are based on carbon atoms, which can form chains.

Polymerization

Polymers are made of repeating units called monomers. The plastic polyethylene, for instance, is made of monomers called ethylene, which is a gas. Ethylene is converted to polyethylene by a chemical reaction called polymerization. The double bonds between carbon atoms break open, and the atoms connect in a chain of single bonds, forming polyethylene, a transparent solid.

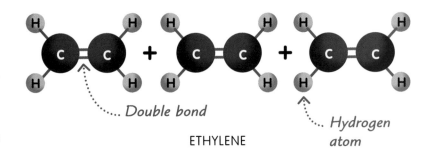

Double bond

ETHYLENE

Hydrogen atom

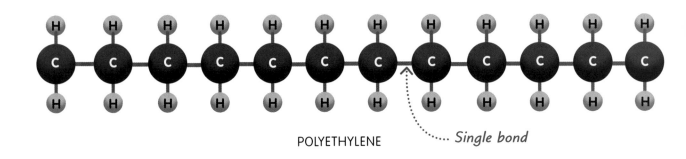

POLYETHYLENE   *Single bond*

Natural polymers

Many biological molecules are polymers, including proteins, carbohydrates, and fats. When we digest food, our bodies break down the polymers into monomers that our bodies can absorb.

1 Meat is rich in proteins, which are polymers made of monomers called amino acids.

2 The DNA molecule is made of two polymers coiled around each other to form a shape called a double helix.

3 Cellulose is a fibrous material made of sugar molecules linked together. It is found in wood and paper.

4 Starch is also made of sugar molecules. Potatoes and bread contain a lot of starch.

Plastics

Plastics are artificial polymers made from the chemicals that we get from crude oil (see pages 168–69). There are two basic types. Thermoplastics, such as polyethylene, melt when they're heated and harden again when they cool. Thermoset plastics stay hard when they're heated and don't melt.

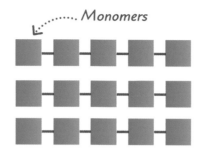
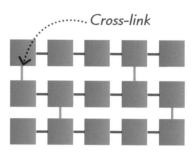

1 Thermoplastics can melt because they're made of separate polymer molecules that can slide over each other.

2 Thermoset plastics can't melt because their polymer molecules are linked by bonds called cross-links.

Plastics and their uses

We use different types of plastic to make all kinds of everyday objects, including packaging, toys, windows, containers, phones, and even clothes.

1 Polyethylene comes in soft forms, used to make plastic bags and food wrap, and harder forms used to make drink bottles, toys, and many other things.

2 PVC (polyvinyl chloride) is one of the hardest plastics and is used to make gutters, drainpipes, and window frames.

3 Polystyrene is used to make things like CD cases because it's very easy to mold. It can also be filled with tiny gas bubbles to make the light, soft foam used in disposable cups.

4 Polycarbonate plastic is very hard to break and can be made into transparent objects. It's used to make phones, sunglasses, safety goggles, and windows.

TRY IT OUT

Turn milk into plastic

You can make your own plastic objects from a naturally occurring polymer called casein, which is found in milk.

1 Heat 10 fl oz (30 ml) of whole milk in a pan until it steams. Add a tablespoon of vinegar to make it separate into solid lumps (curd) and a liquid (whey).

2 Let the milk cool and then pour it through a towel to separate the curds. Squeeze the curd in the towel to remove excess liquid.

3 Add food coloring to the rubbery curd that's left in the towel. Then knead it into shapes and leave it to harden.

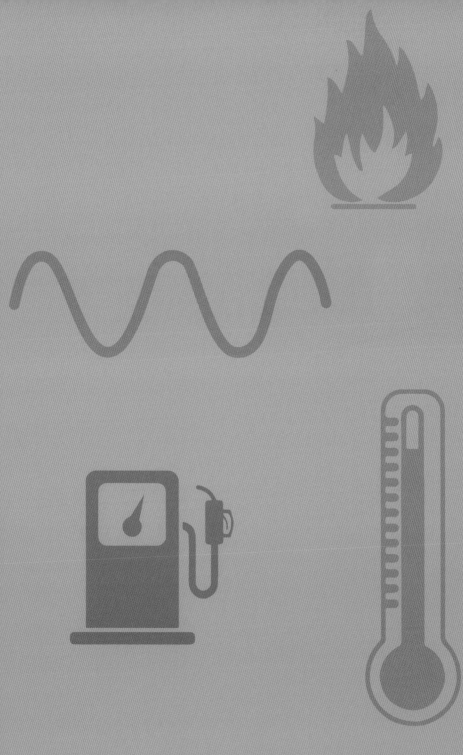

ENERGY

Energy is what makes everything happen. Without it, nothing would move and the world would be pitch black, freezing cold, and completely silent. Energy can be stored and transferred in different ways, from the electricity that powers your phone to the chemical energy stored in the food you eat. You can't destroy energy when you use it—it merely transfers from one place to another.

What is energy?

Energy is what makes everything happen, from the dazzling explosion of a firework to the roar of a jet engine or the movement of your muscles. Energy can be stored or used, but it can't be destroyed. When you use energy, it doesn't disappear—it only gets transferred from one thing to another.

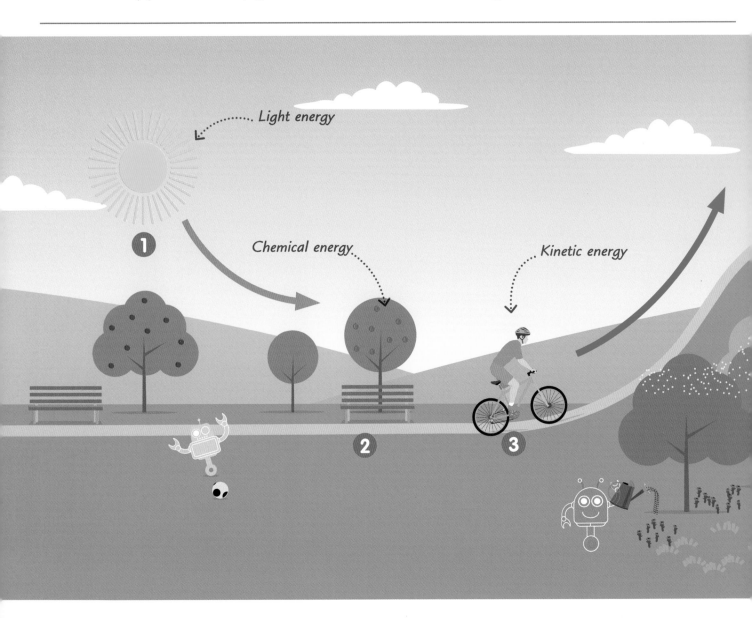

1 Most of the energy we use on Earth comes from the Sun. The Sun's energy takes only eight minutes to travel through space to Earth as heat and light.

2 Plants capture the Sun's energy and use it to make new chemicals. The food we eat contains chemical energy stored by plants.

3 Powered by the food you eat, your muscles transfer chemical energy into kinetic (movement) energy, enabling you to walk, run, or ride a bike.

Forms of energy

Energy can take many different forms, from heat and light to sound and electricity. Some of these, such as light, transfer energy from place to place or from one object to another. Others act as a store of energy. A battery and a compressed spring both store energy, for instance.

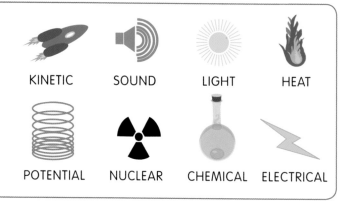

KINETIC   SOUND   LIGHT   HEAT

POTENTIAL   NUCLEAR   CHEMICAL   ELECTRICAL

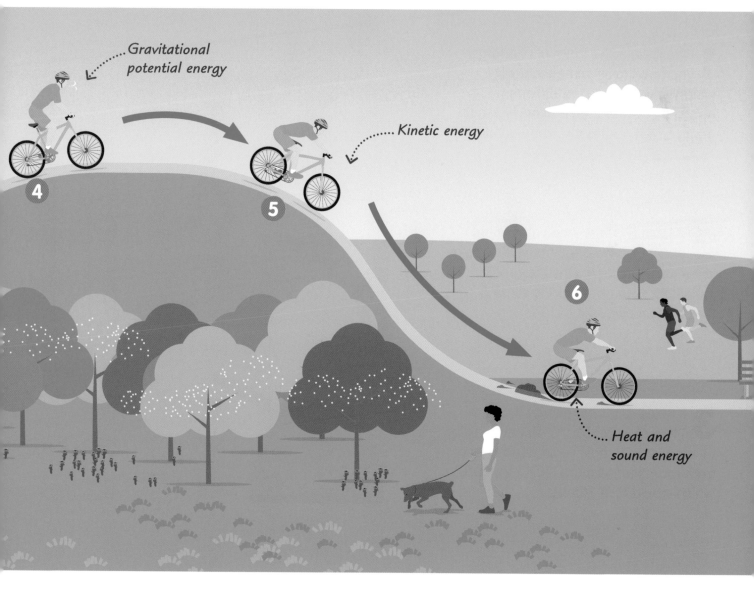

Gravitational potential energy

Kinetic energy

Heat and sound energy

4 When you ride uphill, your muscles transfer energy into a stored form of energy called gravitational potential energy. Anything high up has this energy.

5 When you cycle downhill, gravitational potential energy transfers to kinetic energy, making your bike speed up—even if you aren't pedaling.

6 When you pull the brakes, the bike's kinetic energy is lost as heat and sound, making the brakes squeal and the bike slow down.

Measuring energy

Energy can take many different forms, so there are many ways of measuring it. The most common unit of energy is called a joule.

A slice of cheesecake contains enough energy to power a 5-watt light bulb for 17 hours.

Energy units

1 One joule is the amount of energy you need to lift something that weighs 1 newton (like a 100-gram apple) by 1 meter. You'd need 10 J to lift a bag of ten apples the same distance.

2 A joule is a very small amount of energy, so we often measure energy in kilojoules instead. One kilojoule is 1,000 joules. You use about 1 kJ to climb a typical staircase.

3 It takes 4.19 kJ of energy to warm 1 liter of water by 1°C. To make a liter of water start to boil, you'd need to heat it from room temperature (20°C) to 100°C, which would take 335 kJ.

4 Gasoline stores a huge amount of energy, which is why it makes such a good fuel for cars. One liter of gasoline stores about 35 mJ (35 million joules) of energy.

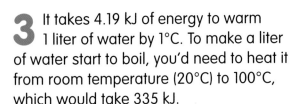

Energy and exercise

The human body needs about 8,000 kJ of energy each day. The amount of energy you use depends on how active you are and how large you are—the bigger your body, the more energy you need.

1 Walking at average speed uses about 970 kJ per hour. You need nearly twice as much energy to walk quickly.

2 Swimming uses about 2,400 kJ per hour. Tiring strokes like the butterfly use more energy than gentle strokes like crawl or breaststroke.

3 Running at average speed uses about 3,700 kJ per hour. A high-speed sprint uses much more energy than a gentle jog.

Power

Power is a measure of how quickly energy is used. The more powerful a machine is, the faster it uses energy. The power of electrical appliances is measured in watts. One kilowatt (1 kW) is 1,000 watts.

1 One watt means using 1 joule of energy every second. A 30-watt TV uses 30 joules of energy every second.

2 A 1,500-watt lawnmower uses energy very quickly, but if you only use it once a week, it doesn't cost a large amount to run.

3 A 200-watt refrigerator is less powerful than a lawnmower. However, it uses more energy because it's on all the time.

REAL WORLD TECHNOLOGY

Measuring electricity

Electricity bills don't measure energy in joules. Instead, they use kilowatt-hours (kWh). One kWh equals 3.6 million joules and is the energy you'd use if you left a 1,000-watt machine, such as a typical iron or microwave, switched on for an hour.

Electric meters show how much electricity a house has used.

Power stations

Power stations produce most of the electricity that powers our homes. Nearly two-thirds of our electricity supply is made by traditional thermal power stations.

Fossil fuels are made over millions of years, from the remains of dead organisms.

Thermal power stations

To generate electricity, most thermal power stations burn fossil fuels, such as coal, oil, and natural gas. Burning fossil fuels harms the environment because it releases carbon dioxide, which contributes to global warming.

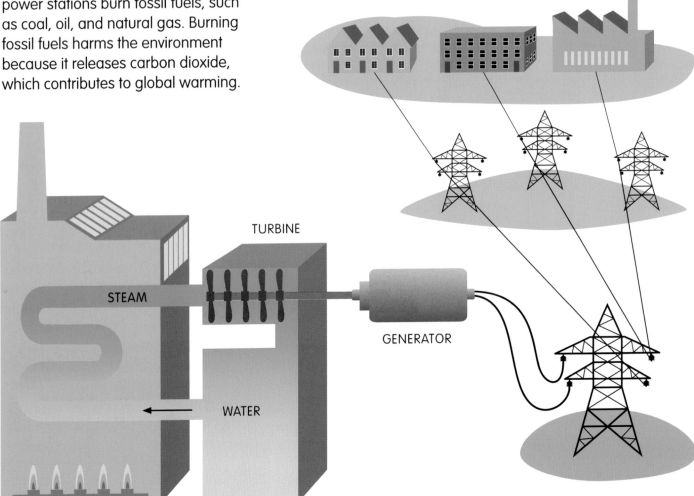

HOMES, SCHOOLS, AND FACTORIES

TURBINE

STEAM

GENERATOR

WATER

BOILER

CONDENSER

ELECTRICITY

1 Water is heated by burning fossil fuels, turning it into steam, which flows through a network of pipes.

2 The steam makes a machine called a turbine spin around. The steam then turns back to water.

3 The spinning turbine turns a generator, which generates electricity as it rotates.

4 Electricity is carried to homes, schools, and factories by cables attached to pylons.

Renewable energy

Our planet's fossil fuel reserves will eventually run out, but other forms of energy, called renewable energy, will last forever. Renewable energy sources contribute less to global warming than fossil fuels, but renewable power stations can harm the environment in other ways.

Incoming tide

Barrier

1 Wind power generates electricity by using the wind to turn giant turbines high in the air. They tend to work best in high areas or out at sea where winds are strong. Some people think they spoil scenic landscapes.

2 Tidal power and wave power both use the motion of seawater to drive turbines placed on the seabed. These power stations are expensive to build, but they can produce large amounts of electricity.

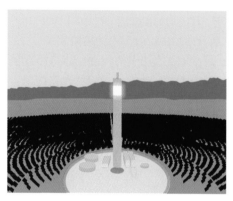

3 Hydroelectric power is generated by channeling rivers through turbines. To ensure a powerful flow of water, huge dams must be built, creating artificial lakes that can damage natural habitats.

4 Biomass-fired power stations burn waste plant material instead of fossil fuels. Carbon dioxide released by burning biomass is offset (canceled out) by growing new crops and forests.

5 Concentrated solar power stations use mirrors to focus sunlight onto a central furnace. It requires large areas of land and only works in places with sunny weather all year.

REAL WORLD TECHNOLOGY

Generators

Generators convert kinetic energy in a moving object into electrical energy. This bicycle's spinning wheel powers its light. Inside the bicycle's generator is a copper coil and a magnet. When the magnet spins, electrons are pushed through the coil by the moving magnetic field, generating electricity.

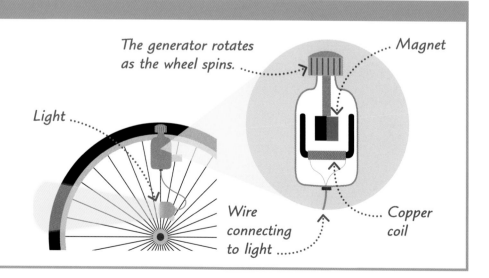

The generator rotates as the wheel spins.

Magnet

Light

Wire connecting to light

Copper coil

Heat

Heat is a form of energy that makes molecules and atoms move faster. The faster they move, the hotter things are. When something heats up, it gives off, or emits, energy as heat. If something is hot enough, it may even emit light.

> The Sun's heat on your skin makes your skin molecules vibrate faster.

Particles and heat

An object might look still, but the particles (atoms or molecules) it's made of are always moving—whizzing, spinning, and vibrating in all directions. The moving particles have kinetic energy, and it is this energy that makes things warm.

1 The atoms in an iron bar at normal temperature are vibrating, but they remain held in place by bonds between them.

2 When iron heats up, the atoms vibrate faster. At 1,742°F (950°C), iron starts to glow red as the atoms emit some energy as light.

3 As the iron gets hotter, its color gradually changes to white. At around 2,800°F (1,538°C), the atoms will separate and the iron will melt.

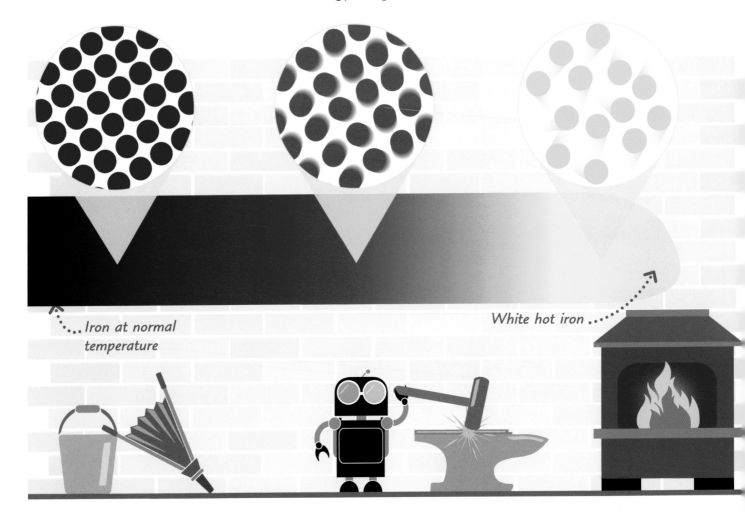

Iron at normal temperature

White hot iron

Temperature

The temperature of a substance tells us the average kinetic energy of its particles: the faster they vibrate, the higher the temperature. Temperature is measured on a thermometer using units called degrees Fahrenheit or degrees Celsius.

Heat and temperature

The heat energy stored in a substance depends on its temperature, but also on how much of it there is. So, because it is so much bigger, a chilly iceberg contains more heat energy in total than a scalding cup of coffee.

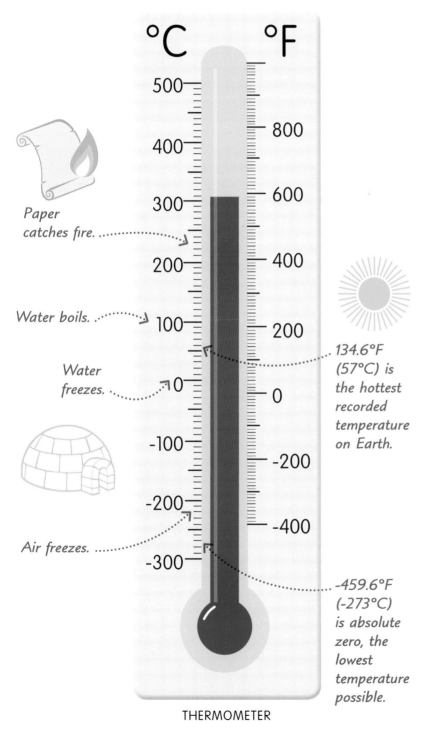

Paper catches fire.

Water boils.

Water freezes.

Air freezes.

134.6°F (57°C) is the hottest recorded temperature on Earth.

-459.6°F (-273°C) is absolute zero, the lowest temperature possible.

THERMOMETER

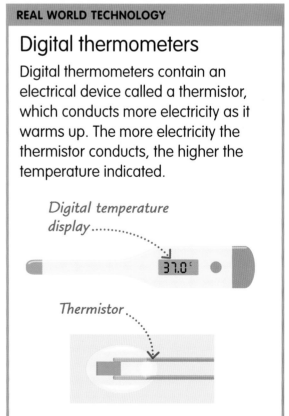

Digital thermometers

Digital thermometers contain an electrical device called a thermistor, which conducts more electricity as it warms up. The more electricity the thermistor conducts, the higher the temperature indicated.

Digital temperature display

Thermistor

Heat transfer

Heat never stays in one place. It is always transferring (moving or spreading) to its cooler surroundings. Heat moves in three different ways: conduction, convection, and radiation.

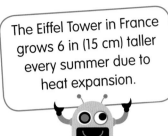

The Eiffel Tower in France grows 6 in (15 cm) taller every summer due to heat expansion.

Vibrating molecules

Conduction

Conduction happens when something warm touches something cooler. Heat spreads from the hotter object to the cooler one until both are the same temperature.

1 A cold metal spoon is placed into a cup of hot coffee.

2 Hot molecules in the coffee vibrate faster than cooler molecules in the spoon. The hot vibrating molecules in the coffee collide with those in the cold spoon and make them vibrate faster. The part of the spoon in the coffee gets warmer.

3 The hot molecules in the spoon bump into their colder neighbors and make them start vibrating faster too, spreading the heat energy along the spoon.

4 The whole spoon becomes warm, as each molecule vibrates and collides with its neighbor.

Conductors and insulators

Some materials, such as metal and water, conduct heat well. They feel cool because they conduct heat away from your skin when you touch them. Insulators, such as fabric, plastic, and wood, are poor heat conductors. They help stop heat from escaping from your body.

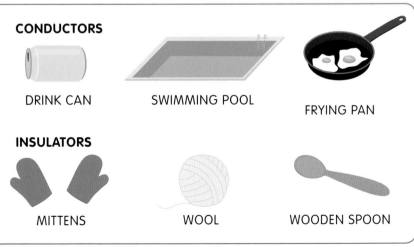

CONDUCTORS

DRINK CAN   SWIMMING POOL   FRYING PAN

INSULATORS

MITTENS   WOOL   WOODEN SPOON

As the water warms, it rises. .....

When the water cools, it sinks. ....

Convection

Convection moves heat through fluids—any type of liquid or gas. It is a cyclical motion. Warm water rises because it is lighter and less dense than the cool water around it. The warm water then cools, becomes denser, and sinks back down again.

Radiation

Unlike conduction and convection, radiation is a form of energy that travels in waves. These waves are also known as infrared rays. They are invisible but you can feel them on your skin, which is why you feel warm in bright sunshine or if you hold your hands close to a fire.

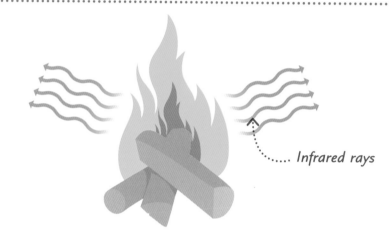

..... *Infrared rays*

TRY IT OUT

Convection currents in water

When a liquid's temperature changes, its density changes. Hot water is less dense than cool water, making it lighter, so it rises. This movement is known as a convection current. Try out this simple activity to see it in action.

1 Put some hot water and a few drops of food coloring in an egg cup or small teacup. Put a piece of plastic wrap over the cup and secure it with a rubber band.

2 Place the egg cup at the bottom of a jar of cold water. Pierce the plastic wrap with the sharp end of a pencil.

3 Take the pencil out. The hot, colored water will start to rise in a plume to the top.

How engines work

Most cars, planes, ships, and rockets are powered by engines that burn fuel to release heat and then turn that heat energy into kinetic energy. We call these heat engines.

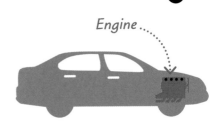

The scientific word for burning is combustion.

Internal combustion engines

Car engines are called internal combustion engines because they burn fuel inside the engine, within small metal cylinders. Hot gases from the burning fuel push metal pistons up and down in the cylinders about 50 times a second. Levers on these pistons then turn the rapid up-and-down motion into rotation to drive the wheels.

Engine

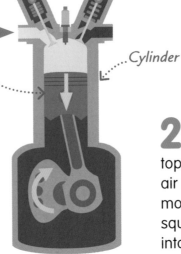

Air and fuel →

The piston moves down.

Cylinder

1 Suck
The cylinders in a car engine work in four stages. In the first stage, air and fuel are sucked into the cylinder as the piston moves down.

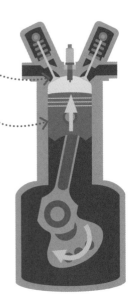

The inlet valve closes.

The piston moves up.

2 Squeeze
The inlet valve at the top closes, trapping the air and fuel. The piston moves back up and squeezes the gases into a small space.

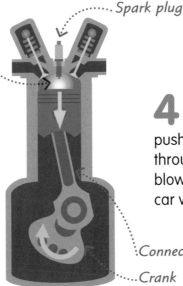

Spark plug

Burning fuel

3 Burn
A spark sets fire to the fuel. It burns, releasing hot gases that expand and push the piston down with great force. A connecting rod and crank under the piston turn the vertical motion into rotation.

Connecting rod

Crank

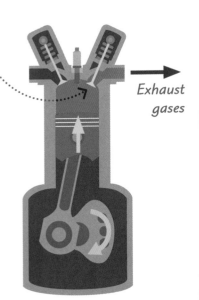

The outlet valve opens.

Exhaust gases →

4 Blow
The piston rises and pushes the burned gases through an outlet valve, blowing them out of the car via the exhaust pipe.

Jet engines

Large aircraft are powered by jet engines. These do not have pistons and cylinders. Instead, they have fans that spin inside a tube, sucking in air and squeezing it into a combustion chamber.

Jet engine

PASSENGER JET

1 A large fan at the front sucks in air, and a set of smaller compressor fans then squeeze the air so it will release more energy when it burns and expands.

2 Jet fuel is injected into the compressed air and the mixture is set alight. The heat makes the compressed air and gases from the burned fuel expand.

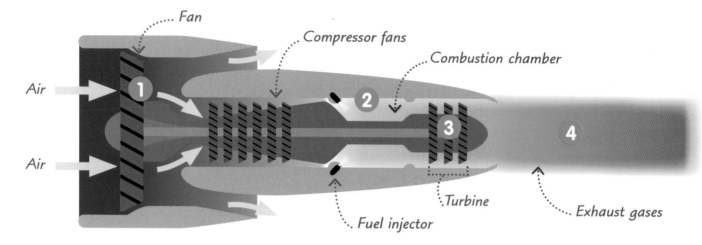

Fan

Compressor fans

Combustion chamber

Air

Air

Turbine

Fuel injector

Exhaust gases

3 The expanding gases rush through a fan called a turbine, spinning it around. This makes the fan and compressors at the front spin around too.

4 Hot exhaust gases roar out of the back at high speed. This powerful movement creates a force called thrust that pushes the plane forward.

Rocket power

There's no air in space, so rockets must carry oxygen (see page 171) with them as well as their fuel. The oxygen reacts with the fuel to power the rocket.

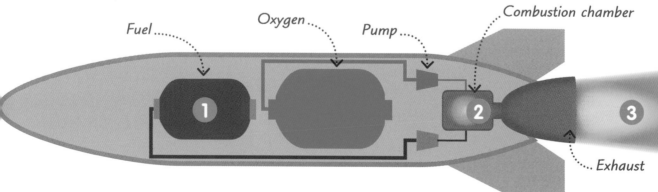

Fuel

Oxygen

Pump

Combustion chamber

Exhaust

1 Fuel (usually liquid hydrogen) and liquid oxygen are pumped from two large storage tanks to the engine.

2 The oxygen and fuel mix and burn in a combustion chamber. This creates a hot blast of exhaust gases from the back of the rocket.

3 The force of the exhaust gases rushing backward creates an equal and opposite force that pushes the rocket forward.

Waves

It might look as if waves move water from one place to another, but this isn't the case. Waves in water don't move the water forward and sound waves don't move air forward. They just transfer energy from one place to another.

Water waves transmit energy, not water, across the ocean.

How waves work

Waves are an important part of our lives. We send and receive information with them, cook with them, and even surf on them, so it is helpful to understand how they work.

The rope is motionless. It has no energy.

1 Let's look at this rope. The robot is holding one end of the rope and the rest is lying along the floor.

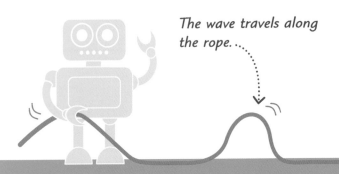

The wave travels along the rope.

2 The robot creates a wave in the rope by flicking its hand. This transfers energy into the rope. The wave transfers the energy along the rope.

This part of the rope is motionless. It has no energy.

3 The robot can produce many waves by moving its hand up and down. All the waves travel along the rope.

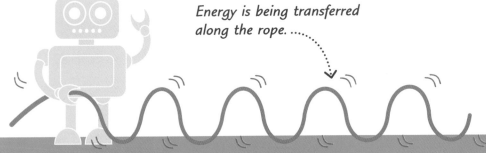

Energy is being transferred along the rope.

Wave machine

Build a wave machine from gumdrops pushed onto wooden skewers and use it to investigate what happens when you change the size and speed of waves.

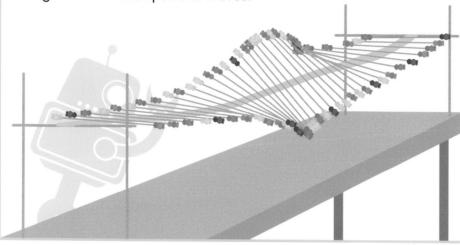

1 Attach a length of duct tape between two points. You could use the backs of two chairs, or clamps attached to the end of a long bench. The tape's sticky side should face upward.

2 Position skewers 2 in (5 cm) apart along the length of the tape. Add another layer of tape on top, to hold the skewers in place.

3 Push a gumdrop onto each end of each skewer. Make sure the tape is horizontal, then flick any part of it to set off the wave and watch it travel back and forth.

Measuring waves

All types of waves can be measured in the same way. To measure a wave, you need to know its wavelength (the distance between two peaks), its amplitude (the wave's height), and its frequency (the number of waves per second).

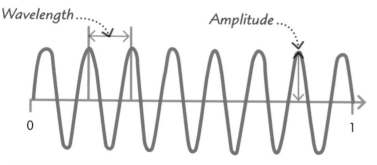

Wavelength ......   *Amplitude* ......

0   1

LOW FREQUENCY

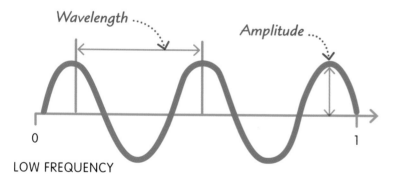

Wavelength ......   *Amplitude* ......

0   1

HIGH FREQUENCY

Optical fibers

Engineers have developed some amazing ways of transmitting information using waves. Optical fibers are long strands of glass or plastic that are as thin as human hair. Light waves are sent along these fibers, traveling at incredible speeds. Pulses of light carry digital data, providing homes with high-speed internet connections.

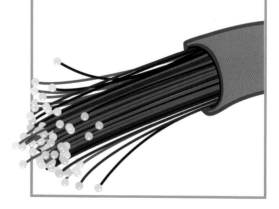

How waves behave

Waves travel smoothly and evenly when left alone. But when they hit an obstacle or pass from one medium to another, such as from water to air, the way they move changes.

The fastest thing known to science is a light wave. It is impossible to go any faster.

Reflection

When waves hit a solid obstacle, they're reflected, which means they bounce back. The shape of a reflected wave depends on the shape of the incoming waves and the shape of the obstacle.

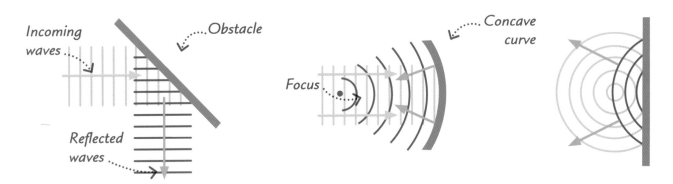

1 When straight waves hit a straight obstacle, they are reflected without changing shape. Light waves behave this way when they hit a mirror.

2 When straight waves hit a concave curve, the reflected waves travel inward toward a focus. Satellite dishes have this shape to focus radio waves.

3 When circular waves hit a straight obstacle, they bounce back as circular waves again. Ripples in a pond behave this way if they hit a wall.

Refraction

Waves travel at different speeds in different substances. When light waves pass from air to water, for instance, they slow down. This change in speed makes the waves change direction if they hit the new substance at an angle. This is called refraction. A straw in a glass of water looks bent because light from the straw refracts as it leaves the water.

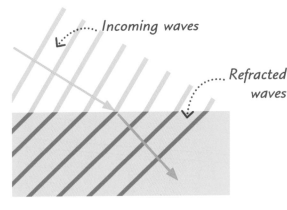

1 When light waves travel from air to water, they slow down, which makes them bend.

2 Light from the straw bends as it travels from water to air, creating a distorted image.

Diffraction

When waves pass through a gap, they sometimes spread out. This is called diffraction. Diffraction only happens when the gap is small relative to the size of the wavelength.

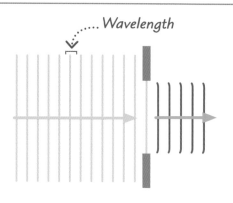

Wavelength

Sound waves

1 If short waves pass through a wide gap, little diffraction occurs. There are shadows where waves are blocked. This is what happens when light goes through a doorway.

2 When long waves pass through a small gap, they are diffracted. This is how sound travels through a doorway. There's no shadow, so the sound fills the room on the other side.

Interference

When waves meet, they can combine to form larger or smaller waves. This is called interference. Interference in light waves produces the iridescent (shimmering) colors seen on soap bubbles and butterfly wings. Stormy weather can make ocean waves interfere, producing giant waves.

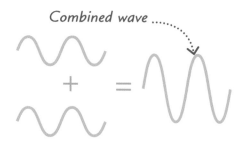

Combined wave

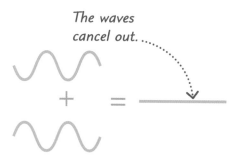

The waves cancel out.

1 If the peaks of similar waves arrive at the same time, the two waves add together to make a new, larger wave. This is called positive or constructive interference.

2 If the peaks of one wave coincide with the troughs (low points) of another, the two waves cancel each other out. This is called negative or destructive interference.

TRY IT OUT

Make waves

It's easy to see interference at work by throwing pebbles into a pond on a still day. Time your throws carefully to make two sets of concentric ripples. Watch where the waves meet and look for positive interference (larger waves) and negative interference (flat water).

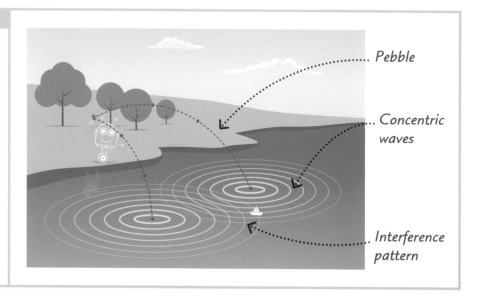

Pebble

Concentric waves

Interference pattern

Sound

The sounds you hear are simply air in motion. When a sound is made, it causes the air to vibrate (move back and forth). These vibrations are then picked up by your ears as sound.

A supersonic jet plane flies faster than the speed of sound.

Sound waves

All sounds start as vibrations. These vibrations spread through the air, as sound waves, until they reach your ears.

The robot plucks the guitar string.

Sound travels through the air in waves.

1 If you pluck a guitar string, it will vibrate. This vibration pushes the air molecules around the guitar string back and forth, making them vibrate, too.

2 Each air molecule bumps into its neighbor, and so on, spreading the vibrations through the air.

3 The sound waves spread out in all directions, growing quieter as they travel farther from their source.

Speed of sound

Sound waves can travel through gases, liquids, and solids. They travel faster in liquids than air because the molecules are packed more tightly, so the vibrations are passed on faster. Sound waves travel even faster in solids.

1 In space
Space is completely silent because it is a vacuum—there is no air. Sound cannot travel in space because there are no air molecules for sound waves to move.

2 In air
Sound travels about 1,080 ft (330 m) per second through air, but that's about a million times slower than light. That's why you see a lightning bolt strike a few seconds before you hear the rumble of thunder.

Sound travels more slowly than light.

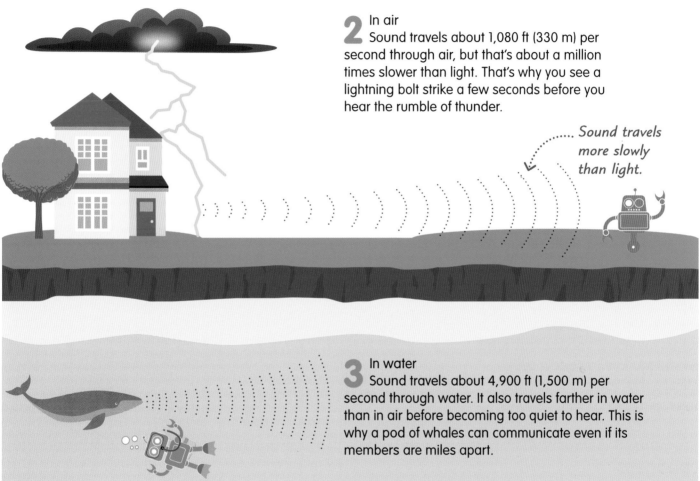

3 In water
Sound travels about 4,900 ft (1,500 m) per second through water. It also travels farther in water than in air before becoming too quiet to hear. This is why a pod of whales can communicate even if its members are miles apart.

TRY IT OUT

Yogurt pot phones

Tie a piece of string between two yogurt cartons and ask a friend to pull one of the cups until the string is tight. Put your ear to your pot and ask your friend to whisper into theirs. You should be able to hear their voice carried as sound waves through the string.

Measuring sound

Sounds can be loud or quiet, high-pitched like a whistle or low-pitched like thunder. These differences are caused by differences in the shapes of the sound waves that reach your ears.

> Babies and children can hear sounds that are too high-pitched for adults to hear.

Frequency

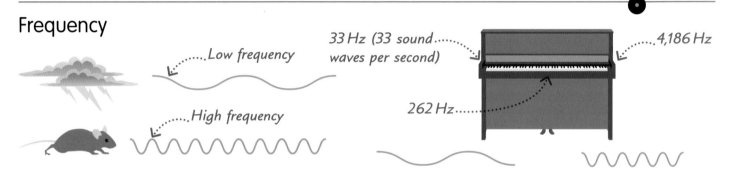

....*Low frequency*

....*High frequency*

33 Hz (33 sound waves per second)

262 Hz....

....*4,186 Hz*

1 The number of sound waves that reach your ears each second is called the frequency. The higher the frequency, the higher-pitched the sound.

2 Frequency is measured in hertz (Hz). The frequency of most pianos ranges from 33 Hz (lowest note) to 4,186 Hz (highest note).

3 Human ears can hear frequencies between 20 and 20,000 Hz. Sound too high for us to hear is called ultrasound. Sound too low to hear is called infrasound. Some animals can hear ultrasound or infrasound.

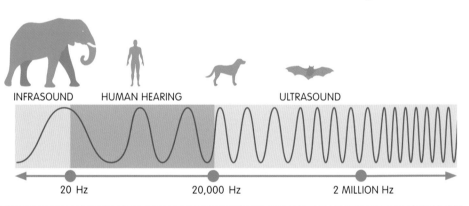

INFRASOUND   HUMAN HEARING   ULTRASOUND

20 Hz   20,000 Hz   2 MILLION Hz

Loudness

The loudness (volume) of sound depends on how much energy is in the wave. This is usually shown by the height of a wave in a wave graph. Loudness is measured in units called decibels (dB).

The quietest sound humans can hear is a 0 dB whisper.....

The rustle of leaves is about 10 dB.....

A mosquito's buzz is about 20 dB.....

Laughter is about 60 dB.....

A washing machine is about 80 dB.....

Tone

Very few sounds contain just one pitch. Most have a basic, or fundamental, pitch, as well as a range of additional pitches called overtones. Overtones help us tell the difference between sounds, and they give each musical instrument its distinctive sound.

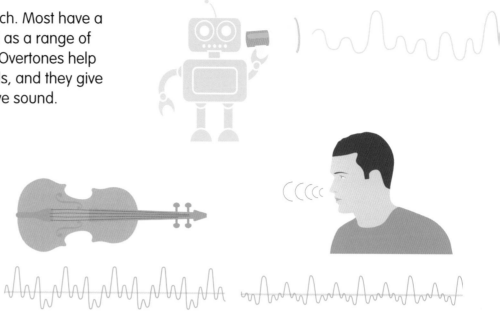

1 A tuning fork produces a pure sound with almost no overtones, so its wave is simple.

2 A violin has a jagged waveform, with lots of sharp overtones on top of the main wave.

3 The human voice has the variety of a violin, but with more marked wave peaks.

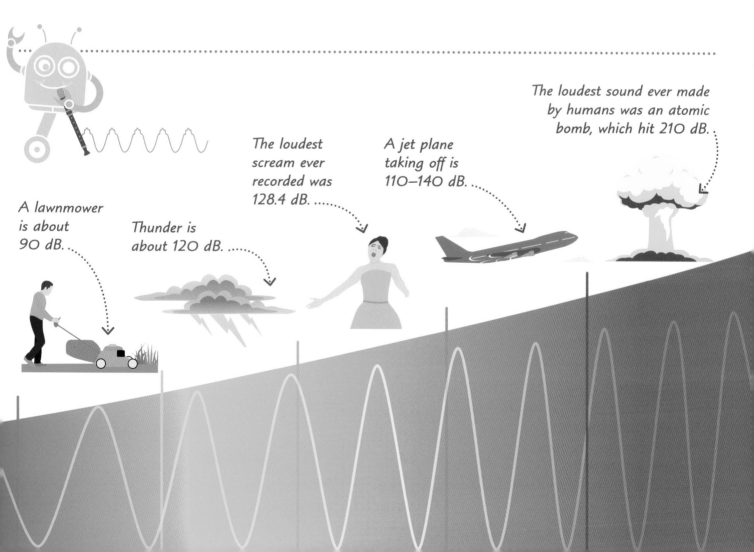

The loudest sound ever made by humans was an atomic bomb, which hit 210 dB.

The loudest scream ever recorded was 128.4 dB.

A jet plane taking off is 110–140 dB.

A lawnmower is about 90 dB.

Thunder is about 120 dB.

Light

Light is a form of energy that our eyes can detect. Light travels in waves. It moves so quickly that a beam of light can light up a whole room in an instant.

> Never look directly at the Sun. It is so bright that it can very quickly damage your eyes.

1 The Sun, the stars, candles, and electric lights send out light, so we call them luminous objects or light sources. You see luminous objects when light from them shines directly into your eyes.

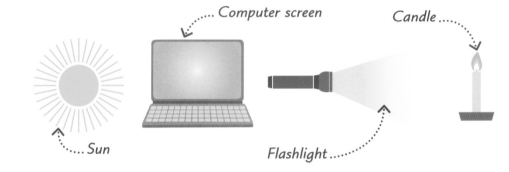

Computer screen

Candle

Sun

Flashlight

2 Most things aren't luminous. You can see them only because light bounces (reflects) off them and back into your eyes. The Moon is not luminous— it only looks bright because it reflects light from the Sun.

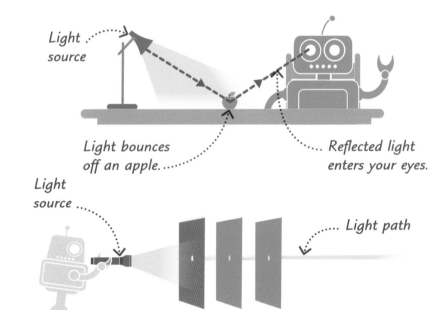

Light source

Light bounces off an apple.

Reflected light enters your eyes.

3 Light moves in straight lines, which we call light rays. If you line up three cards with holes in and shine a flashlight through them, light will only get through when the holes align.

Light source

Light path

4 Because light travels in straight lines, if an object blocks its path it creates a shadow. Shadows aren't usually completely dark because light reflected from nearby objects can still reach them.

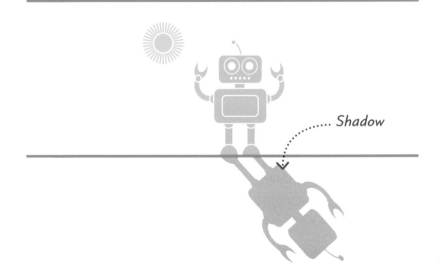

Shadow

5 A small or distant light source casts a sharp shadow, but a large light source casts a softer shadow with different areas. The dark center of the shadow where all the light is blocked is called the umbra. Around this is a paler shadow called a penumbra.

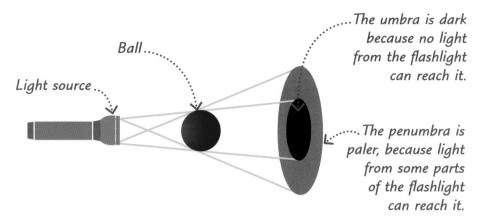

Ball

Light source

...The umbra is dark because no light from the flashlight can reach it.

......The penumbra is paler, because light from some parts of the flashlight can reach it.

Opaque, transparent, and translucent

Most solid objects block light, but some materials, such as water or glass, let light waves pass straight through.

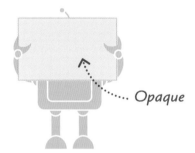

Opaque

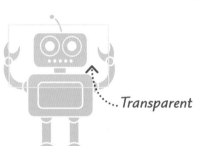

Transparent

Translucent .....

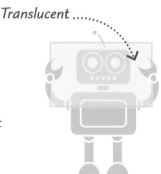

1 An opaque material blocks all light. Materials such as wood or metals are opaque. These materials either reflect light or absorb it.

2 Some materials, such as glass, are transparent. They let almost all light through; a little is reflected, which is why we see can see the surface of the glass.

3 Materials that scatter the light as it passes through, such as frosted glass, are translucent. The light is scattered by tiny particles inside the material.

TRY IT OUT

Sundials and shadows

You can make a sundial to tell the time from the position of shadows.

1 Fill a flowerpot with sand. Then push a long stick firmly upright into the sand.

2 At 8 AM on a sunny day, place a pebble at the tip of the stick's shadow and note the time on the pebble. Repeat every hour.

3 Check your sundial on the next sunny day. What do you think the time is?

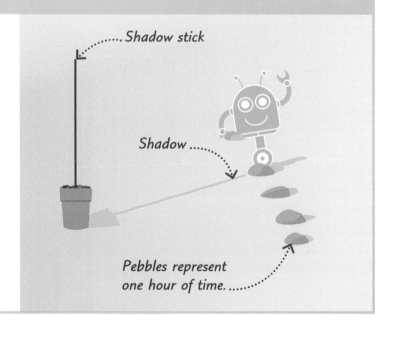

Shadow stick

Shadow ......

Pebbles represent one hour of time. ......

Reflection

When light rays bounce off an object, we say they are reflected. Very smooth objects such as mirrors reflect light so well that we see images in them.

Glass mirrors have a thin coating of silver on the back to reflect light.

1 All objects reflect light, but most objects have a rough surface that scatters rays in many different directions. Objects with a very smooth surface, such as a mirror, reflect rays in a regular way. That's why you can see your face in a mirror.

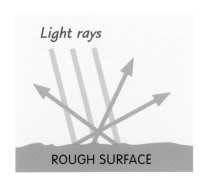

Light rays

ROUGH SURFACE

SMOOTH SURFACE

2 Light rays hitting a mirror are called incident rays, and rays bouncing away are called reflected rays. A reflected ray bounces off at exactly the same angle as the incident ray arrived. We call this the law of reflection.

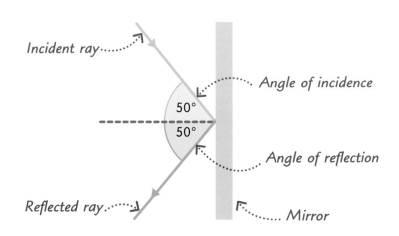

Incident ray

Angle of incidence

50°
50°

Angle of reflection

Reflected ray

Mirror

3 When you look in a mirror, you see an image of an object that appears to be behind the mirror. The image looks the same distance behind the mirror as the object is in front.

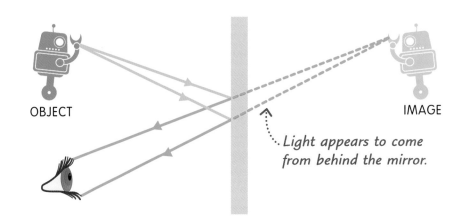

OBJECT

IMAGE

Light appears to come from behind the mirror.

4 Mirrors don't reverse things left to right. Writing looks reversed in a mirror because you've turned it around to face the glass. Mirrors actually reverse images from front to back, along a line through the mirror.

OBJECT   IMAGE

5 On a still day, the surface of a lake is smooth enough to act like a mirror. It reflects the scenery behind the lake, creating a mirror image.

Image

Curved mirrors

Mirrors that have curved surfaces change the size of the image. This is because the light is reflected off different places on the mirror at different angles.

CONVEX

1 A convex mirror curves outward like the back of a spoon. It makes the image smaller, but it gives a wider field of view. Convex mirrors are used in car side mirrors to give a wide field of view behind the car.

CONCAVE

2 A concave mirror curves inward like the front of a spoon. When an object is close to a concave mirror, the image is enlarged. People use concave mirrors for shaving or doing makeup.

REAL WORLD TECHNOLOGY

Extremely Large Telescope

Large space telescopes such as the Extremely Large Telescope (ELT) in Chile use mirrors rather than lenses to collect faint light from deep space. The ELT's main mirror is made up of 798 hexagonal mirrors, each 5 ft (1.45 m) wide, arranged in a honeycomb pattern to form a giant, concave dish.

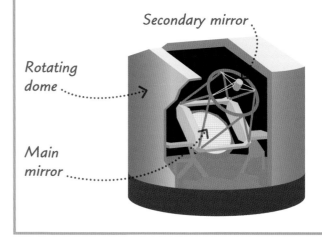

Secondary mirror

Rotating dome

Main mirror

Refraction

When light waves travel from air into water or
glass, they slow down, which makes them bend.
This bending is called refraction.

Sound waves also change
speed when they travel
from one substance
to another.

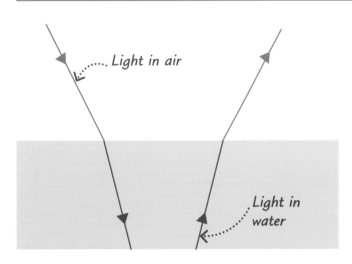

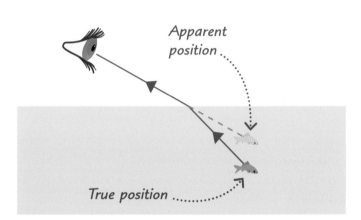

1 Light travels very fast in air but slower in
water. The fall in speed as it enters water
makes the light bend. When it leaves water,
it speeds up and bends the opposite way.

2 When you look at something underwater,
the refracted light from the object creates a
distorted image, making the object look closer
to the surface than it really is.

3 Light rays can be refracted when they travel from cold air to a patch of warm air. This
causes mirages—mysterious pools of "water" shimmering in the distance in deserts or on
hot roads in summer. The mirage is blue light from the sky refracted by air on the hot ground.

Lenses

Lenses are curved disks made of glass or another transparent substance. Their special shape makes light refract in a way that changes what you see through them. There are two main kinds of lenses: concave and convex.

1 Concave lenses
A concave lens is thin in the middle and thicker around the edge, which makes light rays spread out as they pass through. As a result, when you see an object through a concave lens, it looks smaller than it really is.

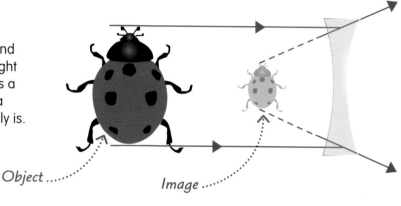

Object ....

Image ....

2 Convex lenses
A convex lens is fatter in the middle, which makes light rays bend inward. They come together, or converge. When you see a nearby object through a convex lens, it's magnified—it looks bigger than it really is.

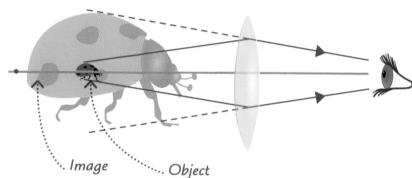

Image

Object

3 Focal point
The point where parallel light rays meet after passing through a convex lens and converging is called the focal point, and the distance between the focal point and the lens is the focal length. The fatter a convex lens is, the more powerfully it focuses light, and the shorter its focal length is.

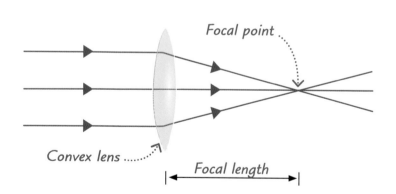

Focal point

Convex lens ....

Focal length

TRY IT OUT

Seeing double

Turn a button into two buttons by dropping it in a glass of water. Light from the button refracts as it leaves the water, creating an image of a second button. Hold the glass at just the right angle to see both: one through the side of the glass and one through the top of the water.

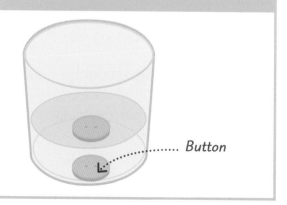

.... Button

Forming images

Lenses can be used to create images of objects. An image is a copy of an object, but it may be smaller or larger than the object or inverted (upside down).

The reflection you see in a mirror is called a virtual image.

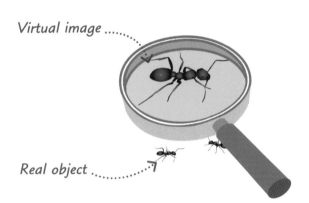

Virtual image

Real object

1 An image that you see by looking through a lens is called a virtual image. When you look at an object through a magnifying glass, the virtual image you see is larger than the real object.

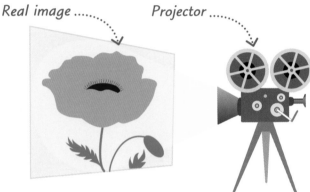

Real image

Projector

2 An image that can be displayed on a screen is called a real image. Projectors, cameras, and the human eye all create real images.

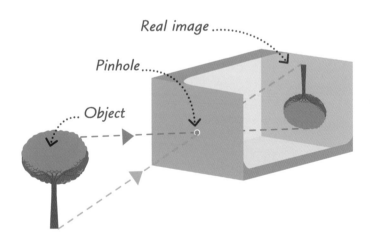

Real image

Pinhole

Object

3 A pinhole camera can create a real image without a lens. Light from each point on an object lands on only one point of the screen, so it forms a sharp image. But the image is very faint because only a tiny amount of light can pass through the hole.

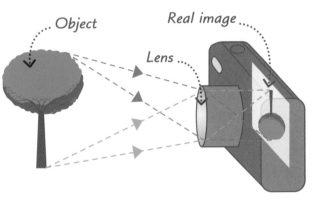

Object

Real image

Lens

4 Cameras and eyes use a lens to create a real image. This means a larger hole can be used, allowing more light through and forming a brighter image. The lens bends light rays so that light coming from each point on the object falls on just one point on the sensor, creating a sharp image.

Digital camera

A digital camera focuses light onto a device called a sensor—a silicon chip that responds to photons (particles) of light by generating an electric charge. On its own, a sensor can't distinguish between colors, so a grid of tiny colored filters is placed on top. Each square of color corresponds to a pixel in the image.

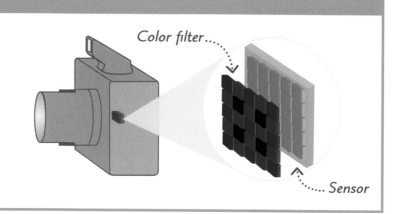

Color filter

Sensor

Ray diagrams

To find out where the image produced by a lens appears, you can draw a ray diagram.

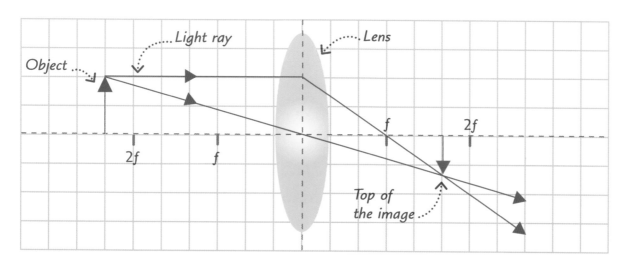

...Light ray

Lens

Object ...

2f

f

f

2f

Top of
the image ...

1 Draw a horizontal axis with the lens in the middle. Mark distances from the lens as multiples of the focal length (see page 207): *f*, *2f*, and so on.

2 Draw the object as an arrow pointing upward.

3 Draw a straight line from the top of the object through the center of the lens.

4 Draw a horizontal line from the top of the object to the lens, then continue this line down through the focal point.

5 Where the two lines meet is the top of the image. The image does not necessarily form at the focal point.

Make a pinhole camera

You don't need a lens to focus light and create an image. You can create an image with just a pinhole in a box by following the steps shown here.

1 Cut a small square hole at one end of a shoebox and a larger hole at the other end.

2 Tape aluminum foil over the small hole and prick it with a pin. Tape tracing paper over the large hole.

3 Place a thick blanket over your head and all of the box except the pinhole end. Point the pinhole at something bright and the image will appear on the tracing paper.

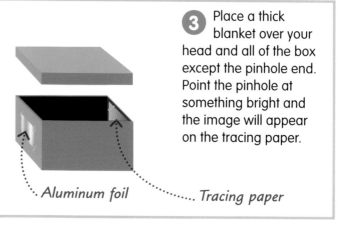

Aluminum foil

Tracing paper

Telescopes and microscopes

Telescopes and microscopes use lenses or mirrors to create magnified images. They work in a similar way, but telescopes create magnified images of distant objects while microscopes create magnified images of tiny nearby objects.

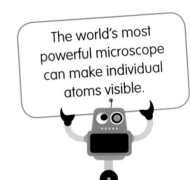

The world's most powerful microscope can make individual atoms visible.

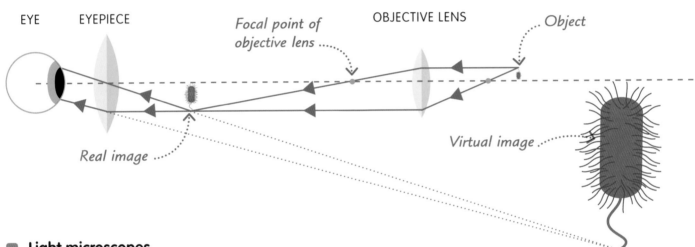

EYE   EYEPIECE   Focal point of objective lens ....   OBJECTIVE LENS   Object

Real image ....

Virtual image ...

1 Light microscopes

A light microscope has two main convex lenses that both work like magnifying glasses. The first lens, called the objective, creates a magnified image of the object. The second lens creates a magnified image of the image. The end result is an image hundreds of times larger than the object (but upside down), which makes it possible to see things too small for the naked eye, such as cells.

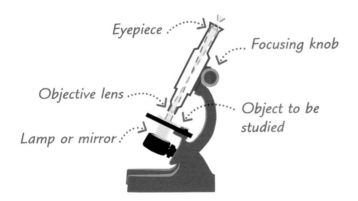

Eyepiece ....

Focusing knob

Objective lens ....

Object to be studied

Lamp or mirror :

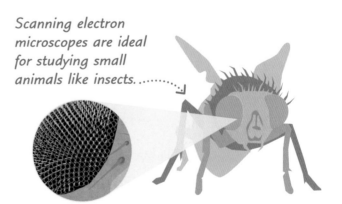

Scanning electron microscopes are ideal for studying small animals like insects. ....

2 Using a light microscope

To use a light microscope, you place the object being studied on a glass slide over a lamp or mirror. Light shines through the object, through the objective lens, and then through the eyepiece.

3 Scanning electron microscopes

Scanning electron microscopes create images not with light but with a beam of electrons focused by magnets. They can magnify 100,000 times and reveal more detail than light microscopes.

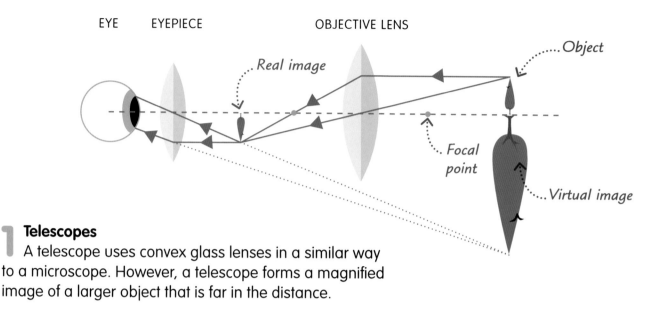

EYE   EYEPIECE   OBJECTIVE LENS

Real image

Object

Focal point

Virtual image

1 Telescopes

A telescope uses convex glass lenses in a similar way to a microscope. However, a telescope forms a magnified image of a larger object that is far in the distance.

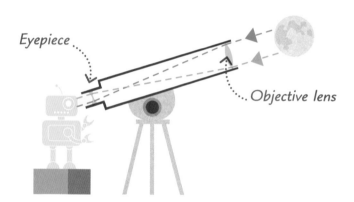

Eyepiece

Objective lens

2 Using a telescope

To use a telescope, you look through the eyepiece and turn the focusing dial, which moves the lens in the eyepiece backward and forward. Many people use a tripod to hold the telescope, which stops the image from shaking.

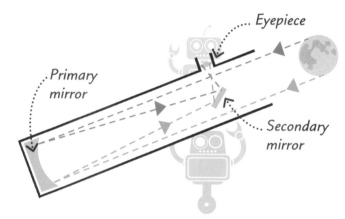

Eyepiece

Primary mirror

Secondary mirror

3 Reflecting telescopes

Reflecting telescopes use curved metal-coated mirrors instead of lenses to create images. These work better in powerful telescopes because, unlike a glass lens, a mirror doesn't cause the light to split into different colors as it bends.

REAL WORLD TECHNOLOGY

Radio telescopes

Most telescopes use visible light, but stars and galaxies emit other kinds of radiation we can't see, including radio waves. Radio telescopes collect and focus radio waves from space with a large dish like a satellite receiver. These telescopes allow astronomers to see through clouds of dust that block visible light, in order to study the heart of our Milky Way galaxy.

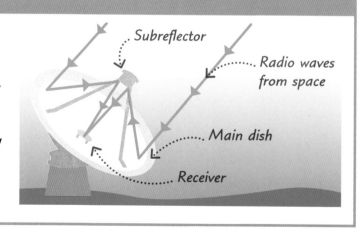

Subreflector

Radio waves from space

Main dish

Receiver

Colors

The world is full of colors, from the bright blue of a clear sky to the deep red of a ripe tomato. All these colors are simply the way our eyes see different wavelengths of light.

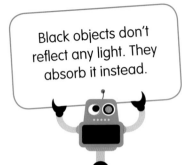

Black objects don't reflect any light. They absorb it instead.

Splitting light

White light appears to have little or no color, but it's actually a mix of all colors of light.

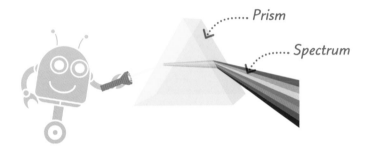

Prism

Spectrum

1 You can split white light by shining it through a triangular block of glass called a prism. The prism refracts (bends) each wavelength differently. Each color has a different wavelength, so the colors fan out into a rainbow pattern—a spectrum.

2 Most colored objects are not emitting (giving off) light, but reflecting it. They get their colors by absorbing some wavelengths and reflecting the rest. A leaf looks green because it absorbs all the other colors in the spectrum but reflects green.

3 The order of colors in the spectrum is always the same: red, orange, yellow, green, blue, indigo, and violet. Red has the longest waves, with wavelengths of around 665 nanometers (nm), or 665 billionths of a meter. Violet has the shortest waves, with wavelengths of around 400 nm.

RED
665 nm

ORANGE
600 nm

YELLOW
570 nm

GREEN
520 nm

BLUE
475 nm

INDIGO
445 nm

VIOLET
400 nm

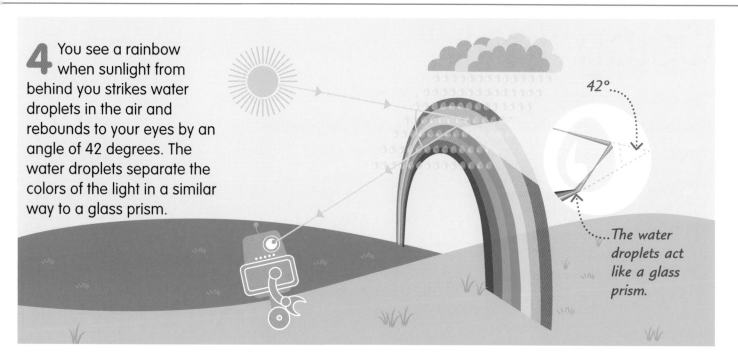

4 You see a rainbow when sunlight from behind you strikes water droplets in the air and rebounds to your eyes by an angle of 42 degrees. The water droplets separate the colors of the light in a similar way to a glass prism.

42°

...The water droplets act like a glass prism.

Adding colors

Our eyes can see millions of different colors, but all of them can be made by mixing light of just three different colors—red, blue, and green—in different proportions. We call these colors the primary colors of light. Mixing paints also creates different colors, but by subtracting colors rather than adding them.

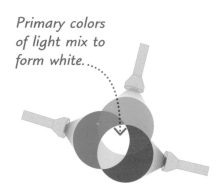

Primary colors of light mix to form white...

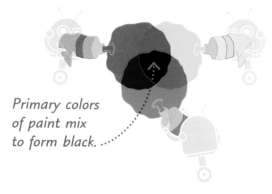

Primary colors of paint mix to form black. ...

1 Adding primary colors creates other colors. Adding all three primary colors of light together creates white light.

2 Mixing paints subtracts colors. A mixture of blue and yellow paint looks green, for instance, because these paints absorb every wavelength except green.

REAL WORLD TECHNOLOGY

Screens

Computer, TV, and phone screens can create every possible hue by mixing the three primary colors of light. Look closely at a screen and you'll see tiny dots (pixels) that are either red, green, or blue. By switching certain pixels on and off, the screen can mix colors in any proportion.

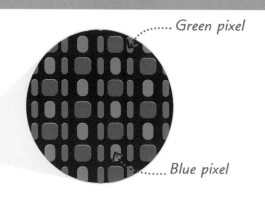

.... Green pixel

.... Blue pixel

Using light

People have found many ingenious uses for light, from looking inside the body or performing surgery on people's eyes to sending high-speed internet data around the world.

Laser beams are used to measure the Moon's exact distance from Earth.

Lasers

Lasers are bright, artificial lights that create a beam so intense it can burn a hole in steel. A laser beam is so straight and narrow that it can accurately hit a mirror left on the Moon by Apollo astronauts.

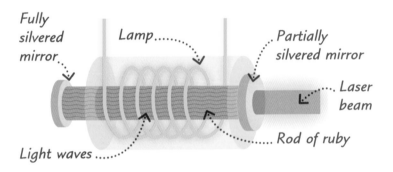

Fully silvered mirror

Lamp

Partially silvered mirror

Laser beam

Rod of ruby

Light waves

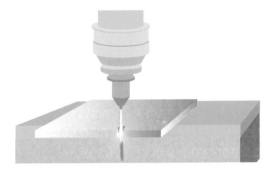

White light

LASER

1 In a ruby laser, a coiled lamp illuminates a rod of synthetic ruby (aluminum oxide). Atoms in the ruby absorb the energy and re-emit it as red light. Both ends of the rod have mirrors that reflect light back and forth, creating an intense beam. One is partially silvered to let the beam escape.

2 White light is a jumbled mix of different wavelengths. Lasers, in contrast, produce light of a single wavelength. The waves are not only equal in size but perfectly in step. This helps keep a laser beam narrow and tightly focused over a long distance.

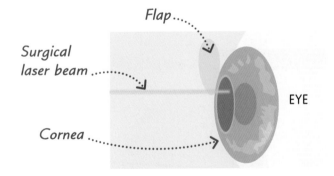

Flap

Surgical laser beam

EYE

Cornea

3 The precision of lasers makes them useful for delicate operations, such as laser eye surgery. A flap is cut in the eye's outer cornea, and a laser is fired in pulses to vaporize small areas of tissue, correcting near-sightedness. The flap is then folded back and allowed to heal.

4 Some lasers produce powerful beams of infrared light that can melt through metal, glass, plastic, and even diamond. Faster and more precise than electric drills, these lasers are used to make cooling holes in engines or the fine holes in shower heads, coffee makers, and food mincers.

Fiber optics

Fiber optic cables are bundles of fine glass threads that can carry digital data as pulses of light. They can transmit data far further and far more quickly than electric wires.

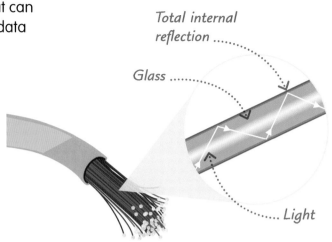

Total internal reflection ....

Glass ....

Light ....

1 Each optical fiber is a fine strand of glass about as thin as a human hair. Light travels through the fiber's glass core, bouncing from side to side. The light beam can't escape because it never hits the side at an angle steep enough to pass through rather than being reflected. This is known as total internal reflection.

2 When you use the internet to connect to a website in another part of the world, data reaches you via fiber optic cables on the seafloor. These are laid by special ships that feed out cable to a plow that runs along the seafloor, digging a trench and dropping the cable into it. Ships lay up to 125 miles (200 km) of cable per day, and the cables have a life span of about a decade.

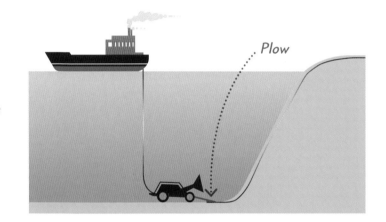

Plow ....

REAL WORLD TECHNOLOGY

Endoscopes

Endoscopes are viewing devices that let doctors see inside a patient's body. An endoscope typically has three cables. One contains optical fibers that carry light into the body, illuminating the area the doctor wants to see. Another carries reflected light back, allowing the doctor to see an image, often on a monitor. A third cable allows tiny surgical devices to be inserted into the body—for instance, to cut out areas of damaged tissue.

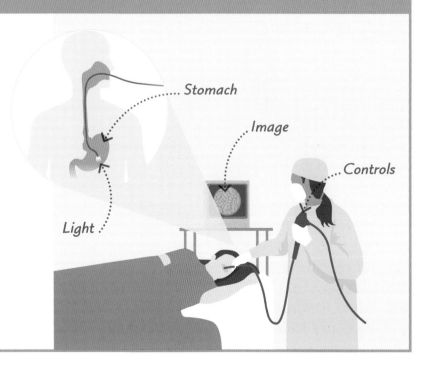

Stomach

Image

Controls

Light

Electromagnetic spectrum

Light energy is a form of radiation that travels in waves that our eyes can detect. Radiation can also travel in waves too short or too long for our eyes to sense. Together with light, all these different wavelengths make up the electromagnetic spectrum.

All electromagnetic waves travel at the speed of light.

Electromagnetic waves

Electromagnetic waves range from radio waves, which can be meters or kilometres long, to gamma rays, which are smaller than atoms.

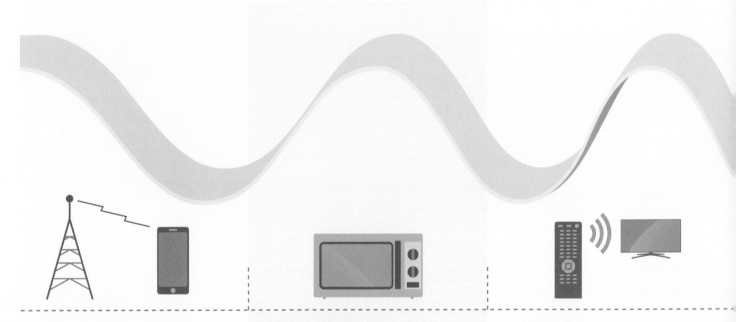

1 Radio waves
Radio waves are used to transmit not only radio shows but also TV programs, phone calls, and internet data invisibly at the speed of light. Long radio waves can bend around obstacles, but shorter waves such as cell phone signals travel best in straight lines.

2 Microwaves
Microwaves are shorter than radio waves (and are sometimes classed as very short radio waves). Microwave ovens produce waves about 12 cm long. These make water molecules vibrate, heating up food, but they pass through glass and plastic.

3 Infrared
Infrared waves are a fraction of a millimeter long and transmit heat energy. Although they're invisible, you can feel them when you warm your hands by a fire or stand in bright sunshine. TV remotes use pulses of weak infrared light to send signals to a TV.

Discovering radio

For many years, the nature of light was a puzzle to science. Unlike sound waves, which travel as vibrations in air, light waves can travel through empty space where there's nothing to vibrate.

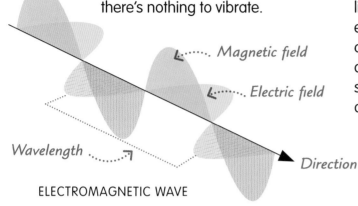

Magnetic field

Electric field

Wavelength

Direction

ELECTROMAGNETIC WAVE

In the 19th century, a Scottish scientist, James Clerk Maxwell, discovered that changes in magnetic and electric fields can travel at the speed of light. He formed a theory that visible light is a kind of double wave in the magnetic and electric fields, and he predicted that there must be other, invisible kinds of electromagnetic waves with different lengths. Sure enough, within a few years, scientists succeeded in creating radio waves—a breakthrough that would change the world.

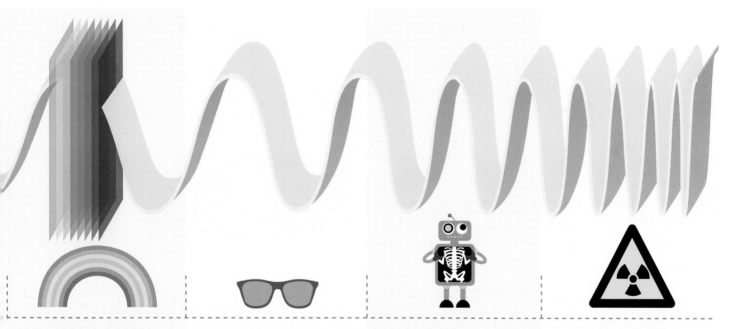

4 Visible light
This is the only part of the electromagnetic spectrum we can see. Visible light includes waves from 0.0004 mm to 0.0007 mm long. The longest visible waves look red, while the shortest waves look violet.

5 Ultraviolet
Ultraviolet (UV) rays come from the Sun and can cause sunburn. Mountaineers and skiers can get sore eyes from high UV levels so they wear sunglasses for protection. We can't see UV light but many birds and insects can.

6 X-rays
These electro-magnetic waves are about the size of atoms. They can pass straight through soft parts of the human body but are blocked by bones and teeth, which makes them ideal for creating images of the skeleton.

7 Gamma rays
These are the most dangerous type of electromagnetic wave. They carry large amounts of energy and can kill living cells. Gamma rays are given off by radioactive substances and can be used to destroy cancer.

Static electricity

If you rub a balloon on a sweater and then hold it to a wall, it will stay there, as if by magic. It's held in place by the same thing that causes lightning: static electricity.

You can see the effects of static electricity best on a dry, sunny day, when there isn't much moisture in the air.

Electricity and electrons

Electricity is caused by something called the electromagnetic force. This force normally keeps electrons trapped inside atoms, but they sometimes escape. If escaped electrons build up in one place, they cause static electricity. If they flow away, they create an electric current.

1 Every atom has a central nucleus and an outer zone of electrons (see page 132). Electrons have a negative charge, and the nucleus has a positive charge. Opposite charges attract each other, like opposite poles of a magnet. This force of attraction normally keeps electrons in place.

2 If you rub certain materials together, electrons can break away from their atoms and transfer from one material to another. Rubbing a balloon on a fuzzy sweater or your hair, for instance, transfers electrons to the balloon. These extra electrons then give the balloon an overall negative charge.

3 Opposite charges attract, and similar charges repel (push each other away). When you hold the balloon on a wall, the negative charge in the balloon repels electrons in the wall. That makes the wall's surface positively charged, so the negatively charged balloon sticks to it.

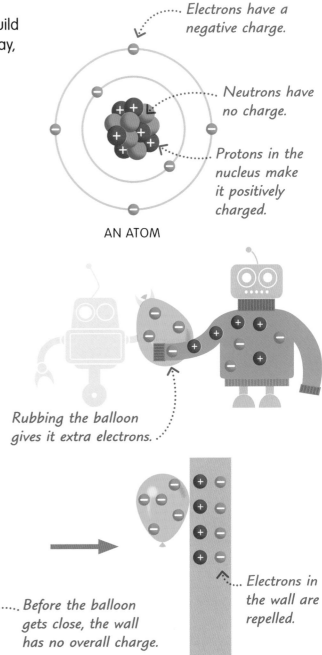

Electrons have a negative charge.

Neutrons have no charge.

Protons in the nucleus make it positively charged.

AN ATOM

Rubbing the balloon gives it extra electrons.

Before the balloon gets close, the wall has no overall charge.

Electrons in the wall are repelled.

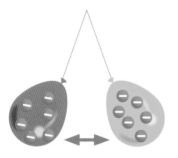

4 If you rub two balloons on a fuzzy sweater, they will both become negatively charged. If you then hang them together from a long loop of string, the balloons will repel each other, leaving a small gap between them.

Electrons transfer from the carpet to your shoes.

5 Plastic-soled shoes can pick up extra electrons just like balloons can. When your shoes rub against a carpet, the extra electrons can make your whole body negatively charged. When you touch something made of metal, the charge escapes and can give you a tiny electric shock.

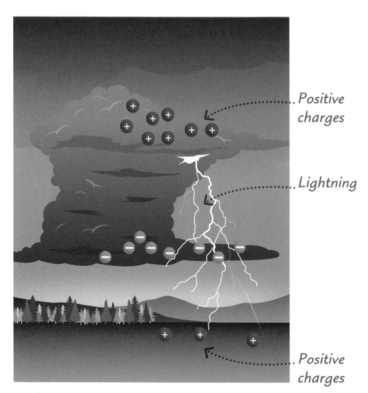

Positive charges

Lightning

Positive charges

Lightning

Lightning is a dramatic display of the power of static electricity. Ice crystals and raindrops inside clouds become charged as they swirl around and crash into each other, swapping electrons. Positive charges and negative charges build up in different parts of the cloud. The charge at the bottom of the cloud creates an opposite charge on the ground. This draws the charge down from the cloud, creating a powerful bolt of light and heat.

TRY IT OUT

Bending water

Try this magic trick to see how static electricity can bend water. Rub a balloon on a sweater to charge it with static electricity. Turn on a faucet and let it run slowly. Hold the balloon close and the charge will attract the water, bending it.

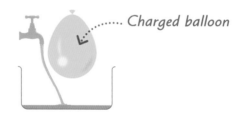

Charged balloon

Jumping paper

Draw and cut out small shapes on pieces of thin paper. Scatter them on a table, then charge a balloon on your hair or a sweater for 30 seconds. Lower the balloon over the pieces of paper and watch them jump up and stick.

Static electricity attracts the paper shapes.

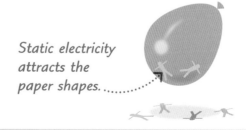

Current electricity

Unlike static electricity, which stays in one place, current electricity moves. All the electrical devices we use rely on flowing electric current.

Electrons in a wire move slower than a snail, but the energy they transmit moves thousands of miles a second.

Moving electrons

Current electricity depends on the free movement of electrons—the tiny, negatively charged particles that form the outer part of atoms. In materials such as metals, some electrons are only loosely held to atoms and can move around. These free electrons can push each other, passing on a charge like runners in a relay race.

1 When an electric wire isn't connected to a power source, the free electrons move around randomly between the metal atoms. There is no movement of charge.

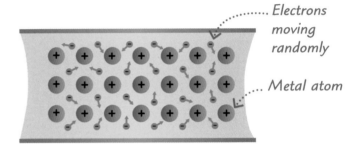

Electrons moving randomly

Metal atom

2 When the power is switched on, the negative charge at the power source repels (pushes away) electrons, because similar charges repel. The electrons move and repel the neighboring electrons, which repel their neighbors, and so on, passing on the charge.

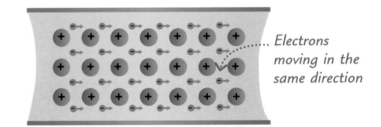

Electrons moving in the same direction

REAL WORLD TECHNOLOGY

Batteries

Batteries use a chemical reaction to create an electric current. A battery has three parts: a negative end (terminal) called an anode; a positive end called a cathode; and a central store of a chemical called an electrolyte. Chemical reactions in the electrolyte cause electrons to build up at the anode. The electrons are naturally drawn to the positive cathode, but their path is blocked. However, when the battery is connected to a circuit, the electrons flow the long way around, creating an electrical current.

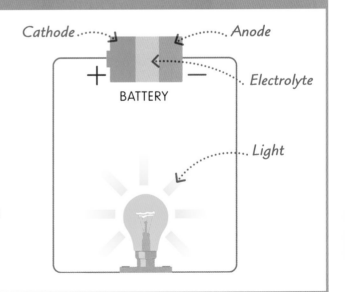

Cathode

Anode

BATTERY

Electrolyte

Light

Conductors and insulators

1 Conductors
Materials that allow electricity to flow through easily are called conductors. Metals such as copper, gold, and silver are good conductors because their atoms have a single outer electron that can separate from the atom easily. Copper is used for most wiring. Gold and silver are expensive and so are only used in small electronic devices. Water contains dissolved ions (charged particles) that conduct electricity, which is why it's dangerous to touch electrical objects with wet hands.

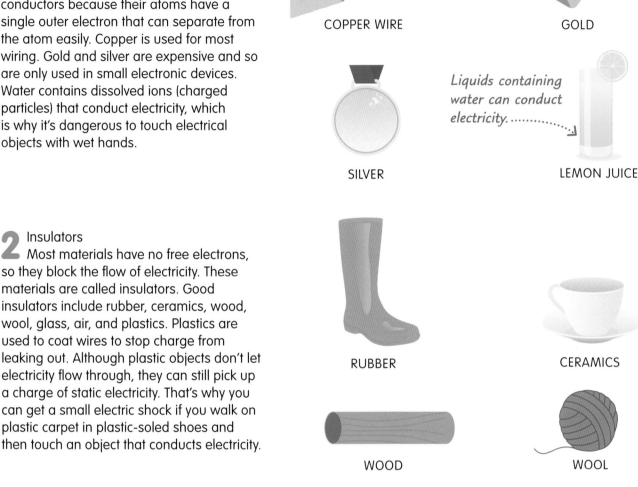

COPPER WIRE

GOLD

SILVER

Liquids containing water can conduct electricity.

LEMON JUICE

2 Insulators
Most materials have no free electrons, so they block the flow of electricity. These materials are called insulators. Good insulators include rubber, ceramics, wood, wool, glass, air, and plastics. Plastics are used to coat wires to stop charge from leaking out. Although plastic objects don't let electricity flow through, they can still pick up a charge of static electricity. That's why you can get a small electric shock if you walk on plastic carpet in plastic-soled shoes and then touch an object that conducts electricity.

RUBBER

CERAMICS

WOOD

WOOL

TRY IT OUT

Electric banana test

To find out whether objects around your home are good conductors or insulators, try this simple experiment. Find an old flashlight powered by AA or AAA batteries. With help from an adult, take it apart and tape three pieces of electrical wire to the battery terminals and bulb connections as shown. You should have two unconnected wire ends. Hold these onto (or push into) different objects such as coins, fruit, and cutlery, and see if the bulb lights.

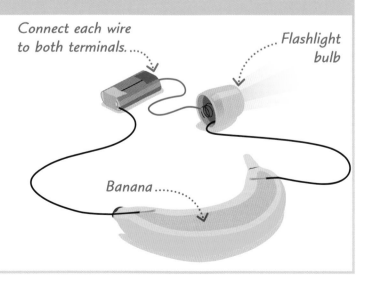

Connect each wire to both terminals.

Flashlight bulb

Banana

Electric circuits

All the electrical devices we use, from phones to TVs, depend on electricity flowing through circuits. When a circuit is switched on, it forms a complete loop without any gaps.

Small devices within an electric circuit are called components.

1 The simplest electric circuits are based on a loop of copper wire. An electric current will only flow if there are two things: a source of energy to push the electrons, such as a battery; and a complete, unbroken loop for the electrons to flow through. Two of the circuits here don't work. See if you can figure out why.

NOT WORKING

NOT WORKING

WORKING

2 If a circuit is broken by a gap, the current will stop flowing. This is how a switch works.

When the switch is open, no current flows.

When the switch is closed, the circuit is complete and the current flows.

3 When two batteries are connected together, they push electrons through the circuit with twice the force. We say they have twice the voltage. (You can find out more about voltage on page 224.) A bulb in the circuit will glow brighter, and a buzzer will make a louder noise.

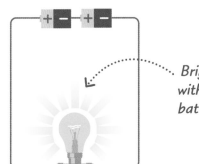

Brighter with two batteries

Series and parallel circuits

Circuits can be connected in two basic ways. If all the components are connected in a single loop, they are said to be connected in series. If the circuit splits into branches, they are connected in parallel.

1 Series circuits

When a circuit is connected in series, the components are connected one after the other on a single loop. The bulbs share the same current, so they glow half as brightly as a single bulb would. If one of them breaks, the circuit is broken and the other bulb stops working too.

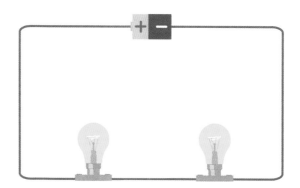

2 Parallel circuits

In a parallel circuit, the components are on separate branches. Each branch receives the full current, so both bulbs glow brightly. There's more than one path for the current to take, so if one bulb breaks, the other will keep working. The wiring in homes is carried by parallel circuits so that different devices can be switched on and off independently.

A break here will only stop one bulb from working.

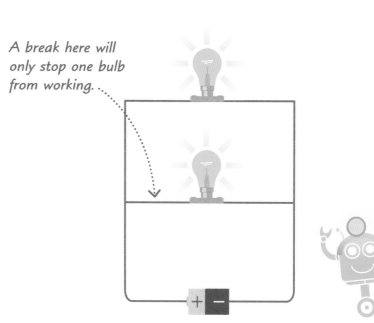

REAL WORLD TECHNOLOGY

Fuses and circuit breakers

If an electrical appliance in your home is faulty, electricity can leak out of its wiring and into its metal body. To protect you from shocks from faulty appliances, their plugs usually contain fuses, and many houses also have fuse boxes or circuit breakers. Fuses contain delicate wires that break if the power flowing through them is abnormally high. Circuit breakers are switches that "trip" and cut the circuit if they detect a surge in power.

Normal fuse

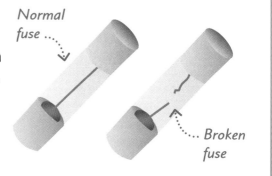

Broken fuse

Current, voltage, and resistance

How much current flows through a circuit depends on how strongly the electrons are pushed (voltage), and on how easily the circuit lets them through (resistance). Current, voltage, and resistance are easy to understand if you think of electricity as water flowing through pipes.

Many devices are powered by currents that reverse direction dozens of times a second. This is called an alternating current.

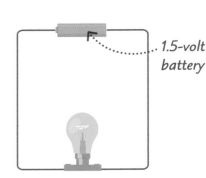

Current

1 The rate at which electrons move through a wire is the current. Measuring current is like measuring how much water flows through a pipe—a large current means lots of electrons are moving past, transferring lots of energy.

...... *Large current*

2 A small current means fewer electrons are on the move. Current is measured in units called amps (A). A current of 1 amp means about 6 trillion electrons are moving past a particular point every second.

...... *Small current*

Voltage

1 A current can't flow unless something is pushing it. In a circuit, the push comes from the difference in electrical potential energy at the start and end of the circuit. This is called voltage and we measure it in volts (V). Voltage works like water pressure. When a water storage tank is high up, the force of gravity creates higher pressure, making water gush from a faucet. When the tank is lower down, the pressure is lower and a smaller current flows from the faucet.

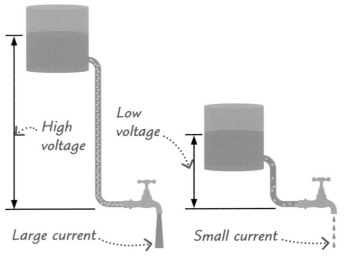

...... *High voltage*

Low voltage ......

Large current ......

Small current ......

2 Voltage is not the amount of current but the strength of the push. However, a higher voltage generates a stronger push and therefore a larger current. A high-voltage battery, for instance, will make a light bulb glow brighter than a low-voltage battery.

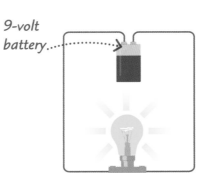

9-volt battery ......

1.5-volt battery

Resistance

LOW RESISTANCE

HIGH RESISTANCE

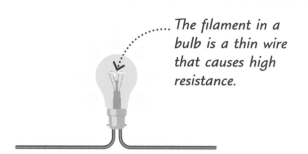

The filament in a bulb is a thin wire that causes high resistance.

1 Even in a good conductor like copper, there is some resistance to the flow of electricity, due to electrons and atoms getting in each other's way. We measure resistance in units called ohms (Ω). The thinner or longer a wire is, the more resistance it causes.

2 Resistance causes energy to be lost as heat or light. A very long, thin wire wound into a coil creates so much resistance that it will glow red or white hot. This is how electric heaters and filament light bulbs work.

3 Anything that increases the resistance in a circuit will reduce the current.

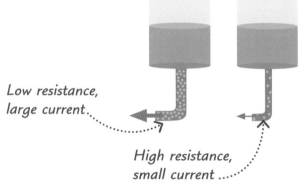

Low resistance, large current.

High resistance, small current

4 High resistance reduces an electric current, but high voltage increases it. The relationship between current, voltage, and resistance can be summed up by an equation called Ohm's law:

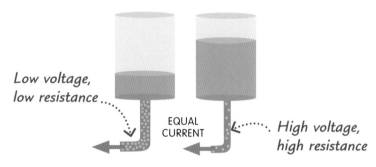

Low voltage, low resistance

EQUAL CURRENT

High voltage, high resistance

current = voltage ÷ resistance

REAL WORLD TECHNOLOGY

Transformers

When current flows through a wire, resistance causes a loss of energy. The greater the current, the greater the loss. To minimize losses, power stations transmit electrical energy over long distances as low current but high voltage. Machines called step-up transformers raise the voltage as electricity leaves the station, and step-down transformers lower it to safer levels before it reaches your home. High-voltage cables are dangerous and are carried high above the ground by pylons.

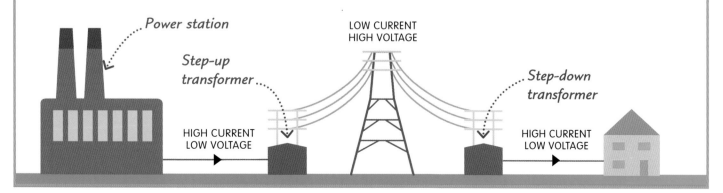

Power station

Step-up transformer

LOW CURRENT HIGH VOLTAGE

Step-down transformer

HIGH CURRENT LOW VOLTAGE

HIGH CURRENT LOW VOLTAGE

Electricity and magnetism

Electricity is closely related to magnetism. Every electrical current creates a magnetic field, and magnets can create electric currents. The branch of science that deals with electricity and magnetism is known as electromagnetism.

Electricity and magnetism are caused by the electromagnetic force, one of four "fundamental forces" that govern the universe.

Electromagnets

1 When electricity flows through a wire, the wire becomes a magnet. It creates an area around it where magnetic forces are felt—a magnetic field. You can see this with a magnetic compass, which swings around when it's next to a wire carrying direct current.

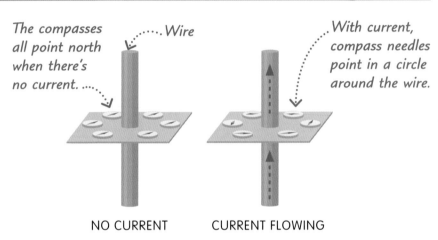

The compasses all point north when there's no current. ·····

····· *Wire*

With current, compass needles point in a circle around the wire.

NO CURRENT   CURRENT FLOWING

2 Electric currents can be used to create strong magnets called electromagnets that can be switched on and off. This works best if the wire is twisted into a coil so the fields around the loops reinforce each other.

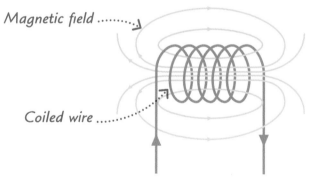

Magnetic field ·········

Coiled wire ·········

3 The effect is even stronger if the coil is wrapped around an iron bar, which becomes magnetized by the field created by a current.

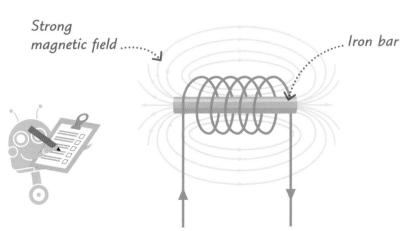

Strong magnetic field ·······

····· *Iron bar*

Generating electricity

1 Just as electricity can create magnetic fields, magnetic fields can generate electricity. This happens when a magnet moves past a wire or a wire moves past a magnet. The magnetic field is said to "induce" a current in the wire, so the effect is called electromagnetic induction.

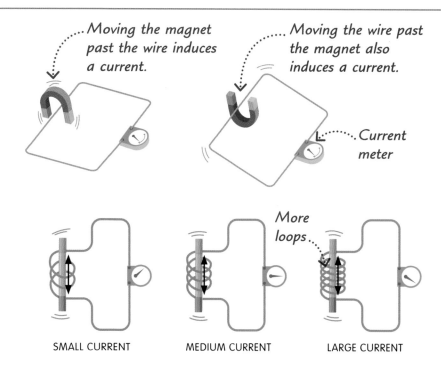

..Moving the magnet past the wire induces a current.

Moving the wire past the magnet also induces a current.

L.....Current meter

2 Moving a magnet back and forth in a loop induces a stronger current. The more loops there are (or the faster or stronger the magnet), the larger the current. But we don't get something for nothing just by adding loops: it's harder work to move the magnet in a dense coil because the induced current creates a magnetic field that repels the magnet.

More loops...

SMALL CURRENT   MEDIUM CURRENT   LARGE CURRENT

3 Nearly all of our electricity is created by electromagnetic induction. In a typical power station, steam from a furnace blows a turbine (a kind of fan), making it rotate. The turbine spins powerful magnets inside a machine called a generator, inducing current in coils of wire.

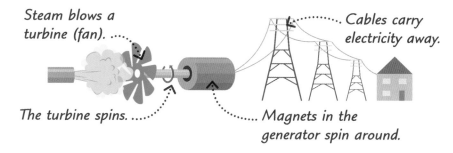

Steam blows a turbine (fan). ....

Cables carry electricity away.

The turbine spins. .....

Magnets in the generator spin around.

Electric motors

Whereas generators turn movement energy into electricity, electric motors do the opposite, turning electromagnetism into movement.

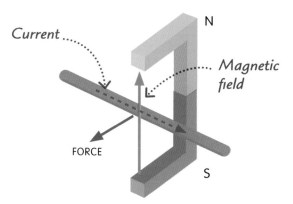

Current ....

N

... Magnetic field

FORCE

S

1 When a current flows through an existing magnetic field, the wire recoils (moves) in reaction because its own magnetic field is repelled by the magnet. This is called the motor effect.

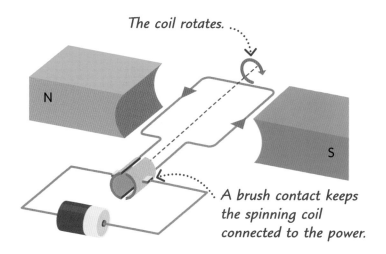

The coil rotates. ...

N

S

A brush contact keeps the spinning coil connected to the power.

2 If the wire is twisted into a loop, the recoil force is upward on one side and downward on the other. This makes the loop spin around, provided it's loosely connected to the power source. This is an electric motor. Motors are used in everything from power tools to electric cars.

Electromagnetism in action

Electromagnets are magnets that can be turned on and off at the flick of a switch. These powerful magnets are used in a huge range of devices, from levitating trains to loudspeakers.

The more coils an electromagnet has, the more powerful the magnet.

Maglev trains

Maglev trains can reach speeds of 375 mph (600 km/h)—as fast as a plane. Instead of rolling on wheels, they float in midair, suspended by electromagnets. This eliminates friction, allowing far higher speeds than in normal trains.

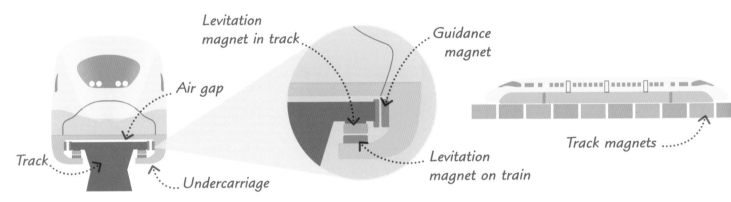

Levitation magnet in track

Guidance magnet

Air gap

Track

Undercarriage

Levitation magnet on train

Track magnets

1 The Transrapid maglev system uses magnetic attraction to lift the base of the train's C-shaped undercarriage, creating an air gap between the train and track.

2 Guidance magnets in the train and the track use magnetic repulsion to stop the train from moving left or right and getting too close to the track.

3 The levitation magnets also drive the train. Computers switch them on and off rapidly to pull the train forward, slow it down, and keep it stable.

Lifting magnets

Lifting magnets are used to pick up scrap iron and steel objects, such as old cars. The magnet is a large iron disk containing an embedded electric coil that magnetizes the whole disk when the current is switched on. It can then lift very heavy loads—and drop them at the flick of a switch.

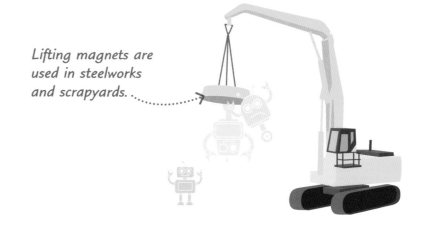

Lifting magnets are used in steelworks and scrapyards.

Loudspeakers

All kinds of loudspeakers, even the tiny ones in earbuds, use electromagnetism to create vibrations in the air—sound waves. Most speakers create sound waves by moving a large paper or plastic cone (a diaphragm) back and forth.

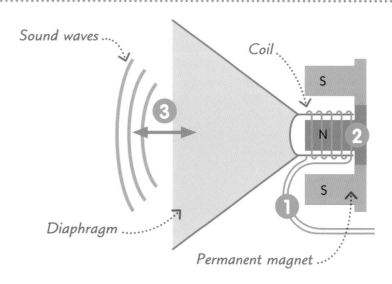

Sound waves

Coil

Diaphragm

Permanent magnet

1 An electric signal is sent to the speaker as an alternating current (a current that rapidly switches direction). The current turns a wire coiled around the diaphragm into an electromagnet.

2 A permanent magnet in the speaker repels the electromagnet, making the diaphragm jerk forward. When the alternating current (AC) reverses, the diaphragm jerks back.

3 The diaphragm vibrates back and forth rapidly, creating sound waves. The frequency of the vibrations is controlled by the frequency of the AC current.

TRY IT OUT

Make an electromagnet

You can make your own electromagnet with a large iron nail, a long piece of copper wire, and a non-rechargeable D cell battery. Be sure to use insulated (plastic-coated or enameled) copper wire because pure copper will conduct electricity into the nail and bypass the coil.

1 Wrap the wire tightly at least 25 times around the nail.

2 Connect the ends of the wire to each terminal of the battery.

3 Try picking up small metal objects, like paper clips.

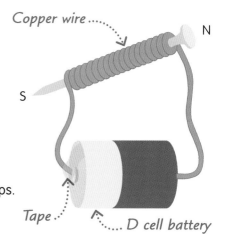

Copper wire

Tape

D cell battery

Electronics

Electronics is the use of electricity not just for power but for processing information. Most modern electronic devices are digital, which means they process information as a stream of digits.

A single computer chip smaller than your fingernail can hold over 3 billion transistors.

1 Digital or analog?

Electronic devices can process information in two very different ways: analog and digital. Analog devices use variations in voltage or frequency to transmit information. Analog radios, for instance, turn variations in the frequency of radio waves into sound waves emitted by a speaker. Digital devices, however, use short pulses of electricity to transmit information as a code of ones and zeroes, called binary code.

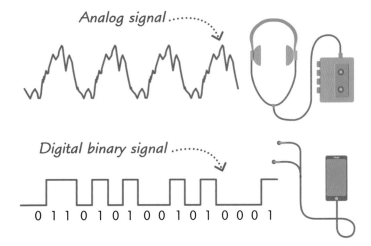

Analog signal

Digital binary signal

0 1 1 0 1 0 1 0 0 1 0 1 0 0 0 1

2 Binary data

The ones and zeroes of binary code are called binary digits, or "bits" for short. With only eight bits, it's possible to represent any letter of the alphabet and any number from zero (00000000 in binary) to 255 (11111111 in binary). Eight bits make up a byte, a million bytes make up a megabyte, and a billion bytes make up a gigabyte.

A	1000001		N	1001110
B	1000010		O	1001111
C	1000011		P	1010000
D	1000100		Q	1010001
E	1000101		R	1010010
F	1000110		S	1010011
G	1000111		T	1010100
H	1001000		U	1010101
I	1001001		V	1010110
J	1001010		W	1010111
K	1001011		X	1011000
L	1001100		Y	1011001
M	1001101		Z	1011010

HEY = 1001000 1000101 1011001

3 Transistors

All digital devices rely on components called transistors, which can work as switches. A typical transistor is a sandwich of three layers of a material called a semiconductor. A semiconductor only conducts electricity in certain circumstances. When current flows to the middle layer of the sandwich, it lets electricity pass between the other two connections, switching the transistor to its "on" state.

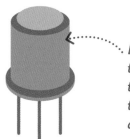

Large transistors have three metal terminals that look like legs. The transistors in silicon chips are far smaller.

4 Logic gates

The transistors in digital devices are joined in groups to form logic gates. These are the building blocks of digital circuits because they can make logical decisions, which means they can do math. Most logic gates have two inputs and one output. The gate compares its inputs and "decides" whether to switch on the output. For instance, an AND gate only switches on when it receives two inputs at once, but an OR gate switches on when it receives either one or two inputs.

AND gate		OR gate		NOT gate	
INPUT	OUTPUT	INPUT	OUTPUT	INPUT	OUTPUT
1 1	1	1 1	1	1	0
1 0	0	1 0	1	0	1
0 1	0	0 1	1		
0 0	0	0 0	0		

Only one input for a NOT gate

5 Flip-flops

Logic gates can be arranged in a clever way that allows them to remember things. This involves connecting their outputs back to their inputs, which is known as feedback. The resulting arrangement can then remember a previous input. This is the basis of all computer memory.

This flip-flop is made of two NOT AND gates.

6 Integrated circuits

All electronic circuits were once made by physically attaching one part after another into a circuit board. Today, circuits containing millions of transistors can be printed onto wafers of silicon, which is a semiconductor. The wafers are then cut into tiny squares called silicon chips or integrated circuits.

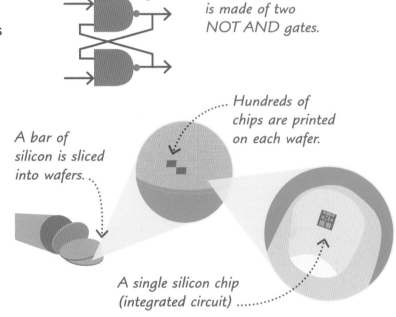

Hundreds of chips are printed on each wafer.

A bar of silicon is sliced into wafers.

A single silicon chip (integrated circuit)

REAL WORLD TECHNOLOGY

Robots

Robots are machines that can carry out complex tasks automatically, without a human operator. Most robots are computer-controlled, and many have a sensory system that allows them to take in information and make decisions about how to respond. Robots can take many different forms.

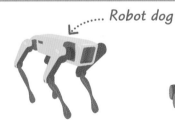

Robot dog

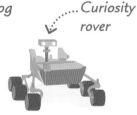

Curiosity rover

1 Some robots are built to resemble humans or animals. Four-legged robots, for instance, can walk on ground that's too steep or rough for vehicles with wheels.

2 Robotic spacecraft and submarines can work in places humans cannot reach. *Curiosity*, a car-sized robot, has been exploring the surface of Mars since 2012.

3 Industrial robots are used to manufacture everything from cars to computers. They carry out tasks such as welding, painting, packaging, and circuit assembly.

FORCES

When a car brakes or a ball rolls downhill, forces are acting on it. A force is simply a push or pull that can make something move, stop moving, speed up, slow down, change direction, or change shape. Forces are at work throughout the universe—gravity, for example, keeps Earth in orbit around the Sun.

What are forces?

A force is simply a push or a pull. When you kick a ball or ride a bike, you're using forces to make something move. Forces can make things start or stop moving, go faster or slower, change direction, or even change shape.

You can't see a force but you can often see or feel its effects.

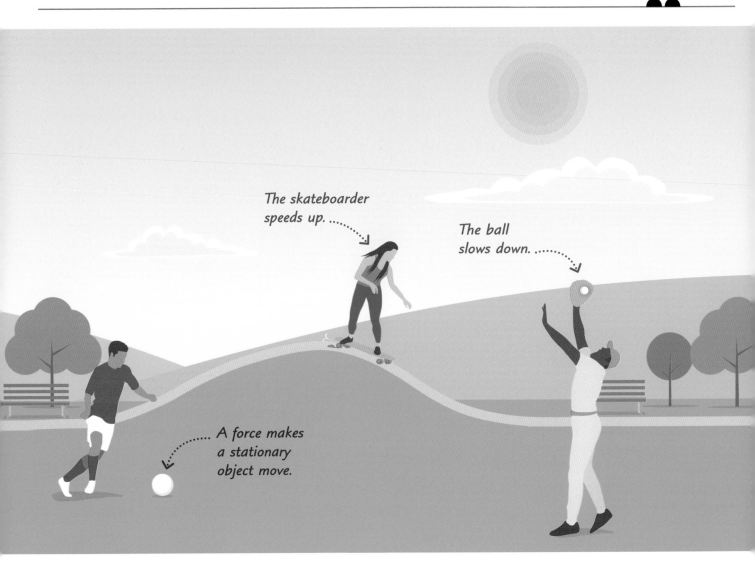

The skateboarder speeds up.

The ball slows down.

A force makes a stationary object move.

1 Making things move
A force can make a stationary object move. When you kick a ball, the force from your foot makes it go flying. The force of gravity pulls the ball back down.

2 Speeding up
Forces can make a moving object speed up. When you skateboard downhill, you go faster because the force of gravity pulls on your body.

3 Slowing down or stopping
Forces can slow an object down or make it stop moving. When you catch a ball, the force of your hands slows the ball and stops it from moving.

Drawing forces

Forces are measured in units called newtons (N) after the English scientist Isaac Newton. One newton is about the force of a large apple's weight. We can show how forces act by drawing a simple force diagram. Forces have size and direction, so they're shown with arrows. The longer the arrow, the stronger the force.

LIFTING FORCE 12,000 N

WEIGHT 8,000 N

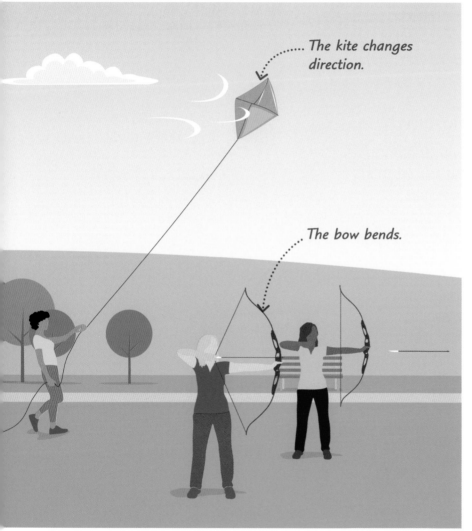

The kite changes direction.

The bow bends.

Distant forces

Some forces only act when objects come in contact with each other, such as when you kick a ball. Other forces (called non-contact forces) can act at a distance.

1 Gravity
Gravity is a very weak force of attraction between all objects. We only notice it from something enormous, such as planet Earth. Earth's gravity makes objects fall to the ground.

2 Magnetism
Magnetism pulls on magnetic materials, such as iron objects. Magnets have north and south poles. Opposite poles attract but similar poles repel (push each other away).

4 Changing direction
Forces can make a moving object change direction. When you fly a kite, the force of the wind on the kite makes it twist and turn in the air.

5 Changing shape
Forces can change an object's shape. When an archer pulls a bowstring, the bow bends. When the string is released, the bow springs back.

3 Electric charge
Objects with positive or negative electric charges can push and pull like magnets. Opposite charges attract, but similar charges repel.

Stretching and deforming

When forces act on an object that can't move, the object may change shape or even break. We call these changes deformations.

> All objects eventually break if enough force is applied to them.

1 Brittle objects can snap or shatter when forces act on them, such as when you break a cracker in two, smash a window, or break open a piggy bank with a hammer.

2 Other objects don't break but change shape instead. We say they "deform." If the shape is changed permanently, like a piece of stretched chewing gum, then the object is said to be plastic.

3 Some objects, like a tennis ball, change their shape for only a moment before regaining their original shape. They are said to be elastic.

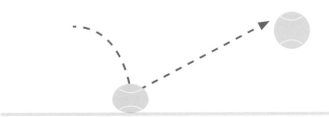

Changing shape

The way objects deform depends on the number and direction of the forces acting on them.

1 Compression
When forces squeeze an object from opposite directions, it compresses. It may bulge at the sides.

2 Tension
Forces pulling in opposite directions create tension, which can stretch an object.

3 Bending
When several forces act in different places and different directions, the object will snap or bend.

4 Twisting
Turning forces (torques) that act in opposite directions on different parts of an object will twist it.

Elasticity

1 Elastic objects spring back to their original shape after a force stops being applied. However, they have their limits. If you stretch an elastic object beyond a certain point, called its elastic limit, it won't return to its original shape.

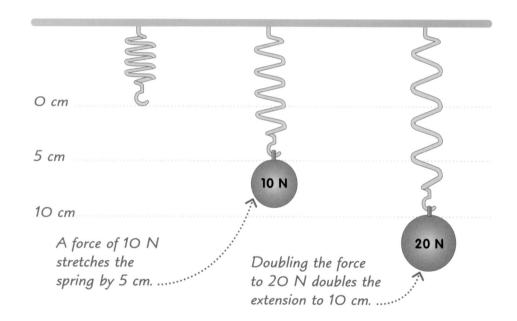

Unstretched spring ....

A spring being stretched ....

Overstretched spring that can't return to its original shape

2 Before an object reaches its elastic limit, the amount it stretches (its extension) is proportional to the force acting on it. We call this Hooke's law after the English scientist Robert Hooke (1635–1703), who discovered it.

O cm

5 cm

10 cm

10 N

20 N

A force of 10 N stretches the spring by 5 cm. ....

Doubling the force to 20 N doubles the extension to 10 cm. ....

REAL WORLD TECHNOLOGY

High fliers

Pole vaulters use a hollow pole made from layers of fiberglass and carbon fiber. The pole is elastic and bends sharply after being planted in front of the bar. As the pole returns to its original shape, it straightens and propels the athlete upward. Top pole vaulters can jump over 20 ft (6 m) high.

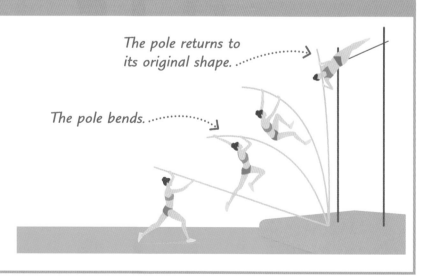

The pole returns to its original shape. ....

The pole bends. ....

Balanced and unbalanced forces

When several forces act on an object at the same time, they combine together and act as a single force. When separate forces are balanced, they cancel each other out.

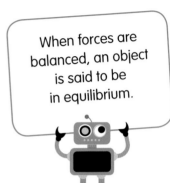

When forces are balanced, an object is said to be in equilibrium.

Balanced forces

1 These tug-of-war teams are pulling with the same amount of force in opposite directions. The forces are balanced and there is no overall force, so nobody moves.

300 NEWTONS   300 NEWTONS

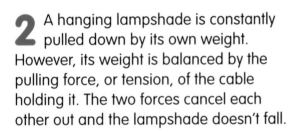

2 A hanging lampshade is constantly pulled down by its own weight. However, its weight is balanced by the pulling force, or tension, of the cable holding it. The two forces cancel each other out and the lampshade doesn't fall.

10 NEWTONS   10 NEWTONS

3 When you place an object on a table, the force of gravity still acts on the object but the object doesn't fall. That's because its weight is balanced by an upward force from the table.

Weight of the book

Force from the table

4 Balanced forces can act on a moving object. When a skydiver reaches maximum speed, the speed and direction of the fall remain constant. The forces of air resistance and gravity that act on the skydiver are balanced.

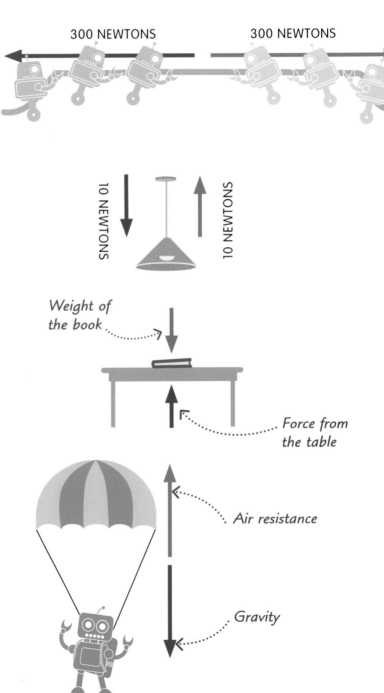

Air resistance

Gravity

Unbalanced forces

When forces aren't balanced, they combine to act as a single force that moves an object or changes the way it's moving. This single force is called the resultant force.

1 You can calculate the resultant force if you know the size and direction of the separate forces. For instance, forces acting in the same direction simply add together.

SEPARATE FORCES

RESULTANT FORCE

2 NEWTONS

2 NEWTONS

4 NEWTONS

2 When the forces act in opposite directions, you subtract the smaller force from the greater force.

4 NEWTONS

2 NEWTONS

2 NEWTONS

3 When the forces aren't in the same or opposite directions, the resultant force is in a direction between them. Here, a box pushed in two directions moves diagonally. You can work out the resultant force by drawing a scale diagram with one force arrow added to the end of the other one.

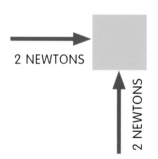

2 NEWTONS

2 NEWTONS

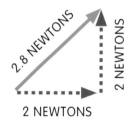

2.8 NEWTONS

2 NEWTONS

2 NEWTONS

REAL WORLD TECHNOLOGY

Suspension bridge

A suspension bridge is built to support its own weight and the weight of any traffic crossing it without collapsing. The bridge's weight pulls it down, but this force is balanced by upward forces from the pillars. A stretching force called tension in the steel cables and suspenders also pulls the bridge upward and supports its weight.

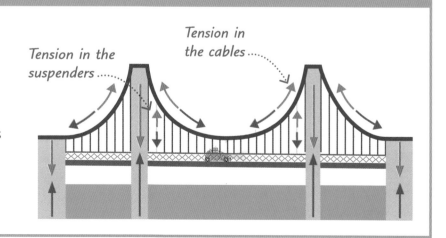

Tension in the suspenders ......

Tension in the cables ......

Magnetism

Magnetism is a force that can push or pull objects without even touching them. Magnets only pull objects made of certain materials, including iron, nickel, cobalt, and steel.

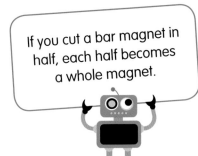

If you cut a bar magnet in half, each half becomes a whole magnet.

How magnets work

The force of magnetism comes from electrons—the tiny, charged particles that make up the outside of all atoms. Every electron acts like a tiny bar magnet, but in most objects the electrons are jumbled around and the magnetic forces cancel each other out.

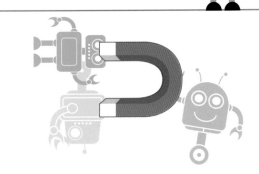

Domains lined up

Domains random

1 In materials that stick to magnets—such as iron—the electrons line up in clusters called domains, which act like mini magnets. However, the domains don't normally line up.

2 In a magnet, all the domains line up together. Their magnetic forces combine, creating a powerful magnetic force around the whole magnet.

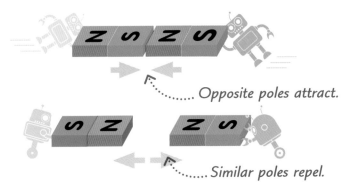

Opposite poles attract.

Similar poles repel.

3 A magnet has two ends: a north pole and a south pole. Two magnets pull each other strongly if opposite poles come close. If similar poles come close, they repel—they push each other away.

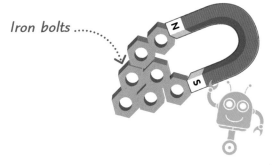

Iron bolts

4 Magnets can also pull objects that aren't themselves magnets. This is because the magnetic force causes the domains inside magnetic materials like iron to line up temporarily.

Magnetic field

Every magnet is surrounded by a magnetic field—a zone in which objects are pulled. The pulling force doesn't reach out in straight lines. Instead, it curves out from one pole and runs back to the other.

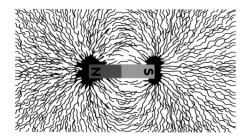

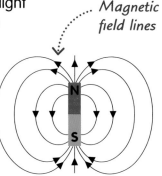

.... *Magnetic field lines*

BAR MAGNET

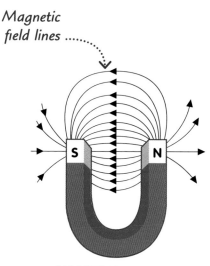

Magnetic field lines ....

HORSESHOE MAGNET

1 A magnetic field is invisible, but you can see its effects by sprinkling iron filings over a bar magnet. The filings will align themselves along the lines of force.

2 The lines show the way a north pole would move, so they point away from the north pole of the magnet and toward the south pole. Where the lines are drawn closest together is where the magnetic field is strongest.

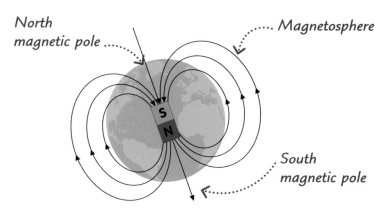

North magnetic pole ....

.... *Magnetosphere*

South magnetic pole ....

3 At the center of Earth is a hot, partially molten iron core that acts like a giant magnet, producing a huge magnetic field. This field extends thousands of miles into space.

4 A compass is simply a magnetized needle balanced on a point. The needle lines up with Earth's magnetic field to show which way is north, helping you find your way.

REAL WORLD TECHNOLOGY

MRI scanner

MRI (magnetic resonance imaging) scanners allow doctors to see inside the human body. When a person lies inside the scanner, a huge, cylindrical magnet causes hydrogen atoms in their body to line up. Pulses of a rapidly changing magnetic field are then fired in short bursts, making the hydrogen atoms turn and realign. When they do so, they emit radio waves that can be processed into an image.

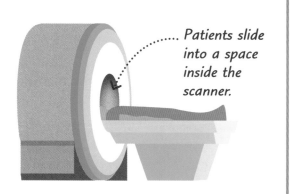

.... *Patients slide into a space inside the scanner.*

Friction

When one object slips, slides, or scrapes across another, a force called friction slows it down. The rougher the surfaces, the greater the friction. Friction is the enemy of motion, but sometimes it's a good thing because it also gives you grip.

A match catches fire when struck because friction heats up the tip.

1 No matter how smooth something looks, in reality it's covered by thousands of tiny bumps and dents. When two objects rub together, these bumps snag each other and slow the objects down. This slowing force is friction.

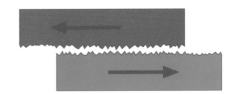

2 There are two kinds of friction: static and sliding. Static friction is much greater and makes it hard to budge an object that isn't already moving, like a heavy box. Once you get it going, it's easier to push along because only sliding friction is slowing it down.

3 Whenever friction happens, some of the energy in moving objects is transferred to heat. You can see this for yourself by rubbing your hands together as hard as you can—after ten seconds or so, your skin will feel hot.

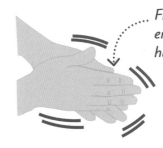

Friction releases heat energy, making your hands warm.

4 Over time, friction wears away parts that rub together, which is why bikes and cars need frequent repairs. Carpenters use tools such as files to deliberately increase friction so they can wear away wood quickly and shape it.

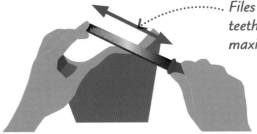

Files have jagged teeth to create maximum friction.

5 Friction gives you grip. Without it, you'd slip and slide across the floor as you walk, and chairs would slide away when you sit down. Outdoor shoes and off-road tires have a deeply patterned tread to increase the force of friction. This gives better grip, helping you walk or cycle on loose or slippery ground.

Knobbly tires increase friction to give better grip.

Fighting friction

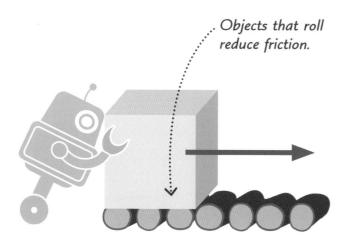

Objects that roll reduce friction.

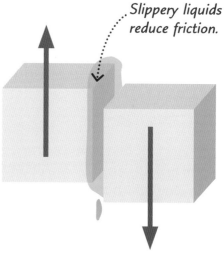

Slippery liquids reduce friction.

1 Objects that roll create less friction than objects that drag. That's why cars and bikes have wheels to move across the ground and bearings to help the wheels turn. However, wheels aren't completely friction-free—they still need enough friction to grip the ground and prevent a skid.

2 A great way to reduce friction between two objects is to put a layer of liquid between them. The liquid, called a lubricant, stops surfaces from snagging. The oil that cyclists put on bike chains is a lubricant. As well as helping the chain move smoothly, it protects the bike from wear.

REAL WORLD TECHNOLOGY

Brakes

Brakes slow down a bike by deliberately creating friction. When you pull the brake lever, a cable squeezes the brake pads against the wheel's steel rim, making them rub together. Used properly, bike brakes should create sliding friction on the wheel. If you brake too hard when riding on slippery ground, the brakes create static friction and the wheel locks, making the bike skid. The solution is to brake little and often.

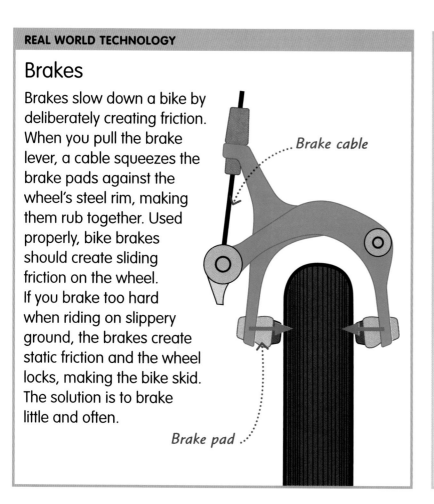

Brake cable

Brake pad

TRY IT OUT

Friction challenge

To demonstrate the surprising power of friction, interleave the pages of two books and then challenge a friend to separate them by pulling the spines. This is very difficult because the combined force of friction between hundreds of pages is too great to overcome.

Interleave the pages.

Drag

When objects move through air or water, they have to overcome a force called drag. Smooth surfaces and streamlined shapes help reduce this force.

Drag in air is also called air resistance, and drag in water is called water resistance.

1 Drag happens because moving objects have to push air molecules out of the way, which transfers energy away from them and slows them down. A long, thin object like a javelin has to push very little air out of the way, so it encounters low drag and flies a long way.

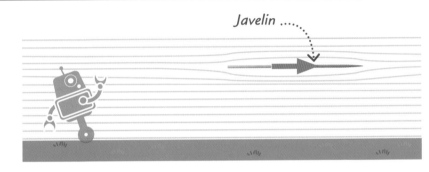

Javelin

2 Large objects have to push much more air out of the way, so they encounter a lot of drag and lose speed quickly. That's why a cardboard box doesn't fly as far as a javelin, no matter how hard you throw it.

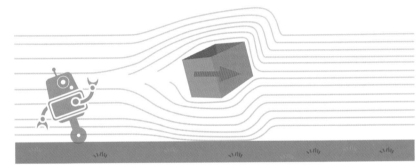

3 Drag is caused partly by friction with air molecules and partly by something called turbulence. Turbulent air swirls around rather than flowing smoothly. This motion takes a lot of kinetic energy from a moving vehicle and makes it less efficient. The faster an object moves and the bulkier its shape, the more drag it causes.

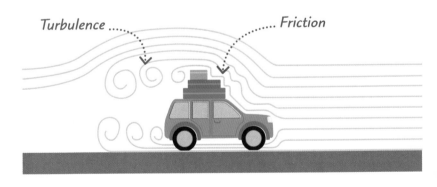

Turbulence

Friction

4 Shapes that move easily through air or water are called streamlined. They have a smooth surface and tapering ends to reduce friction and turbulence. Sports cars, speedboats, and planes are usually streamlined, as are fast-swimming animals like sharks and dolphins.

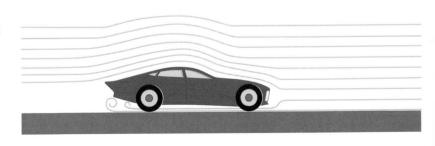

Using drag

Drag is usually bad because it slows things down and wastes energy. However, some objects, such as parachutes, are designed to cause maximum drag.

1 When a skydiver leaps from a plane, he doesn't open his parachute at first. His body accelerates because the force of his weight is greater than the force of drag.

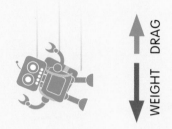

2 As he speeds up, drag increases. Eventually it equals his weight and so he stops accelerating. He is now falling at a steady speed, called terminal velocity.

3 When the parachute opens, drag increases enormously. The drag force is much greater than his weight, so he decelerates.

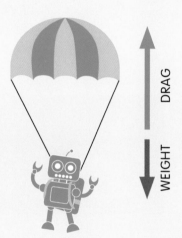

4 As he slows down, the force of drag gradually reduces. Eventually it matches his weight again, and he reaches a new terminal velocity. This is slower than his earlier speed, making it safe to land.

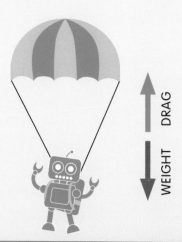

TRY IT OUT

Egg parachute

To see how parachutes work, make one for an egg and see if you can save it from a messy crash-landing.

1 Cut a large square of plastic from a trash bag and tie or tape four lengths of thread to the corners.

2 Make four holes in the top of a plastic cup and tie the thread to them. Put a raw egg in the cup.

3 Launch from a high place. Does the passenger survive its fall? If not, make a larger parachute and try again.

REAL WORLD TECHNOLOGY

Hydrofoil

Because drag in water is much greater than drag in air, some boats reduce drag by lifting their hulls out of the water. A hydrofoil is a boat with underwater "wings" that generate the force of lift (see page 260) raising the boat when it moves quickly.

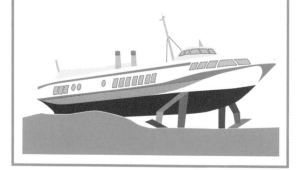

Force and motion

In 1687, English scientist Isaac Newton (1642–1727) published his three laws of motion. These principles describe how an object moves when a force acts on it.

Isaac Newton figured out the laws of motion by studying how objects move in space.

First law of motion

Newton's first law says that if an object isn't pushed by an unbalanced force (see page 239), it will either stay still or keep moving forever in a straight line at a constant speed.

1 A soccer ball sitting on the ground doesn't have any unbalanced forces acting on it, so it stays where it is until someone kicks it.

2 Once kicked, it flies off in a straight line. But not for long…

3 When it's airborne, the ball encounters new unbalanced forces: gravity and air resistance. Its speed and direction change and it falls back to Earth.

4 Newton's first law doesn't sound like common sense because nothing on Earth keeps moving in a straight line for long. However, that's because gravity and air get in the way. In outer space, where there's no air, a moving object will keep drifting away forever.

TRY IT OUT

Balloon rocket

String ····· Peg ··· Straw ··· Tape   ···· *Balloon flies along string*

1 Tie a piece of string or thread to a door handle. Thread a straw onto it and then tie the other end of the string to a firm support, such as a table.

2 Inflate a balloon (a long one is best) and use a clothespin to hold the air in. Use adhesive tape to tape the straw to the balloon.

3 Release the clothespin and watch the balloon zoom along the thread. Air rushing out behind the balloon creates an equal and opposite force pushing the balloon forward.

Second law of motion

Newton's second law says that when a force acts on an object, it makes the object accelerate. This law can be written as an equation. What it means is that the bigger the force, or the smaller the mass of the object, the greater the acceleration.

acceleration = force ÷ mass

1 When you kick a ball, the force makes it move faster—it accelerates.

2 In physics, acceleration means any change in speed or direction—not just getting faster. If you kick a moving ball from the side, it accelerates because it changes direction.

3 If you apply twice as much force to an object, it will accelerate twice as much.

4 The more mass an object has, the more force it takes to accelerate it. So a full shopping cart is harder to accelerate than an empty one.

Third law of motion

Newton's third law says that every force is accompanied by an equal and opposite force. When one object pushes another, the second object pushes back on the first one.

Action force

Reaction force

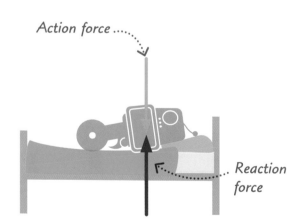

Action force

Reaction force

1 When you paddle in a canoe, pushing the water backward with the paddle creates an equal and opposite force that pushes the boat forward. The force pushing you forward is called the reaction force.

2 The third law even applies to objects at rest. When you lie in bed, your weight pushes down on your bed. However, your bed pushes back up with an equal and opposite force.

Momentum and collisions

A collision is what happens when any moving object bumps into another object, from your fingers tapping a keyboard to a flea landing on a cat. When objects collide, the collision changes their momentum—their tendency to keep moving.

> A moving object keeps moving due to its momentum.

Momentum

Momentum is a measure of a moving object's tendency to keep moving. The more momentum something has, the harder it is to stop—and the more damage it does if it collides with something.

1 It's easy to stop a moving shopping cart when it's empty, but a heavily loaded cart has a mind of its own and takes a lot more effort to stop and start. The more mass a moving object has, the more momentum it has and the harder it is to stop.

Not so easy

Easy to stop

2 Momentum is also related to velocity (see page 256): the faster something is moving, the more momentum it has. A cyclist going at 12 mph (20 km/h) has twice as much momentum as one going at 6 mph (10 km/h).

6 mph (10 km/h)   *12 mph (20 km/h)*

3 You can calculate an object's momentum by multiplying its mass in kilograms by its velocity in meters per second. This equation tells us that a small object traveling very fast (such as a bullet) can have as much momentum—and as much destructive potential—as a large object traveling far more slowly.

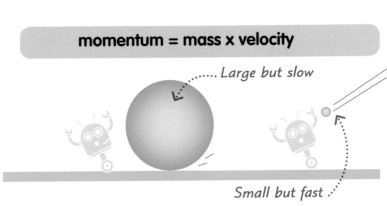

momentum = mass x velocity

...... Large but slow

Small but fast .:

Collisions

1 When objects collide, momentum is transferred from one object to the other. When a moving ball hits a stationary ball, for instance, the first ball loses momentum but the second one gains it.

2 Here, a moving pool ball has struck a line of balls. The momentum has transferred all the way through the balls, making the last one move.

3 When objects collide, their total momentum is the same after the collision as before. This is called the law of conservation of momentum. Here, the white ball has hit a group of colored balls. The total momentum of all the colored balls after the collision equals the momentum the white ball had before.

4 The faster an object gains or loses momentum, the greater the forces involved. When a car hits a stationary obstacle, the change in momentum is very sudden and so the forces can be huge.

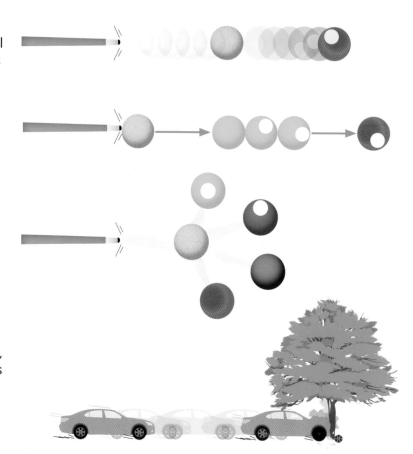

Two-ball bounce

Place a small ball on top of a large ball and drop them to see what happens. When they bounce, the small ball will shoot up far higher than you expect. This happens because the large ball builds up momentum on its fall and transfers a lot of it to the small ball as it rebounds, sending the small ball hurtling upward.

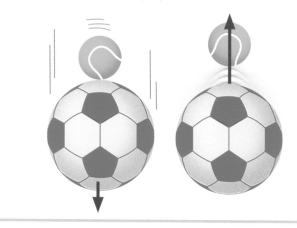

Crumple zones

When cars crash, huge forces act on them as momentum suddenly changes. To reduce these forces, many cars have crumple zones at the front and rear. These are designed to collapse gradually on impact, slowing the change in momentum to protect the passengers.

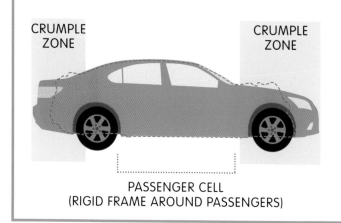

CRUMPLE ZONE

CRUMPLE ZONE

PASSENGER CELL
(RIGID FRAME AROUND PASSENGERS)

Simple machines

Simple machines are tools that work by changing how much force you need to do something. Most of them work by increasing a force, making a tough job much easier.

The human body's muscles and bones work together as levers.

Levers

A lever is a rigid bar that rotates around a fixed point called a fulcrum. The force you apply is called the effort, and the force you're trying to overcome is called the load. If the effort is farther from the fulcrum than the load is, the lever increases the force you put in.

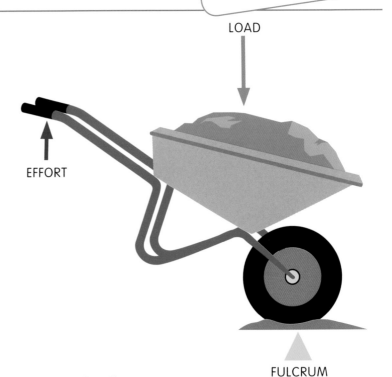

LOAD

EFFORT

FULCRUM

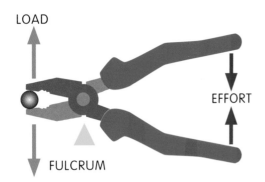

LOAD

EFFORT

FULCRUM

1 Pliers
Pliers give a powerful grip on small objects. Because the effort from your hand is much farther from the fulcrum than the load, pliers magnify the force of your grip.

2 Wheelbarrow
The handles of a wheelbarrow are much farther from the fulcrum (the wheel) than the load, so a wheelbarrow makes it easier to lift a heavy weight.

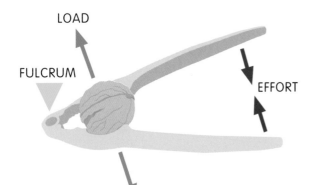

LOAD

FULCRUM

EFFORT

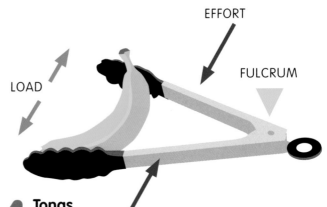

EFFORT

FULCRUM

LOAD

3 Nutcracker
Nutcrackers magnify the force of your hand, making it easy to break open the toughest nuts.

4 Tongs
Tongs reduce the force of your hand because the load is farther from the fulcrum than the effort. This helps give a delicate grip.

Mechanical advantage

The amount by which a machine multiplies a force is called mechanical advantage. For instance, a tool that doubles a lifting force has a mechanical advantage of 2. To calculate the mechanical advantage of a lever, divide the effort's distance from the fulcrum by the load's distance from the fulcrum.

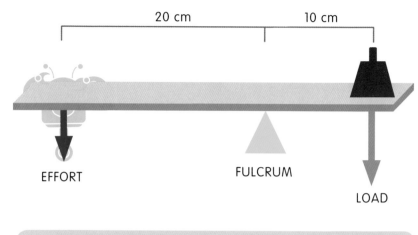

20 cm   10 cm

EFFORT   FULCRUM   LOAD

Mechanical advantage = 20 cm ÷ 10 cm = 2

Ramps

Ramps are another type of simple machine. The sloping surface of a ramp makes it easier to raise a heavy object.

1 A long, shallow ramp reduces the force you need to lift a load upward. However, the load has a longer distance to travel.

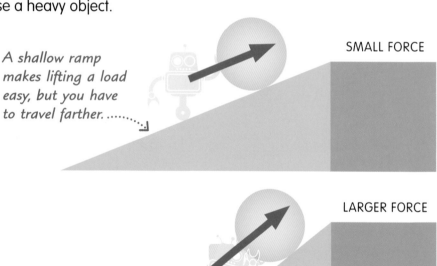

A shallow ramp makes lifting a load easy, but you have to travel farther.

SMALL FORCE

LARGER FORCE

2 Using a shorter, steeper ramp to lift the object to the same height requires more force, but you have less far to travel.

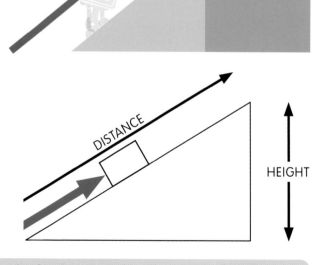

DISTANCE

HEIGHT

3 To work out the mechanical advantage of a ramp, divide the distance traveled along the slope by the height.

Mechanical advantage = distance ÷ height

More simple machines

Levers and ramps aren't the only simple machines. Other simple machines, such as pulleys, screws, and wheels, can also magnify forces and make jobs easier.

Most tools include more than one simple machine. Scissors, for example, have a wedge and a lever.

Wedges

A wedge is thick at one end and thin at the other end. When you apply downward force to the thick end of the wedge, the thin end increases the force and drives it sideways, cutting or splitting an object apart.

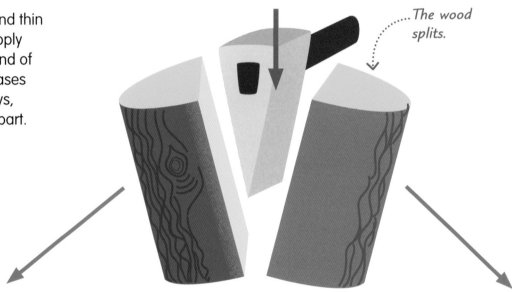

...The wood splits.

Screws

If you tried to push a screw into wood with your bare hands, it would be very difficult. However, when you turn it with a screwdriver, it's much easier. A screw works like a ramp (see page 251) that's been coiled up. Each turn of the screw pushes it a little bit deeper into the wood.

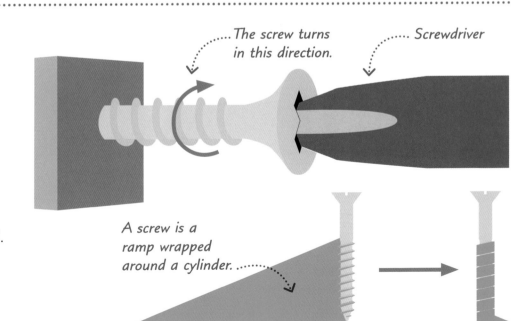

...The screw turns in this direction.

......Screwdriver

A screw is a ramp wrapped around a cylinder. ....

Wheels and axles

A wheel turns around a small central rod called an axle. Together, they work as a circular lever. Just as levers can be used to either magnify forces or increase the distance moved, wheels and axles can be used in two different ways.

1 Magnifying forces
If the effort is applied to the wheel's rim, the force is magnified at the axle, which moves a smaller distance. This is how both a car steering wheel and a screwdriver work.

2 Multiplying distance
When the effort is applied to the axle, the force applied by the wheel is reduced but the wheel moves much farther than the axle because it's bigger. This makes vehicles travel farther and faster.

Pulleys

A pulley is a rope or cable that runs around a wheel. There are different types of pulleys. Some simply change the direction of a force, while others increase the pulling force.

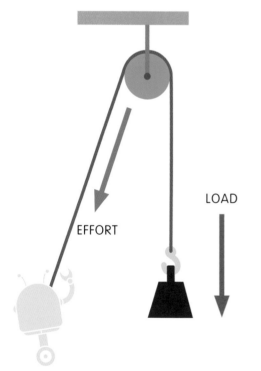

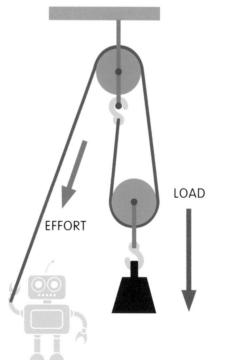

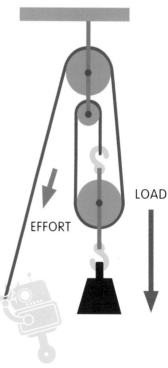

1 A single pulley simply changes the direction of a force. If the effort put into pulling the rope down is greater than the load, the load rises.

2 A double pulley doubles the pulling force, allowing you to lift twice as much, but you have to pull the rope twice as far.

3 We call two or more pulleys working together a block and tackle. A three-pulley block and tackle triples the lifting force.

Work and power

The scientific meaning of the word "work" is different from its everyday meaning. When a force moves an object, the force has done work. Like energy, work is measured in joules (J). Power is a measure of how quickly work is done.

> You do about 1 joule of work when you lift an average apple by 3 feet (1 meter).

1 Work is done when a force moves something. If you push an object but it doesn't move, you haven't done any work. If you push something with a constant force of 1 newton for a whole meter, you've done 1 joule of work.

2 Work always involves a transfer of energy. The energy is either transferred from one place to another, or changed from one form to another. For example, when a golf club strikes a ball, energy is transferred from the club to the ball.

3 You can calculate work with a simple equation. Work is measured in joules, force is measured in newtons, and distance is measured in meters.

work = force × distance

4 For instance, if you push a shopping cart 10 meters with a steady force of 2 newtons, you've done 20 joules of work.

2 NEWTONS

10 METERS

Power

1 Power is a measure of how quickly work is done. The more work done per second, the greater the power. For instance, if a man can do 200 joules of work per second pushing rocks but a bulldozer can do 4,000 joules of work per second, the bulldozer is 20 times more powerful.

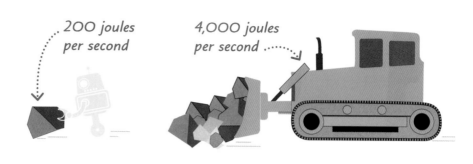

200 joules per second

4,000 joules per second

2 The faster something can work, the more powerful it is. If one person can push a heavy box across a room in ten seconds but a second person needs 20 seconds to push the same box the same distance, the first person has twice the power.

10 SECONDS

20 SECONDS

3 The unit of power is the watt (W), which is 1 joule per second. You can calculate power with this simple equation:

power = work done ÷ time taken

4 Power is sometimes measured in units known as metric horsepower (hp). 1 hp equals 735.5 watts. The more horsepower a car has, the faster it can accelerate to its top speed.

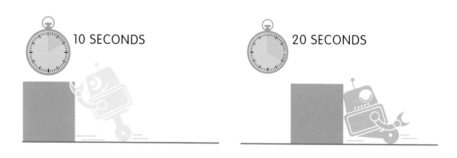

200 horsepower

50 horsepower

REAL WORLD TECHNOLOGY

World's most powerful engine

The most powerful vehicle engines in the world are used to power the huge cargo ships that ferry cargo around the world's oceans. These engines can weigh as much as 2,300 tons and reach the size of a four-story building. They work the same way as a car engine and are powered by diesel, but while a typical car has about 150 horsepower, cargo ship engines can produce up to 109,000 horsepower.

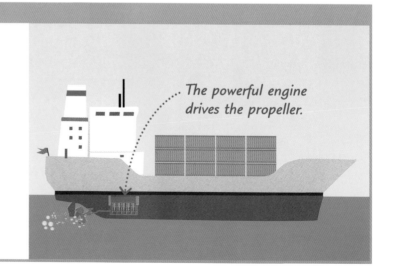

The powerful engine drives the propeller.

Speed and acceleration

Some things move very fast, like a rocket. Others move very slowly, like a snail. Speed, velocity, and acceleration all tell us how an object is moving.

Speed and velocity

200 METERS   20 SECONDS

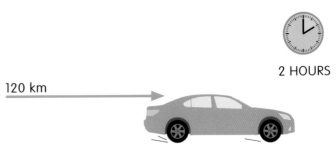

120 km   2 HOURS

1 To work out speed, divide how far something has traveled by how long it took. If an athlete runs 200 meters in 20 seconds, his average speed is 200 ÷ 20 = 10 m/s (meters per second).

2 A car cruises 120 km along the highway in two hours. So its average speed is 120 ÷ 2 = 60 km per hour.

+25 m/s   −25 m/s

3 Velocity is an object's speed in a given direction. If two objects are moving at the same speed but in different directions, they have different velocities. For example, if two cars are moving at 25 m/s in opposite directions, one has a velocity of 25 m/s and the other has a velocity of −25 m/s.

4 If a car drives in a circle at a constant speed, its velocity is continually changing. Its average speed for the whole journey might be 500 meters per second, but its average velocity is zero.

7 m/s   7 m/s

7 m/s   −7 m/s

5 Relative velocity is how fast one object is moving compared to another. Two runners with a velocity of 7 m/s have a relative velocity of 7 − 7 = 0 m/s.

6 If two people are running toward each other at 7 m/s, their relative velocity is 7 − (−7) = 7 + 7 = 14 m/s.

Acceleration

In everyday language, acceleration simply means getting faster. However, the scientific meaning of acceleration is a change in the velocity of an object.

0 km/h   30 km/h   60 km/h

60 km/h   0 km/h

1 Positive acceleration is when something gets faster. This is what happens when a driver puts their foot down in a car.

2 Negative acceleration, or deceleration, is when something gets slower. This is what happens when the driver brakes.

3 Any change in direction is also called an acceleration, even if the speed stays the same. This is because the change in direction means the velocity changes.

4 Acceleration is always caused by a force. When a force acts on an object, its velocity changes, so its speed, its direction, or both will change. For instance, when you throw a ball, it curves back to Earth because the force of gravity makes its velocity change.

Distance–time graphs

A distance–time graph shows the speed an object travels at during a journey. The y-axis (vertical axis) shows the distance, and the x-axis (horizontal axis) shows the time.

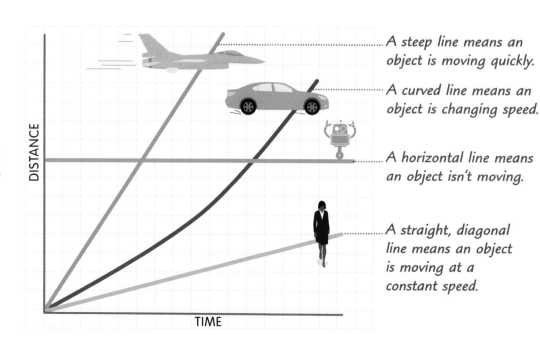

A steep line means an object is moving quickly.

A curved line means an object is changing speed.

A horizontal line means an object isn't moving.

A straight, diagonal line means an object is moving at a constant speed.

Gravity

Whenever you drop something, it falls because it's pulled down by a force called gravity. Gravity works throughout the universe. It holds planets, stars, and galaxies together.

Gravity is the weakest known force in the universe.

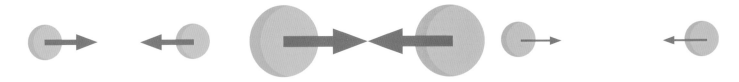

1 All pieces of matter, big and small, pull on each other with the force of gravity.

2 The more mass (matter) an object has, the stronger its gravitational pull.

3 The farther apart two things are, the more weakly gravity pulls them together.

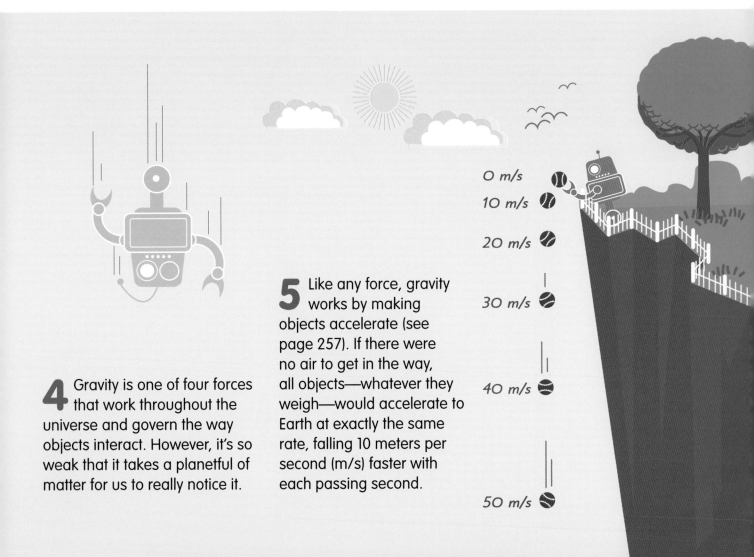

4 Gravity is one of four forces that work throughout the universe and govern the way objects interact. However, it's so weak that it takes a planetful of matter for us to really notice it.

5 Like any force, gravity works by making objects accelerate (see page 257). If there were no air to get in the way, all objects—whatever they weigh—would accelerate to Earth at exactly the same rate, falling 10 meters per second (m/s) faster with each passing second.

0 m/s
10 m/s
20 m/s
30 m/s
40 m/s
50 m/s

Mass and weight

Scientists distinguish between mass and weight. Mass is simply how much matter something contains. Weight is a force—it's how strongly gravity pulls on an object's mass. Your body's mass is always the same no matter where you are, but your weight would change if you left Earth and stood on the Moon.

120.00 kg

20.00 kg

00.00 kg

1 On Earth, an astronaut with a mass of 120 kg sees his weight as 120 kg when he stands on a set of weighing scales.

2 On the Moon, the astronaut's mass is still 120 kg, but his weight is only 20 kg because the Moon's gravity is less than Earth's.

3 In deep space, where there's almost no gravity, the astronaut's mass is still 120 kg but his weight is zero.

REAL WORLD TECHNOLOGY

Off-road vehicles

All objects have something called a center of gravity. This is the midpoint of an object's mass, where all its weight appears to be concentrated. Objects remain stable and balanced if the center of gravity is within their base. Off-road vehicles are designed to have a very low center of gravity and a wide base so they don't topple over on uneven ground.

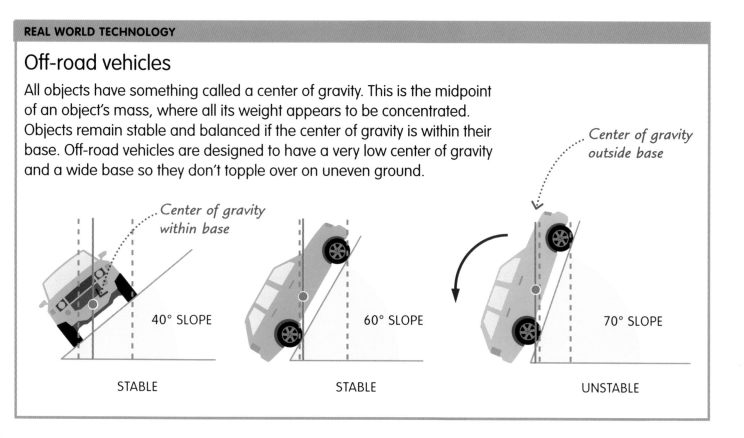

Center of gravity within base

40° SLOPE

STABLE

60° SLOPE

STABLE

Center of gravity outside base

70° SLOPE

UNSTABLE

Flight

Planes seem to defy gravity. They are heavier than air, yet they can take off from the ground and fly above the clouds. Their secret lies in the way they use fast-flowing air to generate a force known as lift.

Some planes can fly faster than the speed of sound.

Wings

A plane's wings generate the force of lift, which counters gravity. However, they can only do so when air is rushing over them at high speed. So before a plane can take off, it must accelerate forward with great power, which is why the plane needs powerful engines and a long runway.

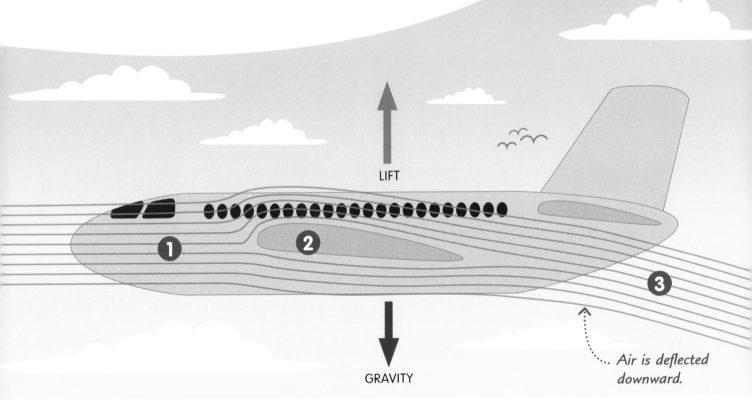

LIFT

GRAVITY

Air is deflected downward.

1 As the plane moves forward, the wing slices through the air. Some air is forced up and over it, but more air is forced down and underneath the wing.

2 The wing is angled so that the front is higher than the back. It also has a special shape called an airfoil, with the top more curved than the bottom. As a result of both its angle and its shape, air pressure under the wing is higher than above it. This difference creates lift.

3 The high pressure under the wing deflects the airflow downward. Newton's third law (see page 247) says that every force has an equal and opposite force. The downward push on the air results in an opposite upward push on the plane: lift.

Angle of attack

The slight upward angle of a plane's wing is called the angle of attack. Up to a point, increasing the angle of attack increases the lift. However, if the angle of attack is too high, the plane will fall.

A very steep angle of attack disturbs the airflow.

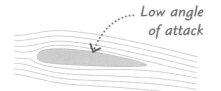

..... *Low angle of attack*

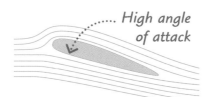

..... *High angle of attack*

1 A wing at a low angle of attack deflects the airflow downward only slightly. This creates a small amount of lift.

2 At a steeper angle of attack, the airflow is forced down further, resulting in increased lift. This makes the plane climb.

3 If the angle of attack is too steep, the air swirls around chaotically. The wing no longer generates lift, so the plane stalls—it begins to fall.

Controlling a plane

Pilots control planes by moving hinged flaps that change how air flows over different parts of the plane. Flaps on the wings change each wing's lift. Vertical flaps steer the plane left and right.

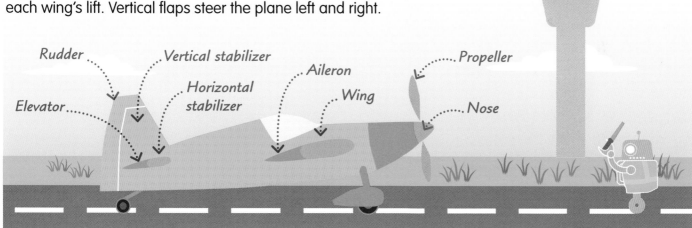

Rudder
Vertical stabilizer
Aileron
Propeller
Elevator
Horizontal stabilizer
Wing
Nose

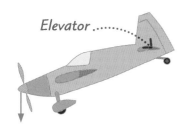
Elevator

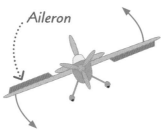
Aileron

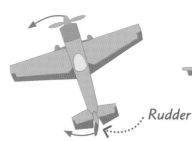
Rudder

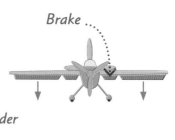
Brake

1 Elevators are flaps that vary the force of lift on the rear of the plane to pitch the aircraft's nose up or down.

2 Ailerons are flaps on the main wings. They move in opposite directions to make the plane roll, which helps it turn.

3 The rudder is an upright flap on the tail. Like a boat's rudder, it steers the plane, making it yaw (turn) left or right.

4 Flaps on the wings or other parts of a plane act as brakes by increasing the force of drag (see pages 244–45).

Pressure

It's easy to press a push pin into a wall, but an elephant's huge weight won't push its feet into the ground. The amount by which a force is concentrated or spread out is called pressure.

Changes in air pressure make winds blow and cause changes in the weather.

Pressure and area

Pressure is the amount of force per unit area. The same force can produce high pressure or low pressure depending on how much area it acts on.

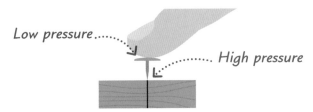

Low pressure

High pressure

1 A push pin concentrates the force of your finger into a tiny point, creating very high pressure. The flat end spreads the pressure on your finger so it doesn't hurt.

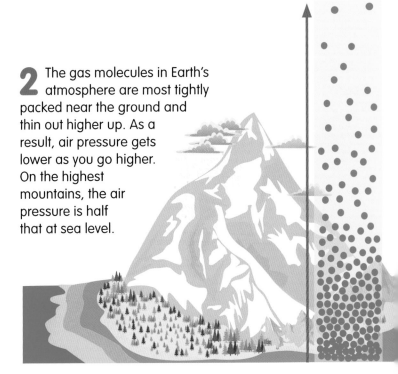

2 Snowshoes do the opposite job of push pins. They spread your weight over a large area, reducing pressure on the snow so you don't sink into it.

Air pressure

Solid objects aren't the only things that can create pressure—liquids and gases can create pressure too.

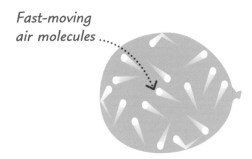

Fast-moving air molecules

2 The gas molecules in Earth's atmosphere are most tightly packed near the ground and thin out higher up. As a result, air pressure gets lower as you go higher. On the highest mountains, the air pressure is half that at sea level.

1 Air molecules are continually flying around at hundreds of miles per hour and bouncing off things. This creates air pressure. When you blow up a balloon, the air pressure inside it stretches the rubber and keeps the balloon inflated.

Water pressure

Water also exerts pressure. The deeper you dive in the sea, the higher the pressure gets. To measure pressure in the oceans, we can use units called atmospheres (atm). 1 atmosphere is the pressure of air at sea level. The pressure in the ocean increases by 1 atmosphere for every 33 ft (10 m) you go down.

1 Scuba divers can safely go to about 130 ft (40 m), where the pressure rises to 4 atmospheres.

2 The deepest a human diver has ever been in a protective suit is 2,000 ft (600 m). The pressure at that depth is 60 atmospheres.

3 Submarines can dive about 0.6 miles (1 km) deep and withstand 100 atmospheres before the pressure begins to crush them.

4 The greatest depth a crewed submersible (underwater vehicle) has reached is 6.8 miles (10.9 km). The reinforced craft had to endure pressures 1,000 times greater than at sea level.

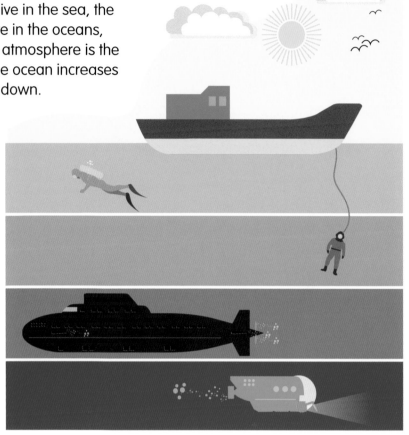

Floating water trick

You can see the power of air pressure by pressing an index card over a glass full of water, turning it upside down, and then carefully removing your fingers. Despite the weight of the water, the index card won't fall off—air pressure keeps it pressed on the glass.

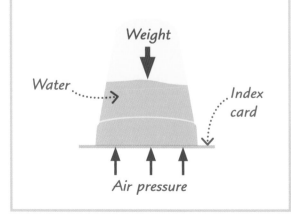

Weight

Water

Index card

Air pressure

Hydraulic jack

A hydraulic jack magnifies forces, making it easier to lift a heavy load. When you press the pump, the force is transmitted through a fluid that is incompressible (can't be squeezed) and so transmits equal pressure in every direction. At the other end, the pressure acts over a greater area, resulting in a greater force (but a smaller movement).

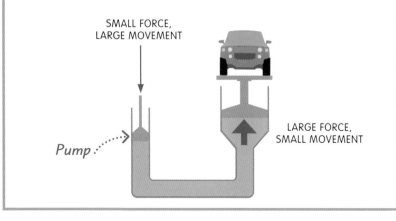

SMALL FORCE, LARGE MOVEMENT

Pump

LARGE FORCE, SMALL MOVEMENT

Floating and sinking

Some things float on water like boats. Others sink like stones. The reason is simple: things that float are lighter than water, and things that sink are heavier.

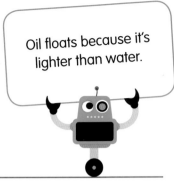

Oil floats because it's lighter than water.

Weight and upthrust

When an object in water is pulled down by its weight, it pushes water out of the way, or displaces it. The water pushes upward with a force that equals the weight of the water displaced. We call this force upthrust.

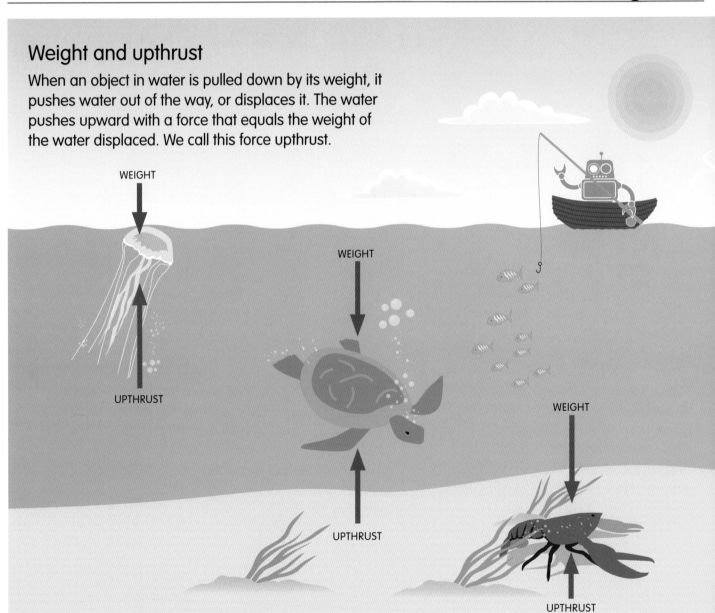

WEIGHT

UPTHRUST

WEIGHT

UPTHRUST

WEIGHT

UPTHRUST

1 If an object weighs less than an equal volume of water, the upthrust is greater than the object's weight. This makes it rise to the surface.

2 If an object weighs the same amount as an equal volume of water, the upthrust equals its weight. The object neither rises nor sinks. We say it has neutral buoyancy.

3 If an object weighs more than water, it sinks. Its weight is greater than the upthrust, so the upthrust can't hold it up.

Archimedes' principle

2,200 years ago, the famous Greek scholar Archimedes discovered that objects weigh less when they're underwater. He realized that this is because the water the object displaces creates upthrust. This is called Archimedes' principle.

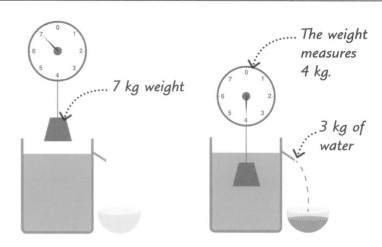

7 kg weight

The weight measures 4 kg.

3 kg of water

1 When this weight is out of the water, the weighing scales show its weight as 7 kg (70 newtons).

2 The weight displaces 3 kg of water as it's lowered, so the scales now show its weight as only 4 kg.

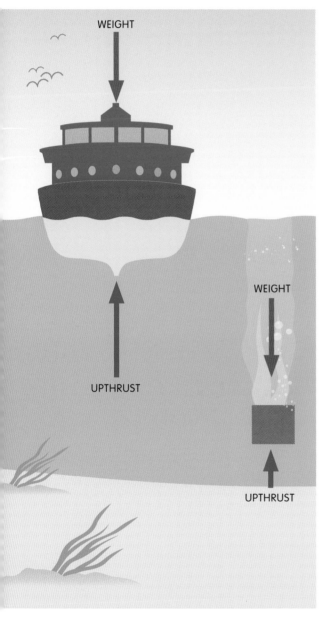

WEIGHT

UPTHRUST

WEIGHT

UPTHRUST

4 A solid block of steel will sink, but a steel ship of the same weight will float. The reason for the difference is that the ship contains a lot of air, so it weighs less per unit volume. We say it is less dense.

REAL WORLD TECHNOLOGY

Submarines

A submarine has large spaces called ballast tanks. When the ballast tanks hold air, the submarine floats on the surface. When they hold water, the submarine can dive because it becomes dense enough to sink.

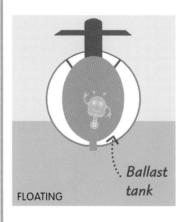
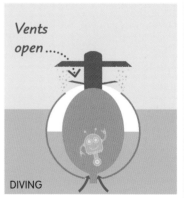

FLOATING

Ballast tank

Vents open

DIVING

1 The ballast tanks are full of air so the submarine floats. Vents at the top of the ballast tanks are closed to keep the air trapped inside.

2 To dive, the submarine lets water into the ballast tanks and the vents open to let air out. This makes the submarine dense enough to sink.

The universe is everything that exists, including planets, moons, stars, galaxies, and the unimaginably huge voids of intergalactic space. Earth is the only place in the universe known to support life. It has just the right climate for water to exist as a liquid on the surface and fall on land as life-giving rain, and its atmosphere shields life from harmful rays from the Sun.

The universe

The universe is everything that exists. It includes planets, stars, galaxies, and the vast expanses of space that stretch farther than we can see.

The size of the universe is a mystery. It may even be infinite in size.

Bigger and bigger

The scale of the universe defies the imagination. Astronomers use light as a yardstick to measure distance because nothing can travel faster. One light-year is the distance light travels in a whole year, or 6 trillion miles (9.5 trillion km).

1 Earth is a small, rocky planet floating in the emptiness of space. Traveling at the speed of light, it would take a seventh of a second to travel once around Earth and about one second to reach our nearest neighbour in space, the Moon.

2 The planets of the solar system orbit the Sun, our local star. The farthest planet—Neptune (shown in blue)—would take only 4.5 hours to reach from Earth at the speed of light.

3 The Sun is just one of 400 billion stars that make up our local galaxy, the Milky Way. This swirling cloud of stars, gas, and dust is 140,000 light-years wide.

4 The Milky Way is one of perhaps 100 billion galaxies that make up the observable universe—the part of the universe we can see. The observable universe is over 90 billion light-years across. What lies beyond it is unknown.

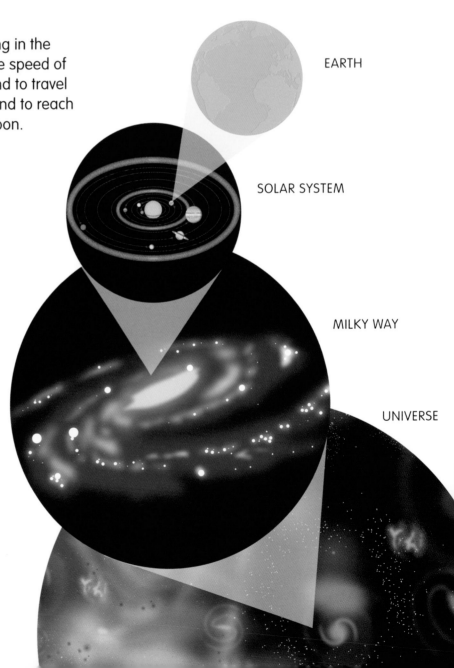

EARTH

SOLAR SYSTEM

MILKY WAY

UNIVERSE

The big bang

Scientists think the universe appeared out of nothingness some 13.8 billion years ago in the Big Bang. At first, the universe was tiny and extremely hot. Over time it expanded and cooled, creating the particles of matter that now form the stars and planets. The universe is still cooling and expanding today.

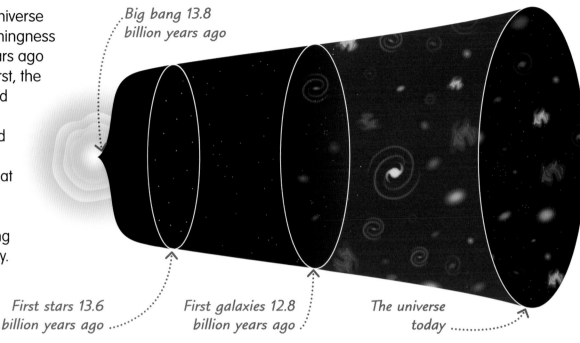

Big bang 13.8 billion years ago

First stars 13.6 billion years ago

First galaxies 12.8 billion years ago

The universe today

Light-years

Light travels at almost 186,000 miles (300,000 km) per second, so one light-year is 6 trillion miles (9.5 trillion km). When we look at distant stars, we see light that has been traveling for years, so we see the stars as they were in the past.

Light travels 9.5 trillion km in 1 year.

LIGHT SOURCE ON EARTH

THE MOON 1 LIGHT-SECOND

THE SUN 8 LIGHT-MINUTES

NEAREST STAR 4 LIGHT-YEARS

TRY IT OUT

Balloon universe

The universe is expanding not because stars and galaxies are flying apart but because the space between them is expanding. To see how this works, try making a model universe with a balloon.

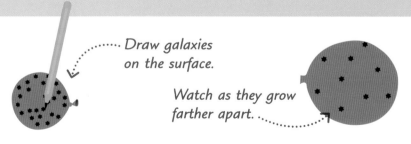

Draw galaxies on the surface.

Watch as they grow farther apart.

1 Partly inflate the balloon. Hold its opening tightly closed, and use a felt-tip pen to draw spots on it. Each spot is a galaxy.

2 Inflate the balloon to its full size. You'll see that the expanding balloon moves the galaxies away from each other.

The solar system

The solar system consists of a star—our Sun—and the objects that orbit (go around) it. It includes eight planets and their moons, as well as asteroids, comets, and dwarf planets.

The Sun contains nearly 99.9 percent of all the matter in the solar system.

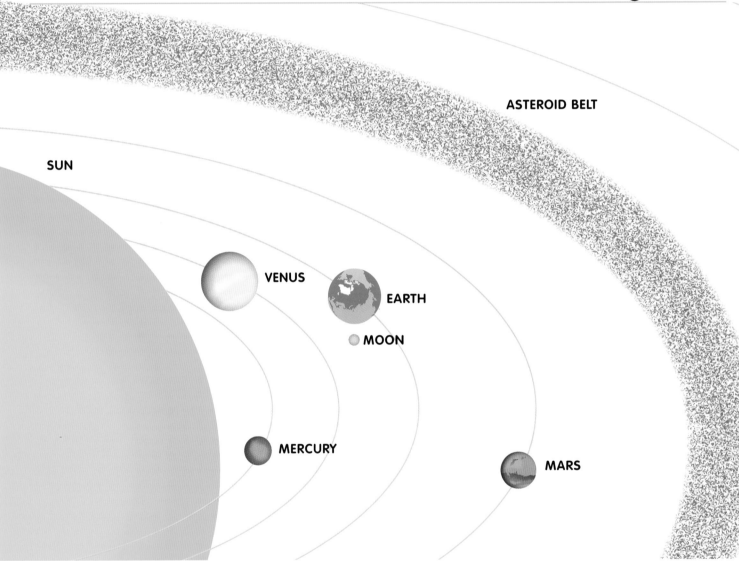

ASTEROID BELT

SUN

VENUS

EARTH

MOON

MERCURY

MARS

1 The Sun
The Sun is an extremely hot, glowing ball of gas at the center of the solar system, and it provides us with heat and light. The pull of the Sun's gravity keeps objects in their orbits.

2 Rocky planets
Mercury, Venus, Earth, and Mars are known as the rocky planets. They are all solid spheres made almost entirely of rock and metal.

3 Asteroid belt
Asteroids are lumps of rock from 3 ft (1 meter) to a few hundred miles across. Most orbit the Sun in a region called the asteroid belt.

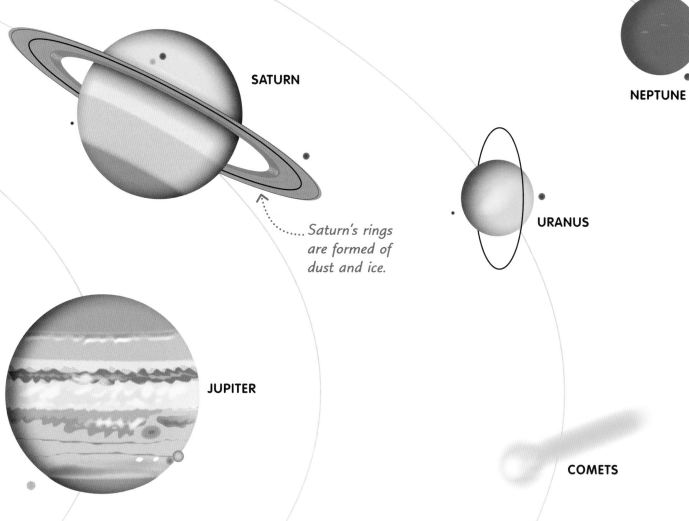

REAL WORLD TECHNOLOGY

Voyager space probes

Voyager 1 and 2 are robots exploring the outer regions of the solar system. They send data, and in the past have sent images, back to Earth.

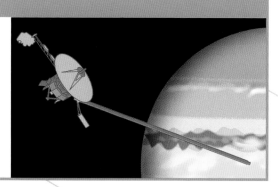

KUIPER BELT

PLUTO

Millions of ice chunks orbit the Sun in a band called the Kuiper Belt.

NEPTUNE

SATURN

URANUS

Saturn's rings are formed of dust and ice.

JUPITER

COMETS

4 Giant planets
Jupiter, Saturn, Uranus, and Neptune are called gas giants because they are made mostly of helium and hydrogen. They are much bigger than the rocky planets, and they orbit the Sun more slowly.

5 Dwarf planets
Dwarf planets, such as Pluto, are much smaller than the rocky planets. Their gravity is only just strong enough to make them form a spherical shape.

6 Comets
These lumps of rock, ice, and dust usually orbit in the solar system's outer regions, but occasionally they pass closer to the Sun and heat up, producing bright tails.

The planets

Our solar system's eight planets are divided into two types. The innermost four are rocky planets—balls of rock and metal. The outer four are giant planets, made of gas, liquid, and ice.

Mercury, Venus, Mars, Jupiter, and Saturn can all be seen from Earth with the naked eye.

Rocky planets

The solar system's rocky planets are Mercury, Venus, Earth, and Mars. They are the four planets closest to the Sun. Each consists mainly of rock but has a core made mostly of iron. Earth and Mars also have moons.

1 Mercury is the smallest planet in the solar system. Its surface is covered in craters. It has hardly any atmosphere and is extremely hot during the day and cold at night.

2 Venus is surrounded by a thick, yellow atmosphere, made mainly of the gas carbon dioxide. Its solid surface is scorchingly hot and dominated by volcanoes.

3 Earth is the only planet with oceans of liquid water on its surface, an oxygen-rich atmosphere, and life. Life on Earth began around 4 billion years ago, soon after the oceans formed.

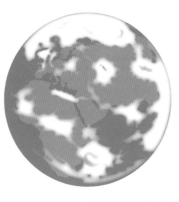

4 Mars is a dusty, desert world with ancient volcanoes, sand dunes, canyons, and many meteorite craters. It has a thin atmosphere made of carbon dioxide, and two small moons.

Size and scale

The planets of the solar system vary hugely in size. The largest, Jupiter, is 87,000 miles (140,000 km) across, while the smallest, Mercury, is just 3,030 miles (4,880 km) across. Earth and Venus are a similar size, as are Neptune and Uranus.

PLANETS SHOWN TO SCALE

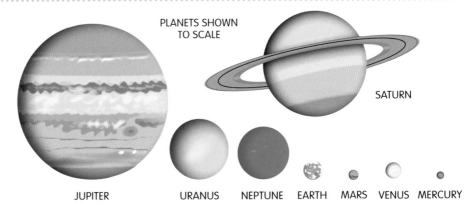

JUPITER   SATURN   URANUS   NEPTUNE   EARTH   MARS   VENUS   MERCURY

Giant planets

The four giant planets are Jupiter, Saturn, Uranus, and Neptune. These planets have no solid surface that we can see. Instead, each has an outer gas layer, mainly made of helium and hydrogen, which surrounds liquid or icy layers and, scientists think, a very small, rocky core. Each giant planet has numerous moons.

1 The bright bands in Jupiter's atmosphere are swirling, turbulent weather systems. It is the fastest-spinning planet.

2 Saturn has vast rings made of ice fragments. It has a banded atmosphere, but a yellowy haze makes it look smooth.

3 Uranus is a pale blue color due to methane gas in its atmosphere. Unlike the other planets, it spins on its side.

4 Neptune is a bright blue color. Winds of up to 1,300 mph (2,100 km/h) blow white clouds of frozen methane around the planet.

Planets outside the solar system

Most stars in our galaxy may have orbiting planets, which means that huge numbers of planets exist outside of our solar system. However, only some of these planets are in the habitable or "Goldilocks" zone around their star, where it is neither too hot nor too cold for life to exist.

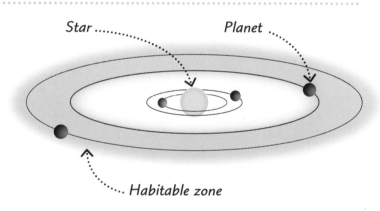

Star ......   Planet ....

.... Habitable zone

Dwarf planets

Dwarf planets are large enough to become spherical through their own gravity. However, they don't have enough gravity to sweep their orbits clear of other objects, such as asteroids. Upon its discovery in 1930, Pluto was classified as a planet, but it was downgraded in 2006. Other dwarf planets include Eris (the most massive dwarf planet known) and Haumea, which is shaped like a football.

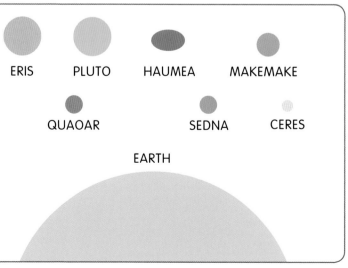

ERIS   PLUTO   HAUMEA   MAKEMAKE

QUAOAR   SEDNA   CERES

EARTH

The Sun

The Sun is our local star and has been shining for about 4.6 billion years. It is a glowing ball of extremely hot gas and consists mostly of hydrogen.

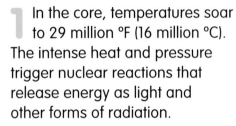

Never look directly at the Sun either with your naked eye or through binoculars—it's dangerous!

Inside the Sun

Like other stars, the Sun has several distinct layers inside. The temperature and pressure rise toward the central core, which is the Sun's source of power.

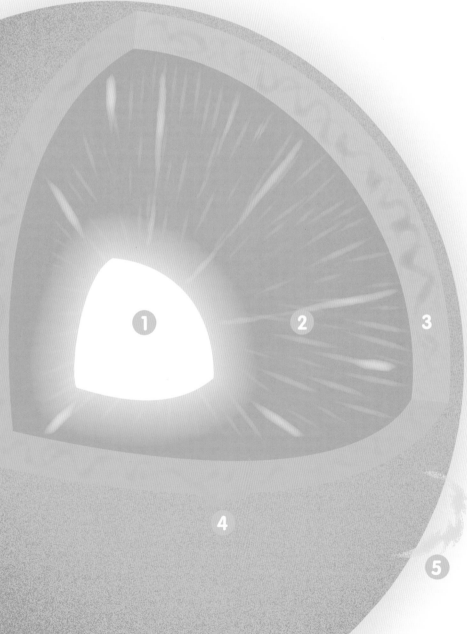

1 In the core, temperatures soar to 29 million °F (16 million °C). The intense heat and pressure trigger nuclear reactions that release energy as light and other forms of radiation.

2 Surrounding the core is the radiative zone. Energy from the core moves up through this layer as radiation, traveling very slowly.

3 Outside the radiative zone is the convective zone. Here, enormous bubbles of hot gas rise to the surface. There they release energy before sinking again.

4 The photosphere is the Sun's visible surface. It emits vast amounts of light, heat, and other radiation. It has a temperature of about 9,570°F (5,300°C).

5 Outside the photosphere is the Sun's atmosphere, which extends thousands of miles into space. Loops of hot gas called prominences often erupt into the atmosphere from inside the Sun.

How the Sun shines

The Sun is powered by a process called nuclear fusion. Inside the core, the nuclei (central parts) of hydrogen atoms collide with such speed that they fuse together and form helium nuclei. This process releases vast amounts of energy, much of which escapes from the Sun as light and makes the star glow.

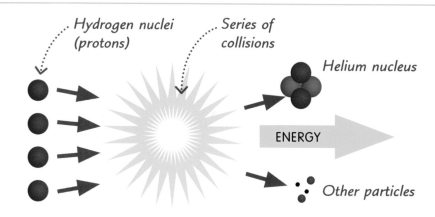

Hydrogen nuclei (protons)

Series of collisions

Helium nucleus

ENERGY

Other particles

NUCLEAR FUSION IN THE SUN

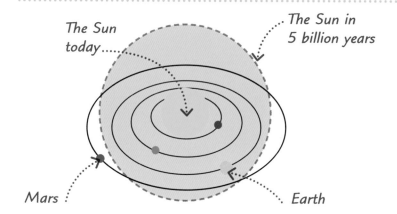

The Sun today

The Sun in 5 billion years

Mars

Earth

The Sun's future

In about 5 billion years, the Sun's core will begin to run out of hydrogen. As a result, the Sun will swell in size, turning into a kind of star called a red giant. It will grow so huge that it will swallow the planets Mercury, Venus, and probably Earth. Later, it will disintegrate to leave just the glowing remains of its core—a white dwarf star.

Auroras

As well as producing light, the Sun emits streams of charged particles that rush through space. When they hit Earth's atmosphere near the poles, they can cause molecules in the air to produce light, resulting in ghostly patterns in the night sky, called auroras.

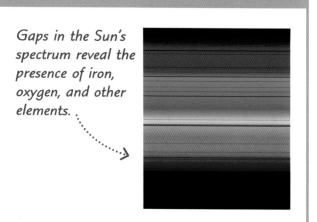

REAL WORLD TECHNOLOGY

Spectroscopy

Astronomers can figure out which chemical elements are present in the Sun or stars by studying their light. White light is a mixture of colors. Astronomers use a device called a spectroscope to split light into a pattern called a spectrum. The spectra of stars have distinctive gaps, caused by chemical elements absorbing certain wavelengths as light leaves the star. Like fingerprints, these gaps reveal which elements are present.

Gaps in the Sun's spectrum reveal the presence of iron, oxygen, and other elements.

Gravity and orbits

Gravity is the force of attraction that pulls falling objects to Earth. Gravity keeps the Moon in orbit around Earth and the planets in orbit around the Sun.

> If you could stand on the Sun, its gravity would make you weigh 28 times your Earth weight.

What does gravity do?

All objects exert the force of gravity, but only things with a huge amount of matter—such as moons, planets, and stars—have enough gravity to pull things strongly. The greater an object's mass, the stronger the pull of its gravity.

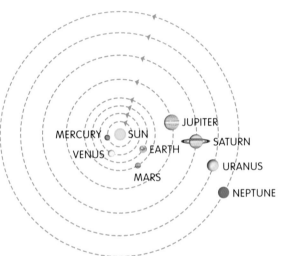

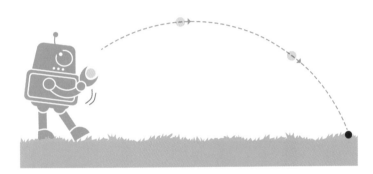

1 Earth
On Earth, gravity makes objects fall to the ground. If you throw a ball, it will follow a curved path as gravity pulls it steadily back down.

2 Planets
The solar system's eight planets, 180 or so moons, and countless comets, asteroids, and dwarf planets are all kept moving around the Sun by its gravity.

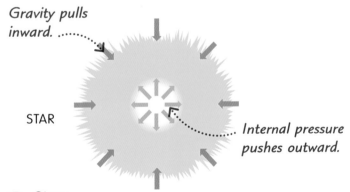

Gravity pulls inward.

STAR

Internal pressure pushes outward.

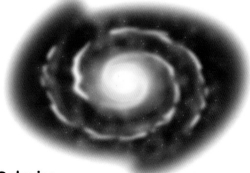

3 Stars
Stars are made of hot gas. Gravity stops the gas from drifting off into space by pulling it inward, forming a sphere. In the center of the star, gravity crushes the gas atoms with such force that nuclear fusion reactions occur, creating heat and light.

4 Galaxies
A galaxy contains millions or billions of stars spread across such a vast expanse of space that it would take billions of years to cross it at the speed of a jet aircraft. The stars are trapped in orbit by huge amounts of matter in the galactic core.

Orbits

An orbit is the curved path that an object in space follows as it travels around another object—such as the path of the Moon around Earth. The English scientist Isaac Newton was the first person to realize that orbits are caused by the force of gravity.

1 How orbits work

Newton realized that an object in orbit moves like a ball a person has thrown. Earth's gravity makes it fall back toward Earth on a curved path. However, if the object is moving fast enough, the curvature of its fall is less than the curvature of Earth, and so it never lands, remaining forever in orbit.

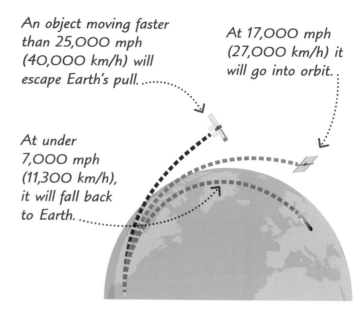

An object moving faster than 25,000 mph (40,000 km/h) will escape Earth's pull.

At 17,000 mph (27,000 km/h) it will go into orbit.

At under 7,000 mph (11,300 km/h), it will fall back to Earth.

2 Shapes of orbits

Orbits aren't perfect circles. Their shapes are called ellipses and are like squashed circles. The orbits of the Moon and the planets are only slightly elliptical. However, comets have very elliptical orbits that take them swooping close to the Sun before flying back out into deep space.

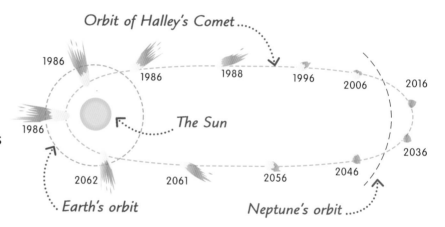

Orbit of Halley's Comet

1986 1986 1988 1996 2006 2016
1986
The Sun
2036
1986
2062 2061 2056 2046
Earth's orbit
Neptune's orbit

TRY IT OUT

Draw an ellipse

You can draw an ellipse with a loop of string, a pencil, two push pins, and a corkboard.

1 Make a loop of string about 8 in (20 cm) long. Place a piece of paper on top of a corkboard, and push the pins through the paper into the corkboard about 3 in (8 cm) apart.

2 Loop the string around the pins and pencil, and carefully draw the ellipse, keeping the string slightly taut.

REAL WORLD TECHNOLOGY

Satellites

Satellites orbit Earth along many different paths. Some are launched so high that they orbit as fast as Earth turns, so they seem to hover at a fixed point (a geostationary orbit).

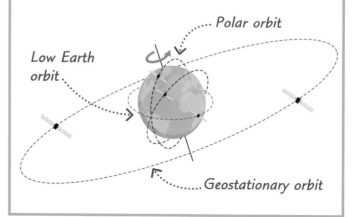

Polar orbit
Low Earth orbit
Geostationary orbit

Earth and the Moon

The Moon is a satellite of Earth, orbiting (circling around) Earth once every 27.3 days. It doesn't produce its own light, but we can still see it because it reflects light from the Sun.

> The Moon is Earth's only natural satellite. It formed 4.5 billion years ago.

The Moon's phases

The Moon sometimes appears as a full circle in the sky and sometimes as a crescent or a semicircle. These changing shapes are called phases. They are caused by changes in the relative positions of the Moon, Earth, and Sun. The full cycle of lunar phases lasts about 30 days.

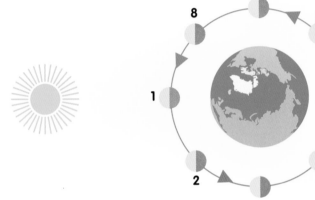

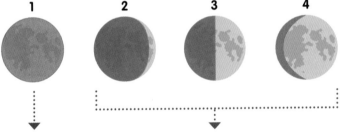

When the Moon is between Earth and the Sun, it cannot be seen from Earth. This is called a new moon.

As the Moon moves, the angle between the Sun, Earth, and the Moon increases, revealing more of the Moon's sunlit surface.

When the Moon is on the opposite side of Earth from the Sun, its whole disk appears lit up. This is called a full moon.

As the Moon continues its orbit, the angle between the Sun, Earth, and the Moon decreases. Less of the Moon's surface is visible from Earth.

Tides

Ocean tides are caused mainly by the pull of the Moon's gravity. The Moon pulls the sea on the near side of Earth, creating a bulge where the water level is higher. On the opposite side of Earth, where the Moon's gravity is weakest, the ocean bulges the other way. As Earth rotates, two high tides sweep around the planet roughly once a day.

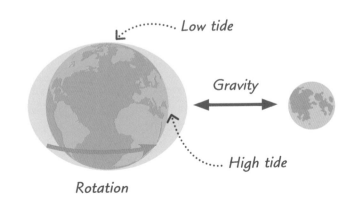

Low tide

Gravity

High tide

Rotation

Eclipses

Eclipses happen when planets or their moons cast shadows on each other. Two main types of eclipses can be seen from Earth: solar eclipses and lunar eclipses.

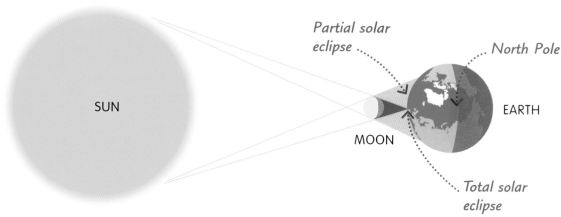

PARTIAL SOLAR ECLIPSE

TOTAL SOLAR ECLIPSE

1 Solar eclipse

A solar eclipse happens when the Moon casts a shadow on Earth. In the center of the Moon's shadow, the Sun is completely blocked for a few minutes and day turns almost to night. This is called a total solar eclipse. If the Sun is only partly blocked, a partial solar eclipse occurs. If you see a solar eclipse, remember never to look directly at the Sun because it can damage your eyes.

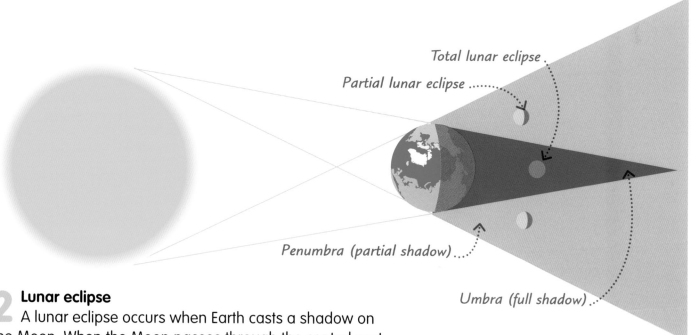

2 Lunar eclipse

A lunar eclipse occurs when Earth casts a shadow on the Moon. When the Moon passes through the central part of Earth's shadow (the umbra), it turns unusually dark. However, some sunlight scattered by Earth's atmosphere still reaches it, giving it a reddish color.

Earth's structure

If you sliced open planet Earth, you'd find four distinct layers inside—the crust, the mantle, and the outer and inner cores. Surrounding all these is a layer of air called the atmosphere.

The temperature at Earth's center is hotter than the surface of the Sun.

1 The atmosphere is a mixture of various gases—mostly nitrogen and oxygen. It is thousands of miles thick, and fades gradually into space.

2 The crust is Earth's solid surface and consists of different types of lightweight rock. Its thickness varies from 3 miles (5 km) to 50 miles (75 km).

3 The mantle is made mostly of dense, solid rock, which is rich in the chemical elements magnesium, silicon, and oxygen. It is about 1,770 miles (2,850 km) thick.

4 Earth's outer core is formed of hot molten (liquid) iron and some nickel. It is about 1,370 miles (2,200 km) thick and its average temperature is 9,000°F (5,000°C).

5 The inner core is an extremely hot ball of solid metal, formed mainly of iron and some nickel. It is about 1,585 miles (2,550 km) across, and the temperature is about 10,800°F (6,000°C).

1 ATMOSPHERE

2 CRUST

3 MANTLE

4 OUTER CORE

5 INNER CORE

REAL WORLD TECHNOLOGY

Geothermal energy

Earth contains an enormous amount of heat energy, known as geothermal energy. In some parts of the world, it can be harvested to produce electricity. Cold water is pumped deep underground, where it is heated by Earth's interior. This hot water is then brought to the surface, where a power station converts the heat energy in the water into electricity.

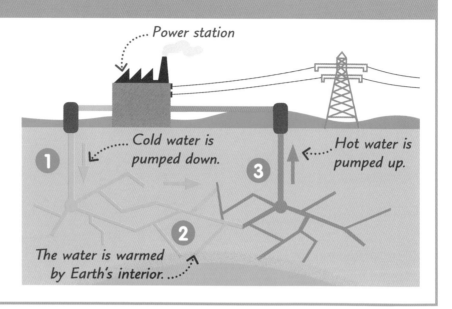

Power station

1 Cold water is pumped down.

3 Hot water is pumped up.

2 The water is warmed by Earth's interior.

TRY IT OUT

Egglike Earth

Crack open a hard-boiled egg and you'll find that the proportions of the eggshell, white, and yolk are similar to the proportions of Earth's crust, mantle, and core.

1 Hard-boil an egg and place it in an egg carton. Crack its pointed end by gently tapping it with a teaspoon.

2 Pick away the top half of the shell. Turn the egg sideways on a hard surface, then carefully cut through it with a knife.

3 Take a look inside your egg. Its structure is very similar to the structure of Earth's layers.

The shell is less than 1% of the egg.

About 45% is made of egg white.

The yolk makes up about 54% of the egg.

Plate tectonics

Earth's rocky outer shell is split into giant fragments called tectonic plates. Their slow movements are continually changing the planet's surface.

Earth's continents move at about the speed that toenails grow.

Tectonic plates

Tectonic plates have irregular shapes and fit together like puzzle pieces over Earth's surface. Each plate has a top layer of rocks—the crust. Below it is a second layer that is actually the top layer of the mantle (see pages 280–81).

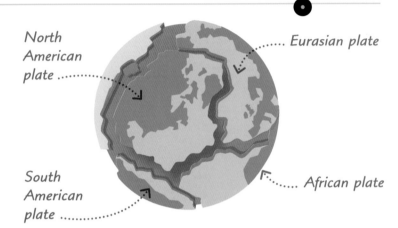

North American plate

Eurasian plate

South American plate

African plate

Plates in action

Tremendous forces are unleashed at the boundaries between plates, causing mountains and volcanoes to form. The picture below shows the boundaries between four different plates.

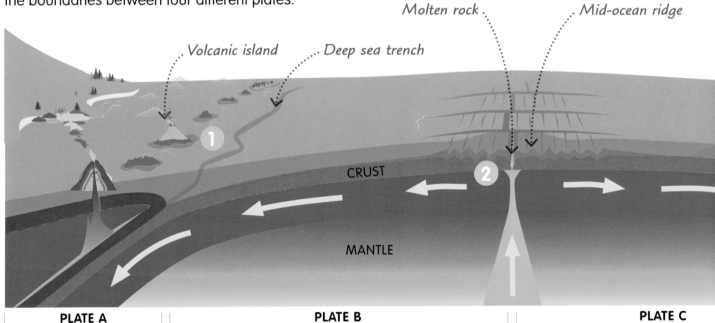

Molten rock

Mid-ocean ridge

Volcanic island

Deep sea trench

CRUST

MANTLE

PLATE A   PLATE B   PLATE C

1 Volcanic islands
In some parts of the world, plates collide under the ocean and one plate moves under another. This causes rock deep underground to melt, and the molten rock erupts at the surface to form volcanic islands.

2 Mid-ocean ridge
Many plate boundaries are in the middle of the oceans. Here, plates move apart, pushed sideways by hot rock rising from deep in Earth's mantle. A chain of undersea mountains— a mid-ocean ridge—forms at these boundaries.

Continental crackers

You can mimic what happens when continental plates collide by placing a couple of graham crackers on a plate of frosting and pushing them together.

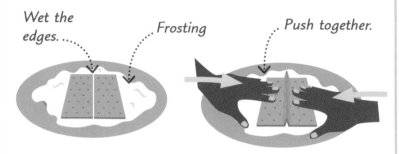

Wet the edges.

Frosting

Push together.

1 Spread freshly made frosting on a large plate. Thoroughly wet one edge of each cracker and place them both on the frosting, with the wet edges together.

2 Push the crackers together to imitate continents colliding. The edges of the crackers will crumple up, mimicking mountain formation.

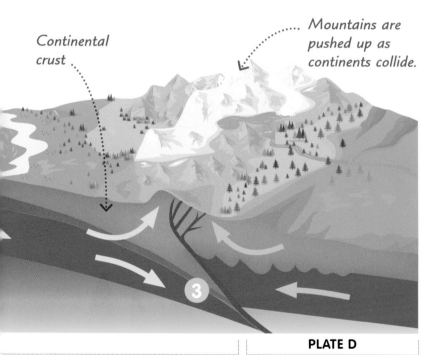

Continental crust

Mountains are pushed up as continents collide.

PLATE D

3 Crashing continents
Where plates collide under continents, one plate may move down under the other. When this happens, the crust in the top plate crumples, creating mountains. The Himalaya mountains and many other major mountain ranges formed this way.

Plate boundaries

Areas where the edges of tectonic plates meet are called plate boundaries. There are three main types of boundaries: convergent boundaries, divergent boundaries, and transform boundaries.

1 At convergent boundaries, plates move toward each other and one plate moves underneath the other.

2 At divergent boundaries, plates move apart, pushed by hot rock welling up from below.

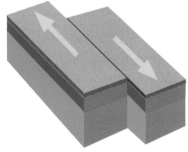

3 At transform boundaries, two plates grind past each other. Sudden movements at transform boundaries cause earthquakes.

Natural hazards

Earthquakes, tsunamis, and volcanic eruptions are natural events triggered by processes happening inside our planet. These events can be terrifying and destructive, but they are very difficult to predict.

During the very largest earthquakes, Earth can move up to half an inch back and forth in space.

Earthquakes

The tectonic plates that make up Earth's crust are constantly moving and pushing past each other. If the plates get stuck, tension builds and can be released suddenly, causing vibrations that travel to the surface. These vibrations cause a violent shaking of Earth's surface—an earthquake.

1 As parts of Earth's crust move past each other, tension may build up. If the strain gets too much, the crust can suddenly shift, releasing huge amounts of energy in the form of seismic waves. The point underground where the earthquake starts is called the focus.

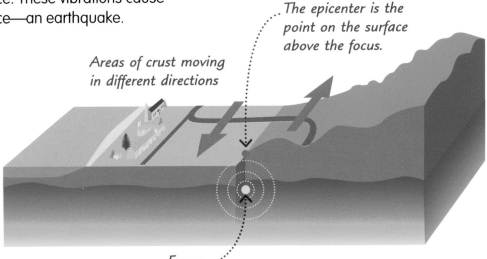

Areas of crust moving in different directions

The epicenter is the point on the surface above the focus.

Focus

2 Seismic waves are felt most strongly at the epicenter, the point on the surface directly above the focus, and this is where most damage occurs. Buildings shake and some may collapse. Aftershocks—smaller earthquakes that happen after the main shock—may cause even more damage.

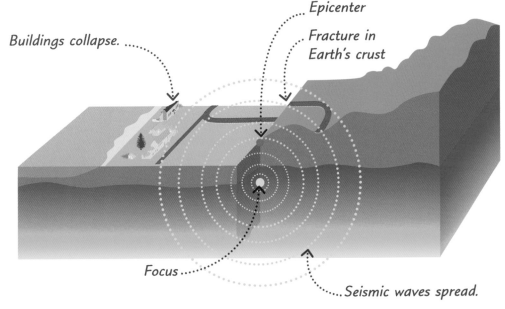

Buildings collapse.

Epicenter

Fracture in Earth's crust

Focus

Seismic waves spread.

Tsunamis

A tsunami is a powerful wave, caused by a sudden movement in the seafloor, that can travel far through an ocean. Tsunami waves can travel at speeds of over 500 mph (800 km/h), but they are hardly noticeable out at sea. Once they reach shallower water, however, tsunami waves can grow as high as 100 ft (30 m).

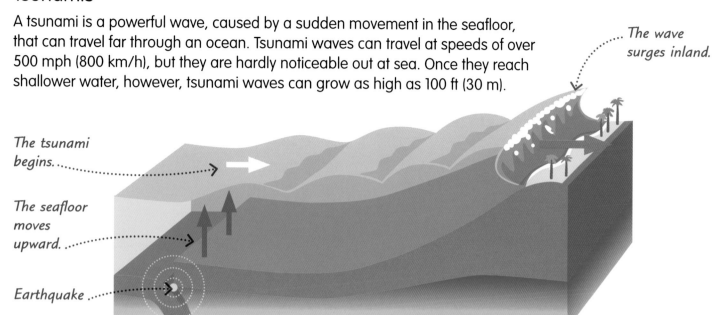

The wave surges inland.

The tsunami begins.

The seafloor moves upward.

Earthquake

1 An earthquake occurs under the seafloor, thrusting a chunk of seafloor several feet upward. This sudden movement of the seafloor pushes up the mass of water above it.

2 The water pushed up from below triggers a series of high-energy waves that travel rapidly across the ocean surface.

3 At the shore, each wave surges inland, flooding the coast and destroying buildings. Boats and cars may be carried a great distance.

Volcanic eruptions

Volcanoes develop in places where magma (hot, liquid rock) from chambers deep underground erupts through an opening at Earth's surface called a vent. Some volcanic eruptions are violent explosions that blast out ash and lava bombs (lumps of rock) that eventually fall to the ground. Others spew lava—molten rock—out of the volcano's vent, which then flows down the sides in a runny stream.

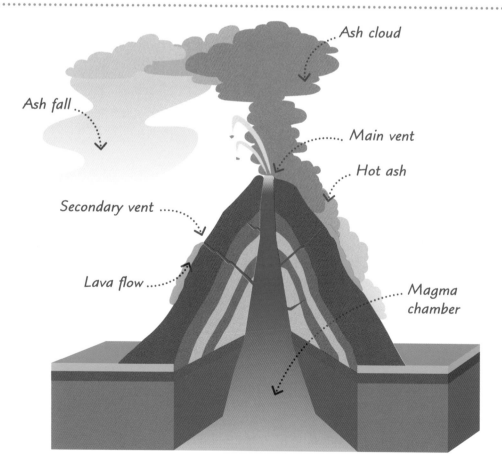

Ash cloud

Ash fall

Main vent

Hot ash

Secondary vent

Lava flow

Magma chamber

Rocks and minerals

Earth's crust is formed of many types of rock, and each rock is made of one or more crystallized chemicals known as minerals. We use them to make all sorts of things, from jewelry to buildings.

> Minerals vary greatly in their hardness—the hardest known mineral is diamond.

What is a rock?

A rock is a collection of mineral grains (little crystals) clumped or cemented together. Some rocks consist mainly of one mineral, but others are made of several different types—for example, pink granite contains grains of feldspar, hornblende, mica, and quartz. Rocks are categorized into three main types based on how they formed: igneous, sedimentary, and metamorphic.

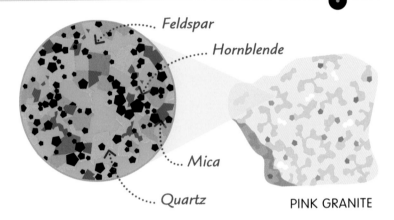

Feldspar

Hornblende

Mica

Quartz

PINK GRANITE

1 Igneous rock

When magma (hot molten, or liquid, rock) cools and becomes solid, it forms igneous rock. If the magma cools and solidifies slowly underground, large crystals form, but if it cools quickly, after spewing out of a volcano, the crystals will be small. Granite is a type of igneous rock.

Some sedimentary rocks contain fossils.

LIMESTONE

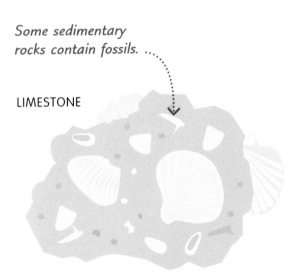

Heat and pressure can create patterns.

GNEISS

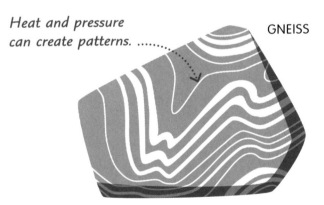

2 Sedimentary rock

These rocks form at or near Earth's surface. Small particles of rock, carried by water or wind, are deposited in sea or river beds, where they are compressed (packed) together. Chalk, limestone, and shale are sedimentary rocks.

3 Metamorphic rock

Metamorphic rock is a rock that has been changed by heat, pressure, or both of these. It forms when magma bakes the rock around it, or when pressure from above squeezes buried rock. Examples include gneiss, marble, schist, and slate.

What is a mineral?

A mineral is a naturally occurring solid chemical. There are more than 5,300 minerals, but only a few are common and these make up most of the rocks on Earth. Each type of mineral has a distinctive shape.

Quartz clock

Quartz is used to make very accurate clocks. When an electric field is moved close to a piece of quartz, the quartz crystals vibrate at a very precise frequency. These vibrations are then used by the clock to measure the passing of time exactly.

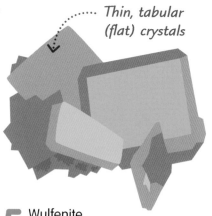

Long, hexagonal crystals

1 Quartz
Quartz is one of the most common rock-forming minerals. It is made of oxygen and silicon. Pure quartz is colorless, but impurities can give it a variety of different colors.

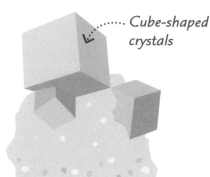

Cube-shaped crystals

2 Pyrite
With shiny, cube-shaped crystals, pyrite resembles metallic dice embedded in rock. It can look like gold, which is much more valuable, earning it the nickname "fool's gold."

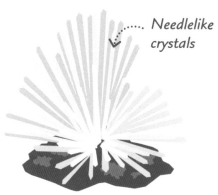

Needlelike crystals

3 Aragonite
Aragonite is a form of calcium carbonate, made of calcium, carbon, and oxygen. It can be white or several other colors, including blue and orange-brown.

Lumpy shape

4 Hematite
Colored silver-gray, reddish brown, or black, hematite is a type of iron oxide (a compound of iron and oxygen). It is the world's main source of metallic iron.

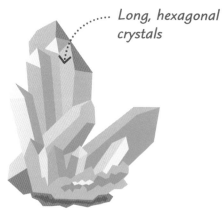

Thin, tabular (flat) crystals

5 Wulfenite
The crystals of wulfenite are typically bright orange-red or orange-yellow in color. This mineral is made of lead, oxygen, and a metal called molybdenum.

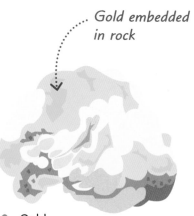

Gold embedded in rock

6 Gold
Gold is bright yellow, highly valued, and rare. Unlike most metals, which occur in a compound with other chemical elements, gold is often found in nature in its pure form.

The rock cycle

Even the hardest rocks don't last forever. Over time, all kinds of rock are broken down into small particles. However, this material is continually recycled to make new rock.

Most parts of the rock cycle happen very slowly, taking place over millions of years.

Recycling rock

Rock can be melted by heat inside Earth or gradually worn away by weathering and erosion (see page 294) on Earth's surface. These processes continually recycle the material in Earth's crust, turning each of the three main types of rock into the others.

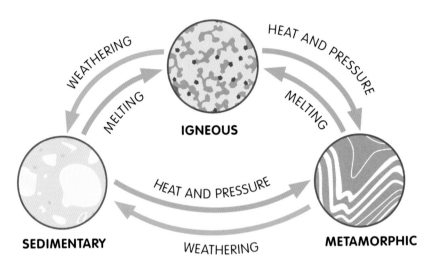

WEATHERING   HEAT AND PRESSURE

MELTING   IGNEOUS   MELTING

HEAT AND PRESSURE

SEDIMENTARY   WEATHERING   METAMORPHIC

REAL WORLD TECHNOLOGY

Oil exploration

The layers of sedimentary rock on the seafloor sometimes trap valuable reserves of oil and gas. Geologists can locate these reserves by beaming sound waves at the seafloor and capturing the echoes with floating microphones. Analyzing the echoes provides information about the different rock layers and whether liquids or gases are trapped between them.

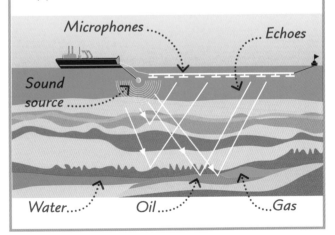

Microphones   Echoes

Sound source

Water   Oil   Gas

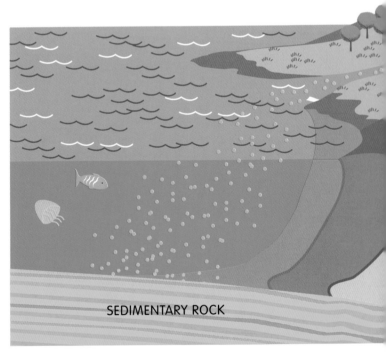

SEDIMENTARY ROCK

2 Particles of rock (sediments) are washed into the sea by rivers and build up on the seafloor in layers. Over millions of years, they are compressed to form sedimentary rock.

1 Sunshine, frost, and rain slowly weaken
and wear away the rock on Earth's surface,
breaking it down into small particles of sand or
clay. These are then washed away by rivers
or blown away by the wind.

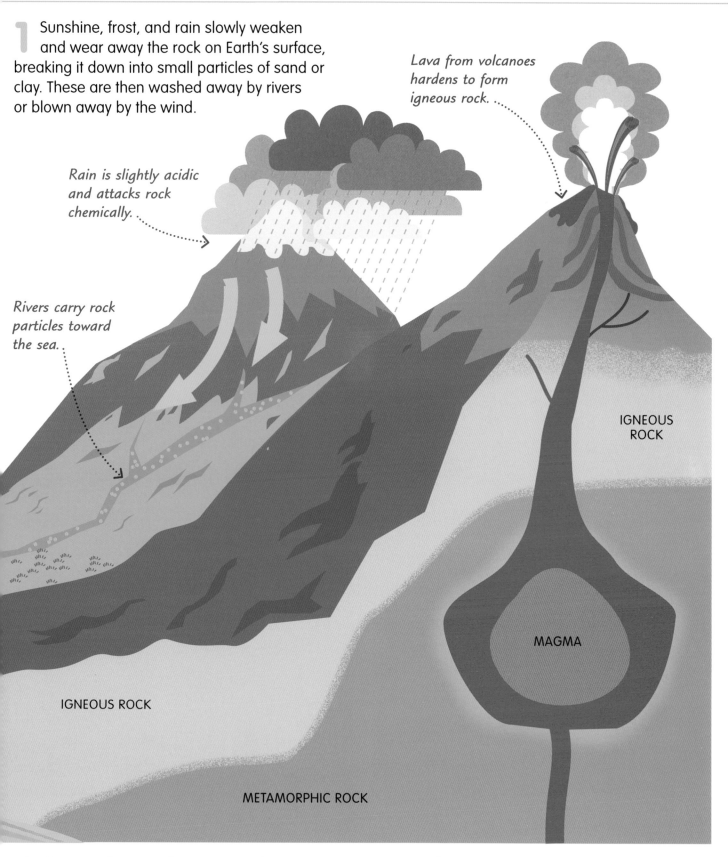

Lava from volcanoes
hardens to form
igneous rock.

Rain is slightly acidic
and attacks rock
chemically.

Rivers carry rock
particles toward
the sea.

IGNEOUS
ROCK

MAGMA

IGNEOUS ROCK

METAMORPHIC ROCK

3 Deep underground, pressure or heat
can change rock both physically and
chemically, turning igneous or sedimentary
rock into metamorphic rock.

4 High temperatures inside Earth melt rock,
turning it into a red-hot liquid called magma.
When magma cools down, it solidifies and forms
a new kind of rock, called igneous rock.

How fossils form

Fossils are the remains of animals, plants, and other living things preserved in rocks. They range from microscopic traces of bacterial cells to gigantic dinosaur bones and tree trunks that have turned to rock.

Most of the animal and plant species that have ever lived on Earth are now extinct.

Fossil formation

Just a tiny fraction of all the animals and plants that have ever lived on Earth leave fossils behind. Fossils are rare because they form by a long and complicated process. When they are eventually exposed, the fossilized remains can tell us about the history of life on Earth.

Sediment sinks to the bottom, covering the skeleton.

1 The animal must die in a place, such as a lake, where it will become buried by sand and mud (sediment). Its soft parts are consumed by scavengers, or they decay, until just hard teeth and bones are left.

2 The animal's skeleton must be quickly covered in a layer of sediment before it decays completely. Over millions of years, many more layers of sediment form on top of the first layer, burying the animal deep underground.

Other types of fossils

Not all fossils form from the bones of dead animals. Below are some other ways fossils can form.

Carbon film fossils appear as a black or brown image.

1 Petrified shell
The shells of marine organisms, turned to rock, are some of the most common and widespread fossils.

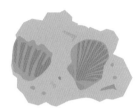

2 Mold fossil
When an organism encased in rock dissolves, it may leave a mold, or impression, of the original shape.

3 Carbon film
This fossil forms when a thin layer of carbon is deposited onto rock over time by a decaying organism.

4 Footprint fossil
A footprint fossil is a type of "trace fossil." It reveals evidence of animal activity, rather than remains.

5 Dung fossil
This trace fossil, called a coprolite, is a lump of ancient animal feces that has become rock.

6 Fossil in amber
These form when the sap produced by trees traps insects and later hardens.

3 The weight of the layers causes the sediment particles to cement together, encasing the skeleton in rock. Water seeps through the rock into the bones, which are slowly replaced with minerals from the water, turning the bones to rock.

The rocks above have eroded away.

Exposed fossil

4 For the fossil to be discovered, the layer it is buried in must be raised upward when Earth's crust moves. Water, ice, or wind must then erode away the layers above, in a process that may take millions of years.

Earth's history

Scientists divide Earth's history into a sequence of periods stretching back billions of years. These are named after ancient bands of sedimentary rock that are found all over the world. Each band has a distinctive collection of fossils, providing a fascinating glimpse into the distant past.

Older layers of sedimentary rock are usually found under younger layers because they formed earlier.

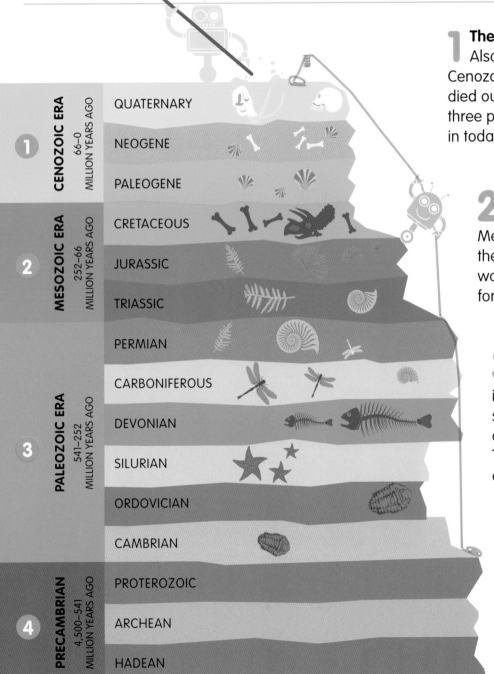

ERA	MILLION YEARS AGO	PERIOD
CENOZOIC ERA	66–0	QUATERNARY
		NEOGENE
		PALEOGENE
MESOZOIC ERA	252–66	CRETACEOUS
		JURASSIC
		TRIASSIC
PALEOZOIC ERA	541–252	PERMIAN
		CARBONIFEROUS
		DEVONIAN
		SILURIAN
		ORDOVICIAN
		CAMBRIAN
PRECAMBRIAN	4,500–541	PROTEROZOIC
		ARCHEAN
		HADEAN

1 The Cenozoic
Also called the age of mammals, the Cenozoic Era began after the dinosaurs died out. Geologists divide this era into three periods, including the one we live in today—the Quaternary.

2 The Mesozoic
Dinosaurs flourished during the Mesozoic Era, which is also called the age of reptiles. Earth's climate was hotter than today, and conifer forests covered much of the land.

3 The Paleozoic
Life was confined to the sea in the early Paleozoic, but later it spread to the land, which became covered in lush, swampy forests. The first fish, insects, and trees appeared during this era.

4 The Precambrian
This "supereon" spans nearly 90 percent of Earth's history, but little is known about it. For most of the Precambrian, the only forms of life were microscopic sea organisms, which left few fossils.

Mass extinctions

At various times in Earth's history, large numbers of animal and plant species have suddenly disappeared from the fossil record. These events are called mass extinctions.

1 Around 252 million years ago, something wiped out 96 percent of marine species and most of the life on land. The cause is unknown, but some scientists suspect that massive volcanic eruptions poisoned the air and seas.

2 Around 66 million years ago, three-quarters of all animal and plant species died out, including most dinosaurs. The cause is thought to have been an asteroid or comet smashing into what is now southern Mexico.

3 Today, Earth may be in the middle of another extinction event, caused by our own species. Deforestation, climate change, and other activities are harming natural habitats, causing many species to disappear.

Changing continents

By studying matching rock strata in different parts of the world, geologists discovered that the planet's continents were once connected. Over time, the continents slowly move, merge, and split. In the Triassic Period, for example, all today's continents were joined into one "supercontinent," called Pangaea.

225 MILLION YEARS AGO

150 MILLION YEARS AGO

TODAY

REAL WORLD TECHNOLOGY

Radiometric dating

Geologists can calculate the age of rocks by measuring the ratio of certain forms of chemical elements in them. For instance, over long periods, a form of uranium called U-235 slowly changes into lead. So if a rock has 39 uranium atoms for every 61 lead atoms, it must be 1 billion years old. Only igneous rocks can be dated this way, but the age of neighboring sedimentary layers can be worked out indirectly.

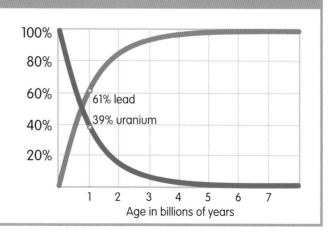

Weathering and erosion

Earth's varied landscapes, from mountains and canyons to valleys and plains, are all shaped by weathering and erosion. These two processes gradually wear away the rock in the planet's crust.

Weathering

Weathering is the breakup of solid rock into small fragments. This can happen in several different ways.

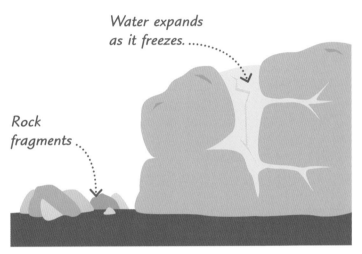

Water expands as it freezes.

Rock fragments

1 Chemical weathering is caused by rain. Rain is slightly acidic and attacks certain minerals in rock, turning them into soft clay. The harder grains of rock left behind crumble into sand.

2 Ice wedging happens when water seeps into cracks in rock and freezes. Water expands when it turns to ice, widening the cracks and splitting the rock into fragments.

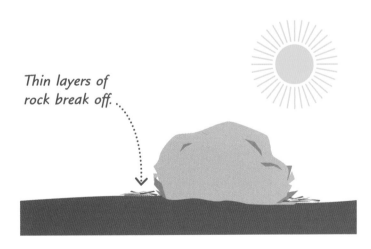

Thin layers of rock break off.

Soil

Mixed soil and rock

Rock

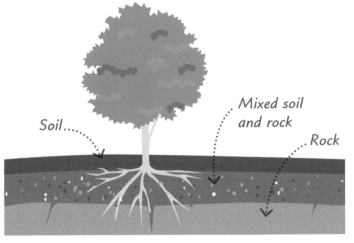

3 Thermal weathering is caused by the Sun's heat. When rocks repeatedly heat up in the Sun and cool down, they expand and contract. This stress makes thin layers break off the surface.

4 Biological weathering is caused by living organisms. Burrowing animals wear away at underground rock, and plant roots work their way into crevices in rock and widen them.

Erosion

Erosion is the removal and carrying away of rock fragments. Water, ice, and wind all cause erosion.

1 As it slowly flows downhill, a glacier carries rocks of many sizes, from sand grains to giant boulders. The debris is dumped at the glacier's end.

2 Rivers carry rock debris as particles of sand, silt, and clay. Over time, a river carves away at the ground to create a wide river valley or a steep-sided canyon.

Weathering breaks down rock, while erosion carries the rock fragments away.

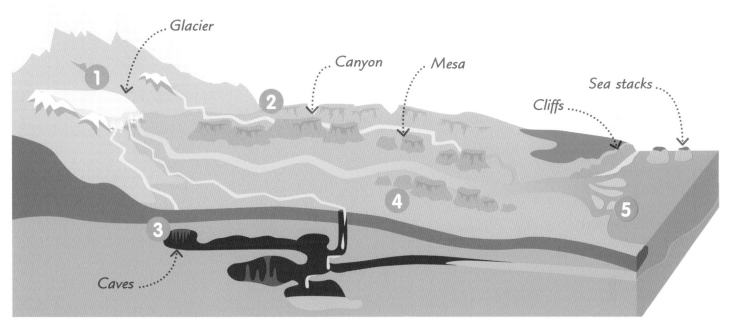

Glacier

Canyon

Mesa

Sea stacks

Cliffs

Caves

3 Rivers don't just flow on the surface. They also find their way underground, where a combination of chemical weathering and erosion can create huge cave systems.

4 In dry places, windblown sand erodes rock, creating flat-topped hills (mesas and buttes), rock arches, and other structures. The sand piles up to form dunes.

5 Ocean waves pounding the coast break up rock, creating cliffs, caves, and towers of rock called sea stacks. The debris is washed away by the sea.

TRY IT OUT

Modeling wave erosion

See for yourself how wave action erodes the coast by making your own wave-maker. For this activity you'll need a paint tray, some sand, small pebbles, water, and an empty plastic bottle with a cap.

1 Put sand at one end of the tray and add a few pebbles on top. Then pour water into the other end.

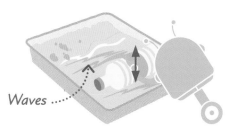

Waves

2 Create waves by bobbing the bottle up and down, and watch what happens to the sand.

The water cycle

The amount of water on Earth never changes; it just gets used again and again. Water is always moving between the sea, air, and land, going around in a never-ending cycle.

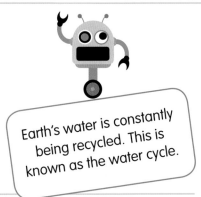

Earth's water is constantly being recycled. This is known as the water cycle.

TRY IT OUT

Make it rain indoors!

This simple experiment shows how evaporation and condensation are at the heart of the water cycle. It uses hot water, so you'll need an adult to help.

1 Put a cup in a deep bowl. Ask an adult to pour hot water into the bowl (but not the cup).

2 Cover the bowl with plastic wrap. Make sure the cover is tight so air can't get in or out.

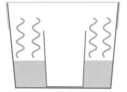

3 Put ice cubes on top, above the cup. Water drops will condense on the bottom of the plastic.

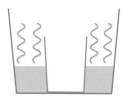

4 When the water drops get big enough, they will fall into the cup. You've made rain!

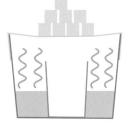

How the water cycle works

The water cycle is powered by the Sun. It starts when water evaporates into the air. Several days later, the water falls back to the ground as precipitation—the scientific name for rain, snow, sleet, and hail.

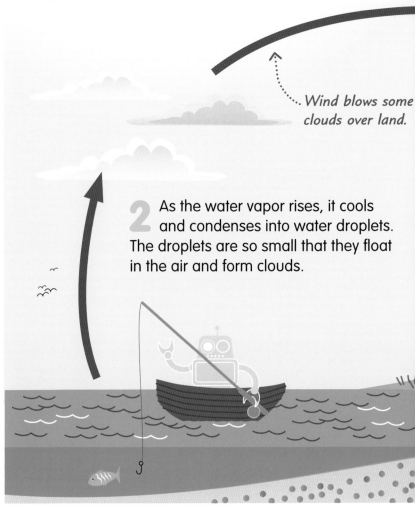

Wind blows some clouds over land.

2 As the water vapor rises, it cools and condenses into water droplets. The droplets are so small that they float in the air and form clouds.

1 Heat from the Sun causes water on Earth's surface to evaporate into the air. The water turns into an invisible gas called water vapor.

REAL WORLD TECHNOLOGY

Salt from seawater

For many centuries, people have made salt from the sea by digging shallow pits by the shore and filling them with salty seawater. When the water evaporates, it leaves behind salt crystals.

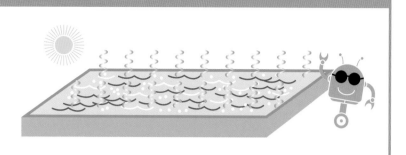

3 Trees and other plants release water vapor from their leaves. This is called transpiration. It adds more moisture to the air, so more clouds form.

Large rain clouds look dark because they block the Sun's light.

4 The water droplets in the clouds stick together to make bigger drops. If these drops get too large or heavy to float, they fall as rain.

Trees release more water vapor.

Rivers run down to the sea.

6 Some water soaks into soil and is taken up by trees and other living things. Water also seeps underground and makes its way to the sea.

5 The water from rain or melted snow runs over the land until it joins streams and rivers. It eventually flows out into the sea.

Rivers

Most of the rain or snow that falls on land finds its way into rivers. Over time, rivers transform Earth's landscapes, carving out valleys and depositing sediment in floodplains and deltas.

Rivers provide food, energy, recreation, transportation routes, and water for drinking.

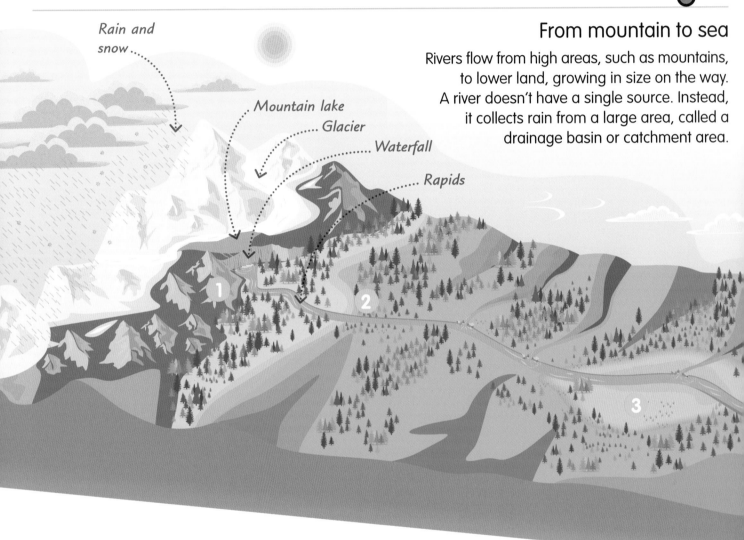

Rain and snow

Mountain lake

Glacier

Waterfall

Rapids

From mountain to sea

Rivers flow from high areas, such as mountains, to lower land, growing in size on the way. A river doesn't have a single source. Instead, it collects rain from a large area, called a drainage basin or catchment area.

1 Rapids
Many rivers start as fast-flowing streams tumbling down rocky slopes. Meltwater from snow feeds violent torrents called rapids that erode the ground. Waterfalls form where the river wears away soft ground but leaves a shelf of hard rock on top.

2 Valley
Over millions of years, rivers gradually wear away the ground below them to form valleys. Steep-sided, V-shaped valleys form in highlands, while wider, shallower valleys form farther downstream.

3 Floodplain
A floodplain is a flat, low-lying area surrounding a river. It gets covered with water when the river overflows, allowing sediment to settle on either side of the river.

Oxbow lakes

The meanders that develop in rivers are continually changing shape as fast-flowing water in the outsides of bends erodes the ground more quickly. Over time, a meander may get cut off to form an oxbow lake.

1 Here, erosion is gradually causing the neck of a meander to narrow (**1**), while the loop itself is enlarging (**2**).

2 Eventually, the neck becomes so narrow (**1**) that at times of flood, some water crosses it.

3 Finally, part of the loop becomes cut off, leaving an oxbow lake (**1**), while the river becomes temporarily straightened out (**2**).

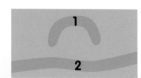

Hydroelectric power

The energy of a flowing river can be harnessed to make electricity. To do this, a dam is built to create a reservoir. Water is then allowed to flow through the dam via a channel, where it spins a machine called a turbine, which is connected to an electricity generator. The electricity is then carried away by power lines.

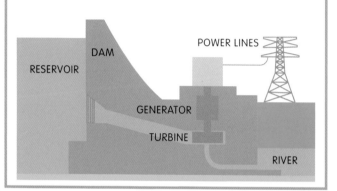

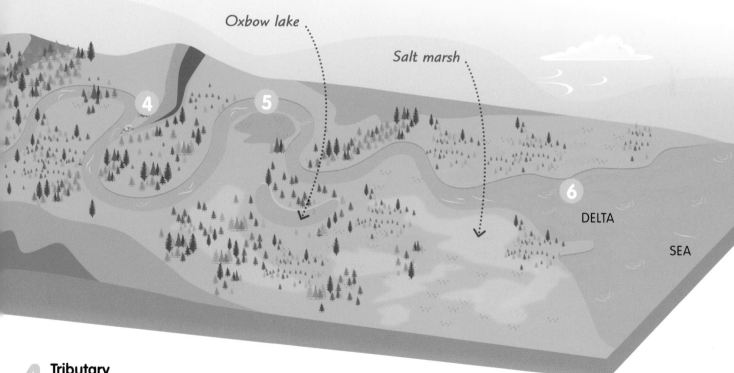

Oxbow lake

Salt marsh

DELTA

SEA

4 Tributary
A tributary is a smaller river that flows into a main river. Each tributary adds more water, causing a river to swell in size on its journey toward the sea.

5 Meanders
S-shaped loops, called meanders, form as a river nears the sea and the slope becomes more shallow.

6 Mouth
The mouth of a river is where it meets the sea. Sediment deposited here may build up to form an area of flat land and channels—a delta.

Glaciers

Glaciers are masses of ice found in mountain ranges and polar regions. As they flow slowly downhill, they wear away the ground below and gradually change the landscape.

About 10 percent of Earth's land is covered by glacial ice.

1 In the accumulation zone near the top of a mountain, snow piles up. Deep layers of snow are compressed to form ice. The ice erodes (wears away) a bowl-shaped hollow in the mountain, which may later become a lake.

2 The main body of the glacier flows slowly downhill, typically moving by about 3 feet (1 metre) a day.

3 Rocky debris from the valley becomes embedded in the glacier. It gets dragged along by the ice, scraping the ground and the sides of the valley like a giant piece of sandpaper.

4 Giant cracks, known as crevasses, and channels of meltwater crisscross the upper surface of the glacier.

5 In an area called the ablation zone, ice begins to melt as conditions get warmer farther down the valley. The glacier starts to break up.

6 At the foot of the glacier is a crescent-shaped mound of rocky debris (a terminal moraine), dumped by the melting ice. Streams of meltwater flow away from the glacier.

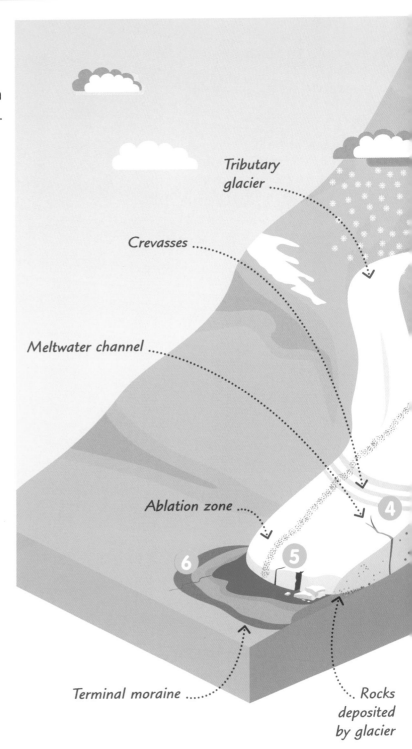

Tributary glacier

Crevasses

Meltwater channel

Ablation zone

Terminal moraine

Rocks deposited by glacier

Shaping the land

Over time, glaciers turn steep-sided river valleys into wide, U-shaped valleys (right). These are common in Earth's northern hemisphere and show that glaciers once covered far more of the planet than they do today.

1 Before a glacier passes through, the main valley is V-shaped. Tributary valleys descend down to the floor of the main valley.

2 A glacier forms and moves through the main valley. The glacial ice and rocky debris erode the bottom and sides of the valley, deepening and widening it.

3 Thousands of years later, the glacier has melted. The main valley is now U-shaped and its tributary valleys "hang," meaning they end high above the main valley.

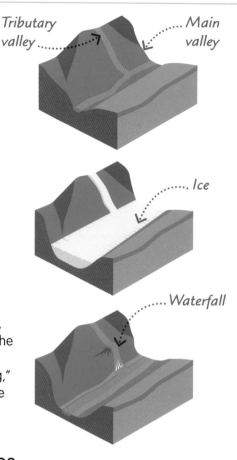

Tributary valley

Main valley

Ice

Waterfall

Other glacial features

As well as U-shaped valleys, glaciers leave behind a variety of other geological (land) features after they melt. These become visible once the glacial ice melts.

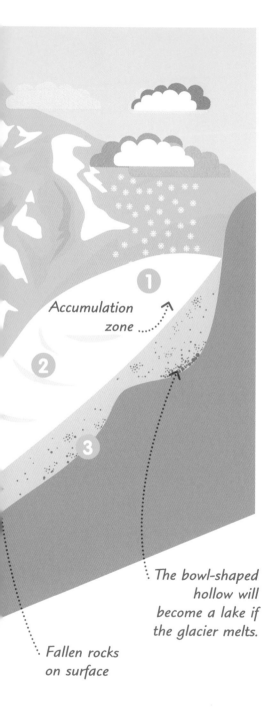

Accumulation zone

The bowl-shaped hollow will become a lake if the glacier melts.

Fallen rocks on surface

1 Drumlin
An egg-shaped hill made of loose rock debris deposited by a glacier and then sculpted by movement of the glacial ice.

2 Kettle lake
A small, shallow, circular lake left by a large chunk of melted glacier ice.

3 Erratic
A huge, isolated boulder that has been transported a long way and then dumped by a glacier.

4 Esker
A winding ridge of gravel deposited by a stream running beneath a glacier.

Seasons and climate zones

Many parts of the world have four seasons: spring, summer, fall, and winter. These seasons bring changes in day length, sunlight intensity, and average temperatures.

Seasonal changes cause many animals to hibernate or migrate.

Why we have seasons

The line, or axis, around which Earth spins is tilted. Due to this tilt, Earth's northern and southern hemispheres lean toward the Sun at different times of the year. This results in the cycle of seasons.

Earth's path around the Sun

Earth rotates around an imaginary line called an axis.

SUN

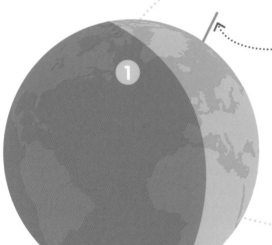

1 June
The northern hemisphere tilts toward the Sun in June, giving northern lands the long days and sunny weather of summer. The southern hemisphere tilts away and has the opposite: winter.

2 September
In September neither hemisphere tilts toward the Sun, so days and nights are the same length everywhere. It's fall in the northern hemisphere and spring in the southern hemisphere.

3 December
In December the southern hemisphere tilts toward the Sun and experiences summer. The northern hemisphere tilts away, giving it the long nights and cold weather of winter.

Beach ball climate model

To see why Earth's equator is much warmer than the poles, try this experiment. Place a beach ball about 12 inches (30 cm) from a desk lamp and leave it for a few minutes. Then feel the surface of the ball with your hand. It will be warm around the equator but cooler at the poles. This is because the equator faces the lamp directly and feels the full force of its beam, while the light at the poles hits the ground at a shallow angle and so is spread out over a much wider area.

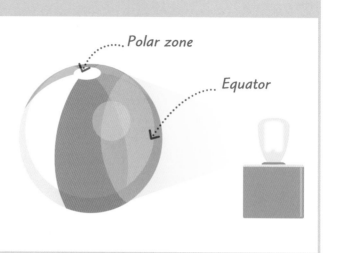

Polar zone

Equator

Climate zones

Earth's shape and tilt cause different amounts of sunlight to reach different parts of its surface. This causes climate zones—large areas of Earth's surface with distinct patterns of weather. There are three main climate zones: polar, temperate, and tropical.

1 There are two polar zones: one around the North Pole and another around the South Pole. They are colder than the rest of the planet and have only two seasons each year: summer and winter.

2 Earth's two temperate zones both have four seasons each year: spring, summer, fall, and winter. Average temperatures are mild, but summers can be very hot and winters bitterly cold.

3 The zone near the equator is called the tropical zone and is warm all year. The northern and southern parts of the tropical zone have rainy seasons and dry seasons instead of summer and winter, but the equator is rainy all year.

4 March
In the northern hemisphere, the days are growing longer and warmer, causing the season of spring. Meanwhile, cooler fall weather and shortening days have arrived in the south.

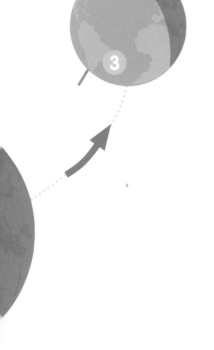

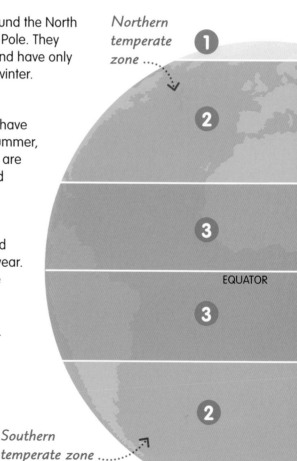

Northern temperate zone **1**

2

3

EQUATOR

3

2

Southern temperate zone ....

1

The atmosphere

Earth is surrounded by the atmosphere, a thin blanket of gases held in place by our planet's gravity. The gases that make up Earth's atmosphere are vital to life on Earth.

All the oxygen in Earth's atmosphere comes from plants.

The atmosphere's layers

The atmosphere has five distinct layers. As you travel from space through the atmosphere toward Earth, each layer becomes thicker (denser) than the layer above.

1 Exosphere
The outer layer extends to thousands of miles above Earth's surface. It merges with space.

2 Thermosphere
This layer is hundreds of miles deep and is home to the International Space Station.

3 Mesosphere
In the upper region of this 20-mile- (30-km) thick layer, temperatures can be lower than −225°F (−143°C), making it the coldest place on Earth. Tiny space rocks burn up here, producing streaks of light called meteors or shooting stars.

4 Stratosphere
About 22 miles (35 km) deep, this layer has a protective band of ozone gas (a form of oxygen) that absorbs harmful ultraviolet radiation from the Sun, shielding the planet's surface.

5 Troposphere
This layer is where all weather occurs. It is 5 miles (8 km) thick above the poles, and 11 miles (18 km) thick above the equator.

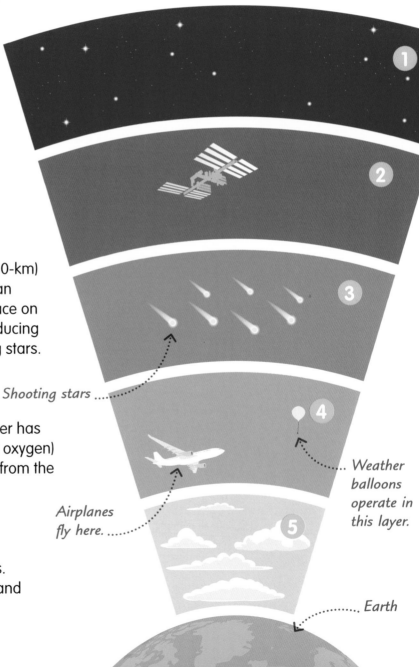

Shooting stars

Weather balloons operate in this layer.

Airplanes fly here.

Earth

Gases in the atmosphere

Nitrogen and oxygen are the two main gases found in the atmosphere, but there are tiny amounts of other gases, too. In the lower layers, water vapor is present, making up about one percent of the air at sea level.

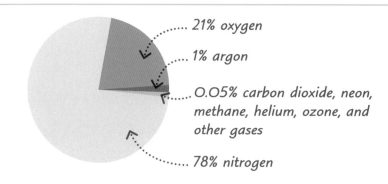

21% oxygen

1% argon

0.05% carbon dioxide, neon, methane, helium, ozone, and other gases

78% nitrogen

Global winds

In the troposphere, air circulates up and down in patterns called atmospheric cells. There are three groups of cells: polar, Ferrel, and Hadley cells. The air movement in these cells, along with Earth's spin (which makes the air veer east or west) creates three global wind patterns that blow over Earth's surface.

1 Winds called polar easterlies blow in polar regions. They blow away from the pole, then Earth's spin makes them swerve from east to west.

2 Westerlies blow in temperate (mild weather) regions. They blow away from the equator, and then from west to east.

3 Trade winds blow in the tropics (near the equator). In the northern hemisphere, they blow from northeast to southwest (northeast trade winds). In the southern hemisphere, they blow from southeast to northwest (southeast trade winds).

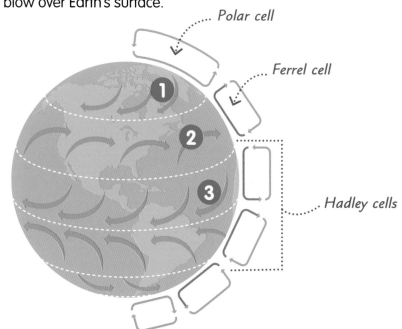

Polar cell

Ferrel cell

Hadley cells

REAL WORLD TECHNOLOGY

Bouncing radio waves

The atmosphere allows people to communicate over long distances by bouncing radio waves around the world. Transmitters emit radio waves, which travel toward a part of the atmosphere known as the ionosphere. The ionosphere reflects the radio waves back to Earth, where they are picked up by receivers elsewhere in the world.

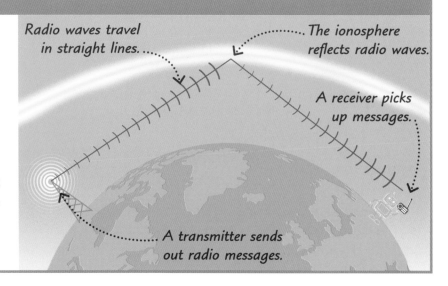

Radio waves travel in straight lines.

The ionosphere reflects radio waves.

A receiver picks up messages.

A transmitter sends out radio messages.

Weather

The air and water in Earth's atmosphere are continually on the move, driven by the Sun's energy and Earth's rotation. These movements create wind, rain, and other types of weather.

> Climate is the typical pattern of weather that a place experiences over a period of time.

Moving air

The changing weather can often be explained by the way large masses of air move and collide in the atmosphere. Clear weather is associated with sinking air, but rising air carries moisture high into the sky and produces clouds and rain.

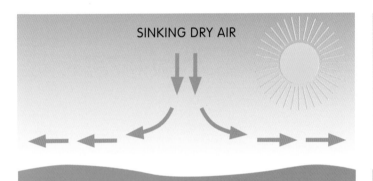

1 High pressure

When air from high in the atmosphere sinks, it presses on the air below, causing high pressure. Air from high altitudes is usually dry, so high pressure brings clear, sunny weather.

2 Low pressure

When air rises, it causes low pressure. The air cools as it rises, and any moisture in the air condenses to form clouds. Rising air usually brings overcast or rainy weather.

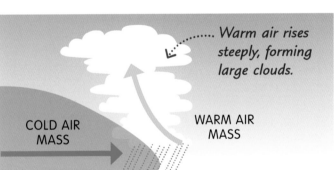
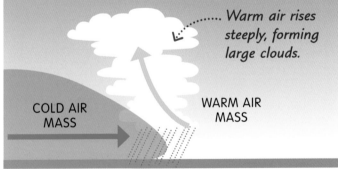

3 Cold front

When a mass of cold air pushes into warm air, it pushes the warm air up strongly. This is called a cold front. The weather gets colder, and moisture in the warm air forms huge rain clouds.

4 Warm front

If warm air pushes into cold air, it slides gently over it, forming a warm front. The moisture in the warm air cools gradually as it rises, forming thin clouds and often bringing light rain.

Extreme weather

The weather is often changeable, but sometimes it is far hotter, colder, or windier than normal. Extreme weather is unusual or violent weather that can threaten lives and damage property.

1 Hurricanes and typhoons are vast, revolving storm systems that form over tropical oceans.

2 A tornado is a rapidly spinning column of air that produces violent and destructive winds.

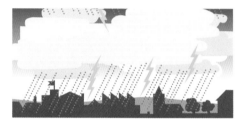

3 Electrical storms bring thunder and lightning, strong winds, and heavy precipitation (rain or hail).

4 Blizzards are severe storms in freezing conditions, bringing heavy snowfall and very high winds.

5 During an ice storm, rain freezes when it touches the ground, coating everything in layers of ice.

6 Heat waves are spells of unusually hot weather that can make people sick and destroy crops.

REAL WORLD TECHNOLOGY

Weather charts

Weather forecasters use charts to display the current weather and their forecasts. The swirling lines on a chart are called isobars and connect areas of equal pressure. Warm fronts are shown by lines of red semicircles, and cold fronts are shown by blue triangles. These fronts often revolve around areas of low pressure, forming a weather system called a cyclone. Although a trained meteorologist (weather scientist) can predict the weather using just a chart, predictions are usually made by supercomputers that model Earth's atmosphere.

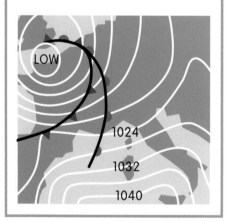

LOW
1024
1032
1040

Cloud types

The names of most clouds are based on three basic shapes: wispy and feather-like (cirrus); lumpy (cumulus); and flat (stratus). Other Latin words are combined with these. For instance, alto means the cloud is medium-high, and nimbo or nimbus means it's likely to cause rain.

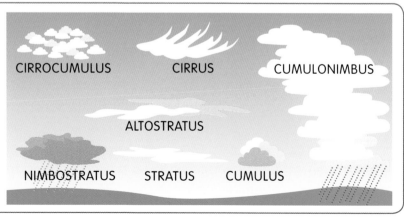

CIRROCUMULUS   CIRRUS   CUMULONIMBUS

ALTOSTRATUS

NIMBOSTRATUS   STRATUS   CUMULUS

Ocean currents

Driven by the wind and by Earth's rotation, the water in the oceans flows around the planet in huge streams called ocean currents. These have a large influence on the climate of many countries.

Turtles use ocean currents as highways to travel long distances.

Surface currents

Some currents flow along the sea surface. On the western sides of the oceans, these surface currents carry warm water from the tropics toward colder regions. On the eastern sides, currents carry cool water back toward the tropics. Many of these currents combine to form huge circular flows called gyres.

1 The California Current carries cold water down the eastern side of the North Pacific. This makes the climate cooler on the west coast of North America.

2 The Gulf Stream carries warm water up the western side of the North Atlantic. It flows very quickly and is one of the world's strongest ocean currents.

3 The North Atlantic Drift carries warm water from the Gulf Stream to Europe. It makes winters in the British Isles and Scandinavia warmer.

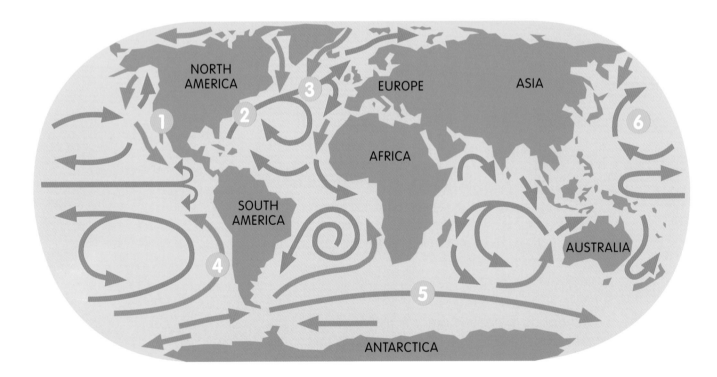

4 The Peru Current is a cold current off the west coast of South America. Cold air carries less moisture than warm air, so it gives this coast a dry climate.

5 The Antarctic Circumpolar Current is a cold current that flows around Antarctica. It keeps warm water away, which helps stop Antarctic ice from melting.

6 The Kuroshio Current carries warm water up the western side of the North Pacific Ocean. It warms the southern part of Japan.

Deep currents

Some currents flow along the seafloor. These are much slower than surface currents, but they play an important role in the world's climate, and they help sustain sea life.

1 Global conveyor
In the North Atlantic, surface water cools and becomes saltier as some of it turns to ice. This makes the water heavier, so it sinks and flows along the seafloor. Some of the deep water can spend 1,000 years flowing slowly over the seafloor before rising again in the Pacific and returning. This giant current is called the global conveyor and plays a key role in the global climate. Some scientists think melting Arctic ice could disrupt it, triggering an ice age in the northern hemisphere.

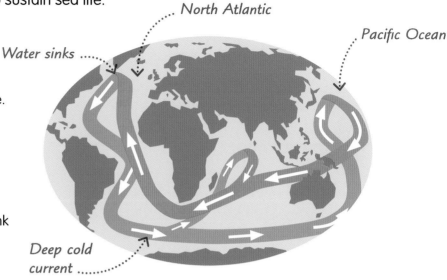

North Atlantic

Pacific Ocean

Water sinks

Deep cold current

2 Upwellings
In some parts of the world, winds push the sea away from the coast, causing water to rise up from the deep. These rising currents are called upwellings. They bring nutrients to the surface, allowing many forms of sea life to flourish. Many of the world's most important fishing sites are near upwellings.

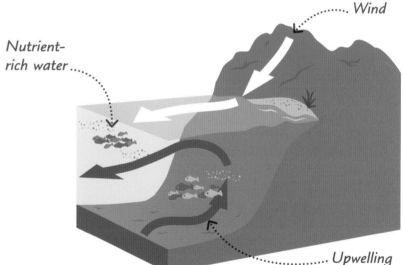

Wind

Nutrient-rich water

Upwelling

REAL WORLD TECHNOLOGY

Underwater turbines

Ocean currents carry vast amounts of energy. If just 0.3 per cent of the energy in the Gulf Stream could be harnessed, it would provide enough power for the whole state of Florida. Engineers are trying to develop technologies that will one day be able to extract energy from ocean currents. One idea is to build turbines on the seafloor that work in the same way as wind turbines on land.

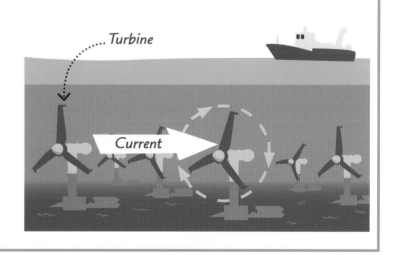

Turbine

Current

The carbon cycle

All living organisms contain carbon, and it's found in many nonliving materials too, such as fossil fuels and some rocks. The movement of carbon between living organisms, the oceans, the atmosphere, and Earth's crust is called the carbon cycle.

> The level of carbon dioxide in the atmosphere has increased by more than 25 percent since 1960.

Parts of the carbon cycle

Some parts of the cycle move carbon around in just a matter of days, while other parts store carbon for millions of years. Human activities can speed up the rate at which carbon dioxide is released into the atmosphere.

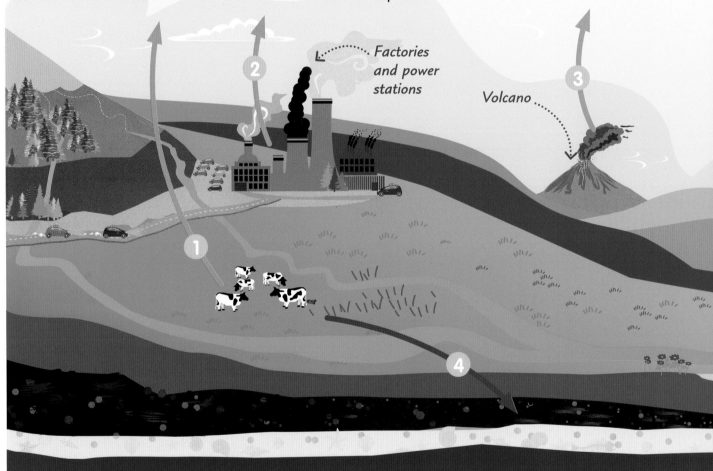

1 Respiration
Animals and other organisms take in carbon through food and release it as carbon dioxide. Carbon is also released when their dung or bodies decompose.

2 Burning fossil fuels
The burning of fossil fuels—whether in factories, power stations, and homes or by cars and planes—releases carbon dioxide into the atmosphere.

3 Volcanic action
Volcanoes and hot springs slowly return carbon from long-term underground stores into the air as carbon dioxide.

4 Fossilization
Some organisms don't decay after dying. Instead, they become buried, trapping carbon in the ground. Over millions of years, their remains form fossil fuels.

REAL WORLD TECHNOLOGY

Climate change

The burning of fossil fuels has dramatically increased the rate at which carbon from underground stores returns to the atmosphere. As a result, the level of carbon dioxide in the atmosphere is rising. Carbon dioxide traps heat in the atmosphere, in much the same way as glass traps heat in a greenhouse, so our planet's average temperature is rising too. Many scientists think the warming climate is causing glaciers to melt, droughts and floods to become more frequent, and coral reefs to die.

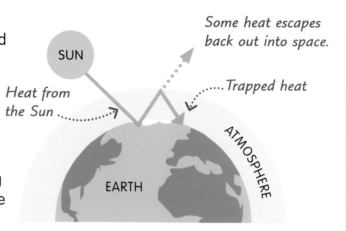

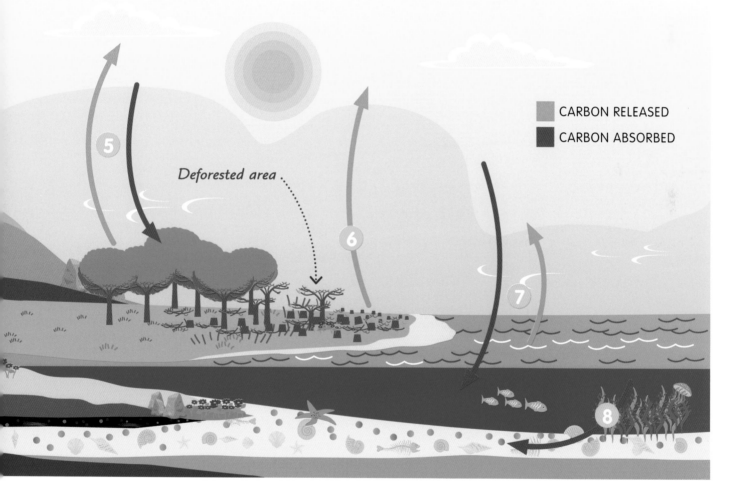

CARBON RELEASED

CARBON ABSORBED

5 Photosynthesis
Plants take in carbon dioxide from the air to make nutrients by photosynthesis. They also release carbon dioxide through respiration.

6 Deforestation
Cutting down forests releases carbon back into the air if the trees are burned or dead vegetation is left to decompose.

7 Ocean exchange
Carbon dioxide passes between the oceans and air. The world's oceans take in more carbon than they release and are known as a "carbon sink."

8 Marine carbon capture
Some marine organisms use carbon dioxide to make shells. When they die, their remains sink to the seabed and fossilize to form limestone, which acts as a long-term carbon store.

Glossary

absolute zero The lowest possible temperature, defined as zero kelvin or −459.67°F (−273.15°C).

acceleration A change in the velocity of a moving object. Speeding up, slowing down, and changing direction are all forms of acceleration.

acid A compound that releases hydrogen ions when it dissolves in water. Vinegar and lemon juice are weak acids.

activation energy The energy needed to start a chemical reaction.

aerobic respiration The process by which living cells use oxygen to release energy from food.

air pressure The force of air molecules pushing against a surface or container.

air resistance A force that slows down an object moving through the air.

algae Simple, plantlike organisms that live in water and make food by photosynthesis.

alkali A compound that releases hydroxide ions when it dissolves in water. Alkalis neutralize acids.

alloy A material made by mixing a metal with another element. Alloys tend to be stronger, harder, and more useful than the pure metal they are based on.

alternating current (AC) An electric current whose direction reverses at regular intervals.

alveoli Tiny air pockets in the lungs of mammals.

amp or ampere (A) A unit used to measure electric current.

anaerobic respiration A type of respiration that does not require oxygen. It releases less energy than aerobic respiration.

anion A negatively charged ion.

anode A positive electrode.

antibodies Proteins in the blood that help the body attack germs such as bacteria and viruses.

artery A thick-walled blood vessel that carries blood away from the heart to other parts of the body.

artificial selection The process by which humans use animal breeding or plant breeding to make changes to a species.

asexual reproduction Reproduction that involves only one parent.

asteroid A large, irregularly shaped rock that orbits the Sun.

atmosphere The layer of air that surrounds a planet.

atom A tiny particle of matter. An atom is the smallest part of an element that can exist.

atomic number The number of protons in an atom.

aurora Wavy patterns of colored light in the night sky, caused by high-energy particles from space hitting Earth's atmosphere.

bacteria Microscopic, single-celled organisms with no cell nuclei. Bacteria are the most abundant organisms on Earth.

base A compound that reacts with an acid to make water and a salt.

battery An energy-storing device that creates an electric current when connected to a circuit.

binary system A number system with only two digits, 0 and 1. Digital devices store and process data in binary form.

biology The study of living things.

boiling point The temperature at which a liquid turns to gas so quickly that bubbles form in it.

bond A force between atoms or molecules that holds them together.

bone Hard tissue that is part of an animal's skeleton.

Brownian motion The random motion of microscopic particles in a liquid or a gas, caused by molecules colliding with them.

buoyancy The upward force on an object in water. Buoyancy can make objects float.

capillaries Tiny blood vessels that carry blood to and from cells.

carbohydrate A biological compound used as a source of energy. Sweet and starchy foods are rich in carbohydrates.

carnivore A meat-eating animal.

catalyst A chemical that speeds up a chemical reaction without being changed itself.

catalytic converter A device in a car that uses a catalyst to change toxic exhaust gases into less harmful gases.

cathode A negative electrode.

cation A positively charged ion.

cell The basic unit from which all living organisms are made.

cell division The process by which one cell splits to produce two cells, called daughter cells.

cellulose A fibrous carbohydrate that forms the walls of plant cells.

Celsius A temperature scale based on the melting point of ice (0°C) and the boiling point of water (100°C), with 100 equal divisions, called degrees, in between them.

chemical A pure element or compound. Water, iron, salt, and oxygen are all chemicals.

chemistry The study of matter.

chlorophyll A green substance used by plants to absorb light energy for making food (photosynthesis).

chloroplasts Tiny bodies in plant cells that contain chlorophyll.

chromatography A way of separating colored chemicals in a mixture by letting them spread through an absorbent material, such as paper.

chromosome A structure in the nucleus of a cell, made from coiled DNA strands, that carries genetic information.

circuit A path that electricity flows around. All electrical devices have circuits inside them.

climate The pattern of weather and seasons a place experiences in a typical year.

climate change Long-term changes in Earth's weather patterns.

clone An organism with exactly the same genes as its parent.

colloid A mixture made up of tiny particles of one substance dispersed in another in which it does not dissolve.

combustion (burning) A chemical reaction in which a substance combines with oxygen, releasing heat energy.

comet A large, icy body that orbits the Sun. Comets develop long tails when they are near the Sun.

compound A chemical consisting of two or more elements whose atoms have bonded.

concentration A measure of the amount of solute dissolved in a solution.

condensation The change of a gas into a liquid.

conduction The movement of heat or electricity through a substance.

conductor A substance through which heat or electric current flows easily.

convection The spread of heat through a liquid or gas, caused by warmer, less dense areas rising.

core The innermost and hottest part of Earth, thought to be made of iron and nickel.

corona A layer of hot gas surrounding the Sun.

covalent bond A type of chemical bond between the atoms in a molecule. Covalent bonds form when atoms share electrons.

crust The rocky outer surface of Earth.

crystal A solid substance with a regular shape. Snowflakes and diamonds are crystals.

decibel (dB) A unit used to measure the loudness of sound.

decomposition Breaking large molecules into smaller ones.

density The mass (amount of matter) of a substance per unit of volume.

detergent A substance that makes droplets of oil or grease disperse in water, making it easier to clean things. Soap and dishwashing liquid are detergents.

diffraction The spreading out of waves after they pass through a narrow opening.

diffusion The gradual mixing of two or more substances as a result of the random movement of their molecules.

digestion Breaking down food into small molecules so that it can be absorbed by cells.

direct current (DC) An electric current that flows in one direction only. See also alternating current.

displacement A chemical reaction in which some of the atoms or ions in a compound are replaced by different ones.

distillation A way of separating chemicals in a liquid by boiling the liquid and collecting the different parts as they condense.

DNA Deoxyribonucleic acid, the chemical that stores genetic information inside living cells.

drag The force that slows down an object as it travels through a liquid or gas.

dynamo An electrical generator that produces direct current.

eclipse The shadow caused by a moon or planet blocking light from the Sun.

ecology The scientific study of interactions between organisms and between organisms and their environment.

ecosystem A community of animals and plants and the physical environment that they share.

elasticity The ability of a material to stretch or bend and then return to its original shape.

electric current The flow of electric charge—for instance, as electrons moving through a wire.

electricity A form of energy carried by an electric current.

electrode A piece of metal or carbon that collects or releases electrons in an electric circuit.

electrolyte A substance that conducts electricity when dissolved in water.

electromagnet A coil of wire that becomes magnetic when electricity flows through it.

electromagnetic spectrum The whole range of different types of electromagnetic radiation, from gamma rays to radio waves.

electron A negatively charged particle that occupies the outer part of an atom. Moving electrons carry electricity and cause magnetism.

electronics The use of electricity to process or transmit information, such as computer data.

element A chemical made of only one kind of atom.

embryo A very early stage in the development of an animal or plant. Animal embryos are microscopic.

emulsion A mixture that consists of tiny droplets of one liquid dispersed in another.

endothermic reaction A chemical reaction that takes in energy from the surroundings.

engine A machine that harnesses the energy released by burning fuel to create motion.

enzyme A protein made by living cells that speeds up a chemical reaction.

equator An imaginary circle around the middle of Earth, midway between the North Pole and the South Pole.

erosion The process by which Earth's surface rock is worn down and carried away by wind, water, and glaciers.

evaporation The change of a liquid into a gas by escape of molecules from its surface.

evolution The gradual change of species over generations as they adapt to the changing environment.

exothermic reaction A chemical reaction that releases energy into the surroundings.

fertilization The joining of male and female sex cells.

fetus The unborn young of an animal.

filter A device that removes the solid material from a liquid.

fluid A substance that can flow, such as a gas or liquid.

food chain A series of organisms, each of which is eaten by the next.

food web The system of food chains in an ecosystem.

force A push or pull that can change an object's speed, direction of movement, or shape.

formula A group of chemical symbols and numbers that shows the atomic makeup of a chemical.

fossil The remains or impression of a prehistoric plant or animal, often preserved in rock.

fossil fuel A fuel derived from the fossilized remains of living things. Coal, crude oil, and natural gas are fossil fuels.

freezing point The temperature at which a liquid turns into a solid.

frequency The number of times something happens in a unit of time. The frequency of a wave is the number of waves per second.

friction A dragging force that slows a moving object down when it rubs against something.

fulcrum (pivot) The fixed point around which a lever rotates.

fuse A safety device used in electrical circuits. Most fuses consist of a thin wire that melts if too much current passes through.

fusion Joining together.

galaxy A vast collection of stars, dust, and gas held together by gravity. Our solar system is part of a galaxy called the Milky Way.

galvanize To coat iron with zinc to protect it from rust.

gamete A reproductive cell, such as a sperm or egg.

gamma rays A type of electromagnetic radiation with a very short wavelength.

gene A length of code on a DNA molecule that performs a specific job. Genes are passed on from one generation to the next.

generator A machine that converts movement energy into electricity.

germination The growth of a small plant from a seed.

glacier A moving mass of ice, formed from accumulated snow.

global warming A rise in the average temperature of Earth's atmosphere, caused by rising levels of carbon dioxide from burning fossil fuels.

gravity A force that pulls all things with mass toward each other. Earth's gravity pulls objects to the ground and gives them weight.

habitat The natural home of an animal or plant.

hemisphere Half of a sphere. Earth is divided into the northern and southern hemispheres by the equator.

hemoglobin A compound in red blood cells that carries oxygen around an animal's body.

herbivore An animal that eats plants.

hertz (Hz) The unit of frequency used to measure waves. One hertz is one wave per second.

hurricane A violent tropical storm with torrential rain and high winds that reach more than 74 mph (119 km/h).

hydrocarbon A chemical compound made up of only hydrogen and carbon atoms.

hydroelectricity The generation of electricity by using the energy in flowing water.

igneous rock Rock formed when molten rock cools and solidifies.

indicator A chemical that shows the acidity of a solution by changing color.

induction The production of an electric current by a moving magnetic field.

infrared radiation A type of electromagnetic radiation produced by hot objects.

insulator A material that reduces or stops the flow of heat, electricity, or sound.

integrated circuit A tiny electric circuit made of components printed on a silicon chip.

interference The combination of two or more sets of waves.

ion An atom or group of atoms that has lost or gained one or more electrons and so become positively or negatively charged.

ionic bond A chemical bond caused by the attraction between positive and negative ions.

joule (J) The standard unit of energy.

kinetic energy The energy stored in a moving object.

laser A beam of intense light consisting of waves that are in step and of equal wavelength.

lens A curved, transparent piece of plastic or glass that can bend light rays.

lever A rigid rod that swings around a fixed point. Levers can multiply forces, making difficult jobs easier.

lift The upward force produced by a wing as air flows past it.

light-year The distance light travels in a year. One light-year is 5.9 trillion miles (9.5 trillion km).

magma Hot, molten rock deep underground. It forms igneous rock when it cools and hardens.

magnetic field The area around a magnet in which its effects are felt.

magnetism The invisible force of attraction or repulsion between some substances, especially iron.

mantle A thick, dense layer of rock under Earth's crust. The mantle makes up most of our planet's mass.

mass The amount of matter in an object.

matter Anything that has mass and occupies space.

melting point The temperature at which a solid turns into a liquid.

metamorphic rock Rock that has been changed by intense heat and/or pressure underground but without melting.

metamorphosis A dramatic change in the life cycle of an animal. Caterpillars undergo metamorphosis when they develop into butterflies.

meteor (shooting star) A small piece of rock or metal from space that burns up as it enters Earth's atmosphere, producing a streak of light.

meteorite A piece of rock or metal from space that enters Earth's atmosphere and reaches the ground without burning up.

microorganism A tiny organism that can be seen only with the aid of a microscope.

microscope A scientific instrument that uses lenses to make small objects appear larger.

microwave A type of electromagnetic radiation. Microwaves are very short radio waves.

mineral A naturally occurring solid chemical. Rocks are made of mineral grains stuck together.

mixture A substance containing two or more chemicals that are not chemically bonded to each other as molecules.

molecule A group of two or more atoms joined by covalent bonds.

momentum The tendency of a moving object to keep moving until a force stops it. Momentum can be calculated by multiplying mass by velocity.

moraine A heap of rocky debris dumped by a glacier.

motor A machine that uses electricity and magnetism to produce motion.

nectar A sugary liquid found in the flowers of some plants.

nerve A bundle of nerve cells that carry electrical signals through the body of an animal.

neuron A nerve cell.

neutralize Make an acid or alkali into a neutral solution (a solution that is neither acidic nor alkaline).

neutron A particle in the nucleus of an atom that has no electrical charge.

newton (N) The standard unit of force.

nucleus The central part of an atom or the part of a cell that stores genes.

nutrients Chemical compounds that plants and animals need in order to survive and grow.

ohm (Ω) A unit of electrical resistance.

omnivore An animal that eats both plants and animals.

opaque Does not let light through.

optical fibers Thin glass fibers through which light travels. They are used to transmit digital signals at high speed.

orbit The path of one body in space, such as a moon, around another, such as a planet.

ore A naturally occurring rock from which metal can be extracted.

organ A major structure in an organism that has a specific function. Organs in the human body include the stomach, brain, and heart.

organic Derived from living organisms or a compound based on carbon and hydrogen atoms.

organic compound A chemical with molecules containing carbon and hydrogen atoms.

organism A living thing.

osmosis The movement of water through a cell membrane (or other semipermeable membrane) from a weak solution to a strong one.

oxide A compound formed when oxygen combines with other elements.

parasite An organism that lives on and feeds off another organism, called the host.

particle A tiny bit of matter.

periodic table A table of all the elements arranged in order of atomic number.

pesticide A substance used to kill pests such as insects.

photon A particle of light.

photosynthesis The process by which plants use sunlight, water, and carbon dioxide from air to make food molecules.

pH A scale used to measure how acidic or alkaline a solution is.

physics The scientific study of forces, energy, and matter.

pitch How high or low a sound is. Pitch is directly related to the frequency of sound waves.

plankton Tiny organisms that live in the water of oceans and lakes.

polymer A carbon compound with long, chainlike molecules made of repeating units. Plastics are examples of polymers.

power The rate of transfer of energy. The more powerful a machine is, the more quickly it uses energy.

pressure The amount of force pushing on a given area.

protein An organic substance that contains nitrogen and is found in foods such as meat, fish, cheese, and beans. Organisms need proteins for growth and repair.

proton A particle in the nucleus of an atom that has a positive electric charge.

radiation An electromagnetic wave (or a stream of particles from a source of radioactivity).

radioactivity The breakdown of atomic nuclei, causing radiation to be released.

reactive Likely to take part in chemical reactions. Highly reactive chemicals react very easily.

real image An image formed where light rays focus. Unlike a virtual image, a real image can be seen on a screen.

reflection The bouncing back of light, heat, or sound from a surface.

refraction The change in direction of light waves as they pass from one medium, such as air, to another, such as water.

renewable energy A source of energy that will not run out, such as sunlight, wave power, or wind power.

resistance A measure of how much an electrical component opposes the flow of an electric current.

respiration The process by which living cells release energy from food molecules.

retina A layer of light-sensitive cells lining the inside of the eye.

salt An ionic compound formed when an acid reacts with a base. The word salt is often used to refer just to sodium chloride, the salt used to flavor food.

satellite An object in space that travels around another in a path called an orbit. The Moon is a natural satellite. Artificial satellites around Earth transmit data and help us navigate.

sedimentary rock Rock formed when sediment (particles of older rock) settles on the bed of a sea or lake and is slowly cemented together over time.

seismic wave A wave of energy that travels through the ground from an earthquake or explosion.

sex cell A reproductive cell, such as a sperm or egg.

sexual reproduction Reproduction that involves the combination of sex cells from two parents.

skeleton A flexible frame that supports an animal's body.

solar system The Sun together with its orbiting group of planets, including Earth, and other smaller bodies such as asteroids.

solute A substance that dissolves in a solvent to form a solution.

solution A mixture in which the molecules or ions of a solute are evenly spread out among the molecules of a solvent.

solvent A substance (usually a liquid) in which a solute dissolves to form a solution.

species A group of similar organisms that can breed with one another to produce offspring.

spectrum The range of different colors in visible light, or the range of different types of electromagnetic radiation.

stalactite A column of rock hanging from the roof of a cave. Stalactites grow slowly from calcium carbonate deposited by dripping water.

stalagmite A column of rock on the floor of a cave. Stalagmites grow slowly from calcium carbonate deposited by dripping water.

stratosphere The layer of Earth's atmosphere above the clouds.

sugar A carbohydrate with a small molecule. Sugars taste sweet.

surface tension A force in the surface of water that creates a delicate skin that can support very small objects, such as insects.

suspension A mixture made of solid particles dispersed in a liquid.

tectonic plate One of the large, slow-moving fragments into which Earth's crust is divided.

temperature A measure of how hot or cold something is.

tissue A group of similar cells, such as muscle tissue or fat.

transformer A machine that increases or decreases voltage.

translucent A term for a material that allows some light through but is not transparent.

transparent A term for a material that allows light through, making it possible to see through it.

ultrasound Sound waves with a frequency too high for human ears to detect. Ultrasound is used for medical scanning.

ultraviolet (UV) A type of electromagnetic radiation with a wavelength slightly shorter than visible light.

universe All of space and everything it contains.

vapor Another word for gas, especially a gas formed by evaporation from a liquid that is not hot enough to boil.

vein A tube that carries blood from body tissues to the heart.

velocity The speed an object moves in a specific direction.

vibration Rapid back-and-forth movement.

volume The amount of space an object takes up.

watt (W) A unit of power. One watt equals one joule per second.

wavelength The length of a wave, measured from the crest of one wave to the crest of the next.

weight The force with which a mass is pulled toward Earth.

work The energy transferred when a force moves an object. Work can be calculated by multiplying force by distance.

X-ray A type of electromagnetic radiation used to create images of bones and teeth.

Index

Acknowledgments

Dorling Kindersley would like to thank Ben Ffrancon Davies,
Christine Heilman, and Rona Skene for editorial help; Louise
Dick, Phil Gamble, and Mary Sandberg for design help; Katie
John for proofreading; and Helen Peters for indexing.

Planets

Punch out the patterns on
these cards and fold them
to create planets.
(These planets are
not to scale.)

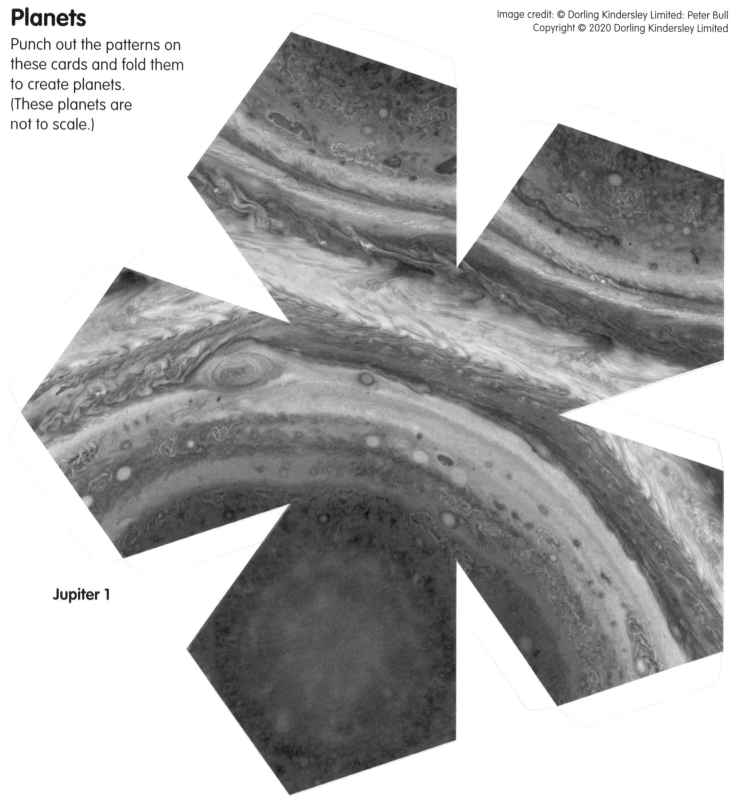

Jupiter 1

How to make your planets

1. Punch out the pattern of the planet. Fold every pentagon and tab downward along the creases.

2. Jupiter and Saturn have two nets, each one like a star shape. For all the smaller planets, if you turn the shape lengthwise, it will look like two stars joined together.

3. In the center of each star is a pentagon surrounded by five other pentagons. Start with one star. Apply glue to all of its tabs.

4. Turn the pattern over so that the printed side is on the table. With the middle pentagon flat on the table, fold up all its surrounding pentagons to form a cup shape. Stick the tabs to the pentagons to hold the cup shape in place. You have now made one hemisphere.

5. Apply glue to the tabs on the other half of the planet and fold up in the same way to make the second hemisphere.

6. Bring together the two hemispheres. Tuck the tabs inside and glue in place to form your planet. If it gets tricky, go slowly, sticking one tab at a time.

Saturn 1

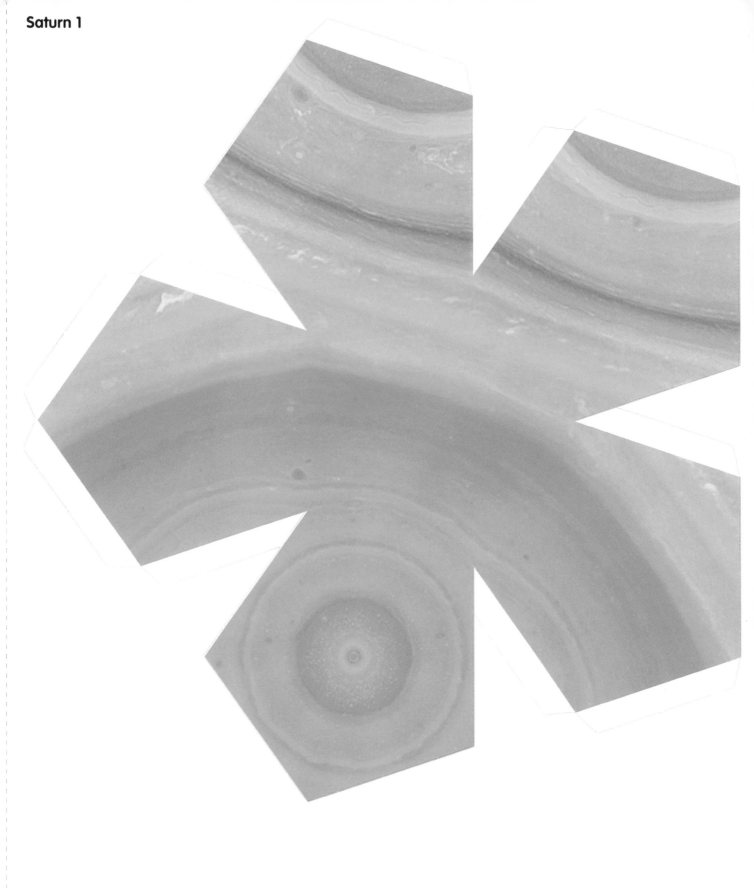

Saturn's ring

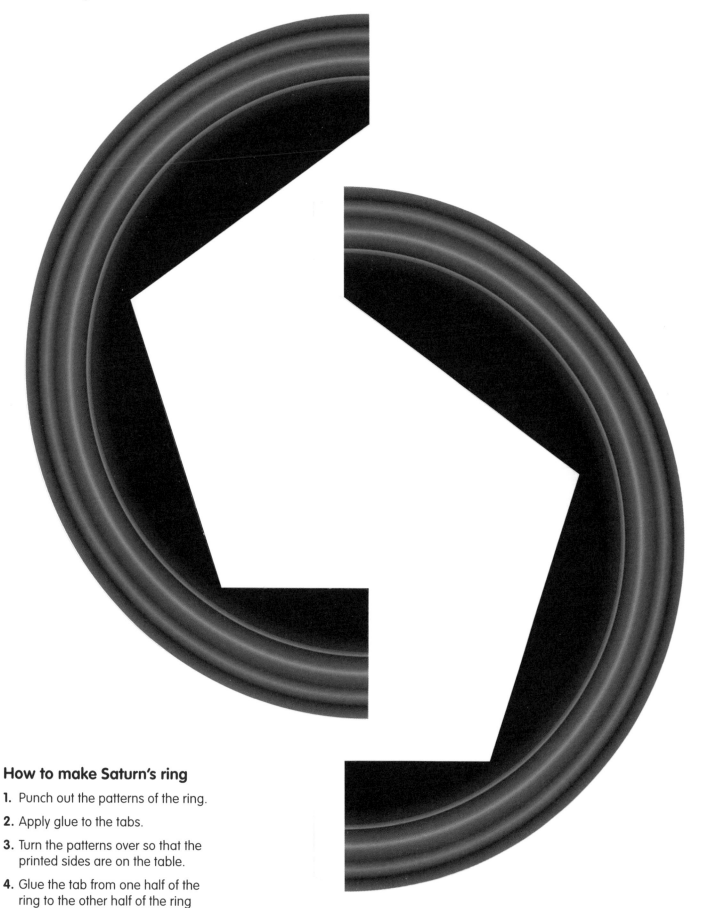

How to make Saturn's ring

1. Punch out the patterns of the ring.

2. Apply glue to the tabs.

3. Turn the patterns over so that the printed sides are on the table.

4. Glue the tab from one half of the ring to the other half of the ring to form a circle.

5. Gently slide the ring over your model of Saturn so that it sits around the middle.

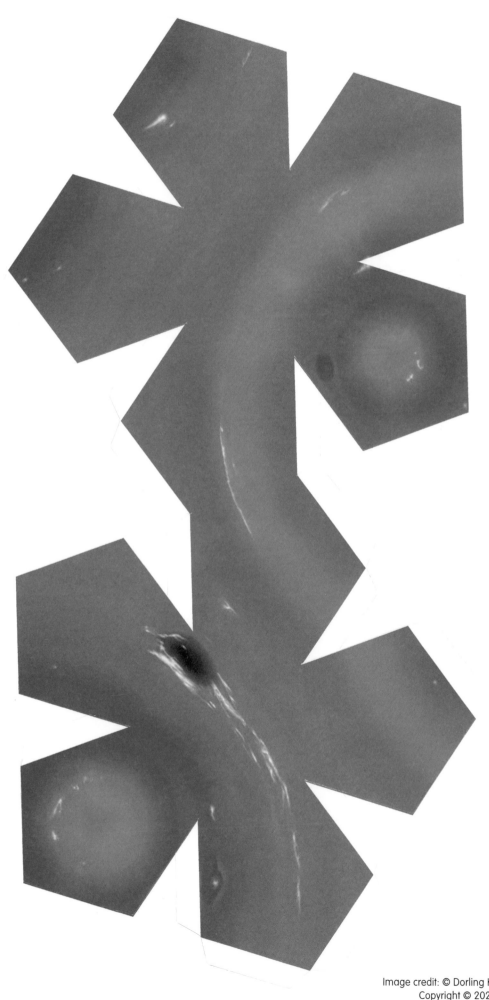

Earth

Mercury

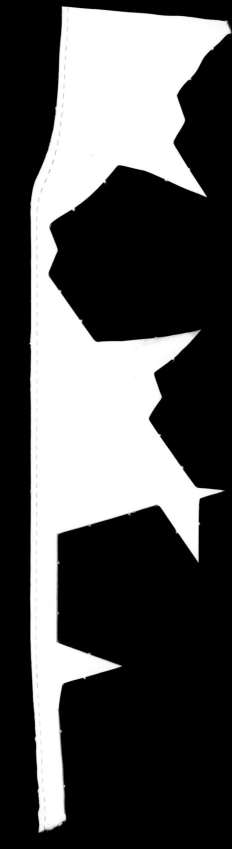

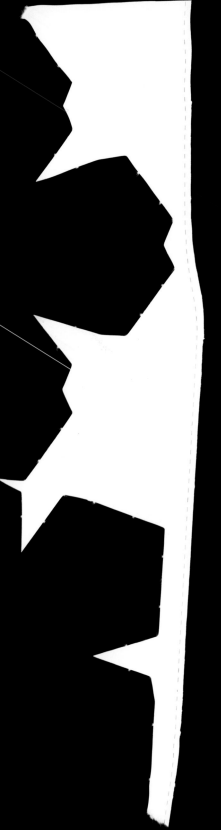

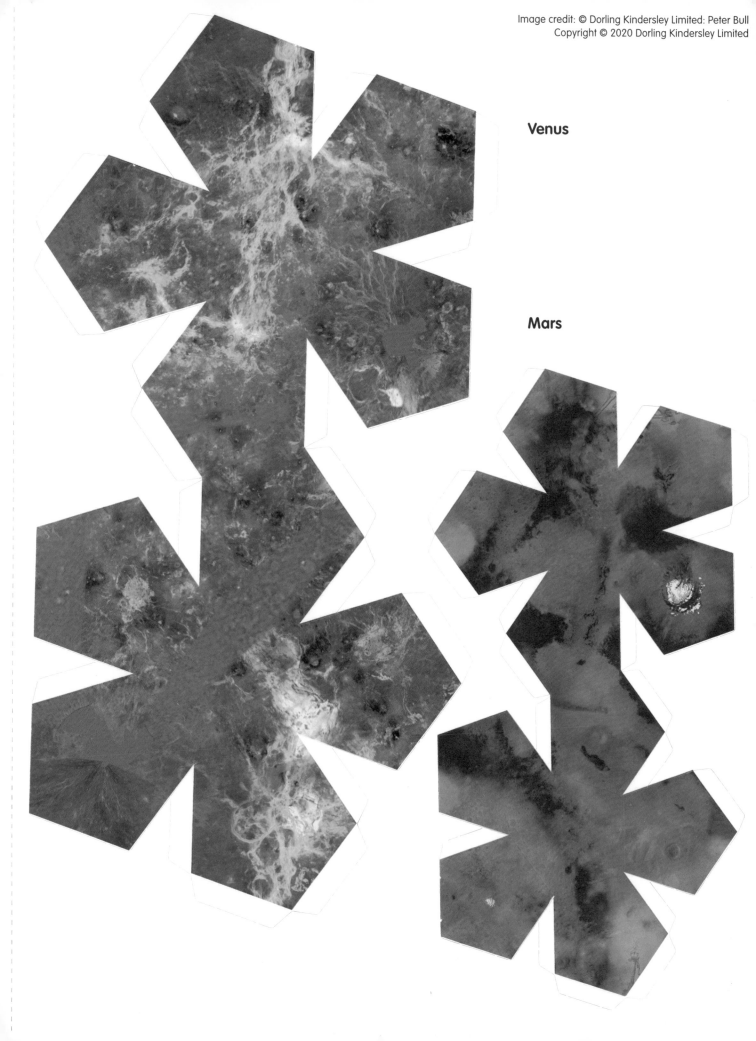

Venus

Mars